WESTERN WINDS

THE BRONTËS'
IRISH HERITAGE

Ever truly and
respectfully Yours,

D. Montès

WESTERN WINDS

THE BRONTËS' IRISH HERITAGE

EDWARD CHITHAM

The History Press Ireland

Frontispiece: Patrick Brontë in old age.
(From R. Scruton, *Thornton and the Brontës*, 1898)

First published 2015

The History Press Ireland
50 City Quay
Dublin 2
Ireland
www.thehistorypress.ie

British Library Cataloguing in Publication Data.
A catalogue record for this book is available from the British Library.

ISBN 978 1 84588 833 6

Typesetting and origination by The History Press
Printed and bound in Great Britain by T J International Ltd, Padstow, Cornwall

CONTENTS

Part 2 Pruntys in Yorkshire

ACKNOWLEDGEMENTS

During the 1980s Alex Flanigan of Belfast supplied me with a great deal of researched material, some of which I used in *The Brontës' Irish Background* (published 1986), but some of which I was not then able to use. I owe a great debt of gratitude to his most generous contributions. The Brontë Society (Irish Section) made it possible for me to visit many of the sites associated with Patrick and his forebears. Thanks are due here especially to Mervyn Patton of Portadown. Helena Haffield enabled me to pay another visit to County Down and reassess Patrick's birthplace and Drumballyroney church. I am particularly grateful to Frank Watters of Poyntzpass who left no stone unturned to try to discover the notes made by John McAllister concerning Hugh Prunty's account of his life. Thanks are also due to Bryan Hooks (*Banbridge Chronicle*), Dr William Roulston of the Ulster Historical Foundation, C.E.F. Trench of Slane for material on Ardagh, Henry McMaster of Holywood, County Down, and Amber Adams of Calgary, Alberta, Canada, for general encouragement and help.

A host of earlier writers on Brontë issues have provided clues to be followed up. In the internet age, thanks are also due to volunteers and institutions which provide useful background material, including the Public Record Office of Northern Ireland (PRONI), the National Archives of Ireland, Fermanagh Genweb, John Hayes, and Ros Davies of County Down.

Internet contributors often use secondary sources or transcripts, which I have tried to check from primary sources where possible. My other sources are listed in the bibliography.

I cannot close this list without a word of posthumous thanks to Dr William Wright, a native of the Brontë 'homeland' in County Down, whose evidence on the family background is priceless, though sometimes overlaid with some romantic exaggeration. Whatever his faults, he rescued this important perspective from total oblivion. Without his account we would know little of this vital story and Brontë studies would be much the poorer.

PRELIMINARY NOTE ON SPELLING

The spelling of Irish names when anglicised took years to be standardised, and even now spelling is not always consistent. The Brontë family in England used accents, a dieresis or no mark at all. Patrick's surname was written Branty when he arrived in Cambridge. In the 1986 predecessor to this work I used the form Brunty for the family name before Patrick standardised on Brontë, but I feel now that Prunty is a more likely form for most of Hugh's life. I am following the principal of writing 'Prunty' until Brunty or Brontë seem more appropriate; this is confusing, but there seems no rational alternative. The townland in which he was born is often written Emdale, but older maps prefer Imdel, and this is the version I shall use; there are arguments for both. Patrick's mother was called 'Ayles', pronounced as a dissyllable, by her friends. I prefer Irish Eilís, partly because this seems to show where Emily got her pseudonym, but also because it links the name with the common name Elizabeth. Patrick's sister was named 'Alice', another approximation. In a partly pre-literate society, sounds matter more than ink marks on paper.

The situation is no better for words in the Irish (Gaeilge) language. I shall use 'Irish' to mean the native language. While on the sometimes fraught subject of terminology, I will mention that 'Ulster' will mean the traditional province, part of which is now in the Republic and part in the United Kingdom. This is because in the eighteenth and nineteenth centuries the name would have been so understood. Words in Irish will be spelt as they appear in documents, which can mean that they are differently spelt on different occasions.

Even anglicised words may sometimes cause trouble: the McAllister family are sometimes McAllister, sometimes McAlister and sometimes McCallister. All I can hope is to be consistent except when quoting.

INTRODUCTION

H as it ever been sufficiently recognised that Charlotte Brontë is first and foremost *an Irishwoman* … ?' asked Mrs Humphry Ward in 1899, writing a preface to *Jane Eyre* in the Haworth edition of the Brontë works. The answer is certainly, 'No'. However, the reading public are not to blame for this, though Mrs Ward's point remains true for many critics and biographers. Even they are not to be held totally responsible, since both Charlotte and her father, Patrick, did their very best to ensure that this would be the case. The purpose of this book and its 1986 predecessor is to redress the balance somewhat, though this may appear a little disrespectful to Charlotte and her father. Not so, however, to Emily Brontë, whose major work, *Wuthering Heights,* and her poems mark her out as an extremely unusual spirit, who observed Yorkshire without becoming integrated there. When one of her Irish uncles visited Haworth, the youngest sister, Anne, said she would like to come 'home' with him to Ireland.

Discovering the Irish background is not easy. As well as penetrating the reserve of Charlotte and Patrick, we shall need to rely for a consistent narrative on an author who sometimes romanticised and didn't quote precisely all his sources: Dr William Wright. Nevertheless, we shall find him most unwarrantably attacked for fleshing out his account imaginatively. He is a priceless witness, despite flaws.

At the end of the nineteenth century there was, unfortunately, a determined effort to keep the Brontës as Yorkshire regional novelists, as indeed in part they were; but not wholly. Some of their ideas and attitudes, and perhaps even storylines, can be traced to eighteenth- and nineteenth-century Ireland.

The question that will be explored in this book is what exactly was the Brontë heritage from Ireland? Can we know anything for certain about the sisters' grandparents? Do we have information about their uncles and aunts? What kind of milieu was that in which Patrick grew up in the County Down of the late eighteenth century? Was Patrick's father really a 'peasant'?

How much did the Brontë sisters and Branwell know about their family past? How did Patrick come to be a clergyman in the Church of England? Is it possible to probe even further back and discover an ancestry that Patrick himself in his terse remarks to the biographer Mrs Gaskell hints at? It will be suggested that Patrick was an extraordinary, forceful person (he honourably called himself an 'eccentrick'), who inherited his character from both parents, but in particular from his own father, Hugh. His power was in turn inherited by his daughters and his eccentricity by at least one of them. Though of course they also inherited characteristics from their Cornish mother, the basis of their fire and single-mindedness was transmitted – in part perhaps even genetically – from the paternal line. So may have been the artistic and verbal versatility, but mercurial temperament, of brother Branwell.

This exploration, then, is only partly literary. By trying to understand the social as well as the cultural background of the Irish Brontës, we may be able to come closer to the influences which, though living in Yorkshire, the younger generation felt intensely. We can see them in somewhat the same light as today's immigrants from the Asian sub-continent, torn between the assumptions of their parental heritage and the world they now live in. Patrick Brontë strove to be English, but never rid himself of an Irishness which was palpable; this is perhaps one reason why he didn't fulfil his full potential. He wanted to be active in politics, but to do so meant rejecting those parts of his own background. His energy demanded outlets, but his status as 'perpetual curate' militated against his ambition. His hopes were only fulfilled by his daughters. This book will try to explain why some of these things were so.

The reconstruction of this Irish milieu of the eighteenth and nineteenth centuries is not easy, but it is fascinating. Irish readers will need to be a little patient while their history is explored for the benefit of readers from other backgrounds. There may be a temptation to remark, 'Of course we know that!', but readers from England and beyond may not. Those who know the Brontë works may love their authors with a passion or may be objectively evaluating their work. In either case the Irish background requires illumination. Patrick Brontë seems to have decided that it was useless to try to explain his early life (about a quarter of his whole life span, in fact) to his adopted countrymen, and so suppressed almost all his story. But if in the twenty-first century we want to understand the minds of the family members, we must unveil what he and Charlotte wanted to leave veiled.

SOUTH DOWN IN THE LATE EIGHTEENTH CENTURY

In order to understand Patrick Brontë's character and his later attitudes, it is useful to begin with the historical, cultural and social background of the area where he grew up. The obstacles are formidable. Not only did many historic records perish in the Four Courts fire of 1922, but records were sparse in the first place. It is often supposed that the early registers of Drumballyroney church were lost, but it is not certain there were any.[1] From time to time the government sought to discover the social and religious make-up of various Irish districts, but these enquiries were not consistent. The native Irish Catholic population was not frequently noticed except statistically.

The following records do survive:

Drumballyroney church registers after 1779
Names of 'freeholders' from about 1780
Glascar Presbyterian Church registers from 1780
A list of growers of flax who qualified for spinning wheel subsidies in 1796
Accounts of the Battle of Ballynahinch in 1798

Apart from these, we have to rely, with caution, on documents produced in the early part of the nineteenth century. Among these are the early Ordnance Survey maps and Ordnance Survey 'Memoirs'. These give a good account of the situation in the 1830s and sometimes note historic details gathered from the local population. Two other important sources, which need to be used with care but can contribute a good deal, are the 'Tithe Applotment' (in the case of the Brontë area dating from 1827/8) and the much later but exhaustive Griffith's 'Valuation', which was based on the newly produced accurate maps of the Ordnance Survey.

One of the difficulties we need to overcome is the matter of names. Ireland was divided into counties, but also 'baronies', parishes and townlands.

The concept of 'manors' was also introduced, with manor courts and dues, but the boundaries of these manors do not coincide with parishes. Parishes were based on Church of Ireland churches, but the Church of Ireland, though influential in the life of Patrick Brontë, was not much of a reality in the lives of the population. It had power, but in some places few adherents. Patrick was born in the townland of Imdel, parish of Drumballyroney, near the boundary with Aghaderg parish, townland of Ballynaskeagh, and divided from it by a brook. To make matters more confusing, the family moved from one to the other. A further issue comes in the closeness of Annaclone parish (variously spelt), which borders Ballynaskeagh and Lisnacreevy to the north.

In Pender's 'census' of Ireland in 1659, there were no Scots in 'Glascermore', Ballynaskeagh or Imdel townlands, but in Derrydrummuck Scots and English outweighed native Irish 23:13.[2] We have no figures at all for the late eighteenth century, but the Ordnance Survey Memoirs of the 1830s consider that there are roughly equal numbers of Catholics and Presbyterians in Aghaderg parish.

Much of the land in the Brontë area had been owned by the Magennis family until 1615. (Quite surprisingly, we shall see in an appendix that some of them remained into the nineteenth century, near Hilltown.) In the eighteenth century large tracts were still in the hands of major landowners, who let it to quite substantial tenants; they in turn sub-let. The major landowners were often Church of Ireland, as were some of the lower tenants, but the majority of the lower tenants were Presbyterian. However, some Catholics were on this rung of the social ladder. Agriculture was far and away the most frequent source of subsistence, but linen production was also very important, the spinners initially spinning with wheels that had to be turned by hand. Some farms were very small as holdings could be divided on a parent's death. Landlords in the Prunty area do not seem to have been especially oppressive but they would of course have directed affairs in their own interest. For example, the Hill family (later the Marquises of Downshire) planted a new village in Clonduff parish in the late 1760s, named Hilltown, which will later become a part of the Brontë story. Into this town they introduced Catholic spinners to stimulate the flax trade.

The population was far from homogeneous. There had been a little intermarriage and some conversions from one branch of Christianity to another, but on the whole the Scots remained Presbyterian, the native Irish remained Catholic, and the English remained Church of Ireland. Socially, the boundaries were blurred, but there could be violent clashes between one group and another.

This matter looms large in the Brontë story. William Wright instanced the infamous brawl at Dolly's Brae near Rathfriland in 1849. From a Westminster point of view, they were all Irish and everyone except some of the Church of Ireland members seems to have felt disadvantaged. Patrick Brontë (still 'Prunty') began life in this disadvantaged group.

Part of South
Down, based
on the 1899
OS plan, with
authorial
additions.

Towns were important as markets. Banbridge was a trading point, with its linen market, post office, and bridge over the River Bann. Here Patrick Prunty brought his finished linen webs to Clibborns' factory. Rathfriland (often 'Rathfryland' in earlier documents) was another nearby market town, and a meeting place of roads. Further off, and a likely place to find employment, was Newry. There was little possibility of transport other than by walking, and it seems most probable that when Patrick went to Banbridge he would have walked there (though we have no evidence). Many years later he said he had been accustomed to walk 40 miles in a day. Horses enter the Prunty story at the time of Patrick's father Hugh's marriage, perhaps indicating that the McClorys, into whose orbit Hugh introduced himself, were rather above the lowest status. We shall later find Patrick in possession of a few books, but it is impossible to say where he acquired them. We know he borrowed some from the Presbyterian Samuel Barber, whose influence on Patrick we shall look at later. Even now Imdel is sometimes thought of as 'remote'; we have to see it in the 1780s as a backwater. We have no direct evidence as to the leisure activities of the population in the eighteenth century, but will try to make informed guesses at a later stage. An account of the diversions of the people in North Down dating from 1752 mentions dancing 'in the village, or in farmhouses, where, in imitation of their superiors, they keep up the revel from eight or nine in the evening until daybreak'.[3]

The name 'Imdel' is ancient and unusual. It has now been influenced by the English 'dale', but records up to the beginning of the nineteenth century, and particularly the very early versions, show an initial I. A discussion of the name can be found in *Place Names of Northern Ireland, Vol. VI*. Most of the Imdel population lived in single-storey houses. These could be quite substantial, being built of stone, but there may have been some less firm houses which were partly or wholly made of mud. As elsewhere in Ireland, they were isolated, not in villages but strung along lanes or in fields. They had two or four rooms. Heat was obtained by burning peat from bogs, a habit which Patrick kept up in Haworth. Food was mainly potatoes with stirabout and milk, with some bacon when the pig was ready. All groups seem to have drunk whiskey freely, a point which needs to be kept in mind when we assess the truth of the allegations that Patrick drank it at Haworth.

2

WILLIAM WRIGHT, PRESBYTERIAN

As has been said, we would know little about the Irish background of the Brontës if it had not been for William Wright's *The Brontës in Ireland*. Wright was born and lived his early life in the 'Brontë Homeland'. He knew some of the Brontë family personally and had seen others; for example, he mentions seeing a later generation mending roads, with 'Brontë' painted on their carts. He was close to the Presbyterians in whose school Patrick taught and he talked with some of Patrick's pupils. However, Wright was a romanticiser, and embroidered his story with imaginative detail which cannot be substantiated, as he had been taught by his tutor, William McAllister. This does not invalidate his main very precious evidence about the life of Patrick's father Hugh and the Prunty brothers and sisters. Elsie Harrison is most misleading when she writes, 'One Brontë enthusiast, named Wright, did indeed go to Ireland to rake over the ashes of the Brontë legend, but he turned up so confused a medley that, to the historian, his work seemed worthless'.[1] Wright had no need to go to Ireland; he lived there for many years in the same area as the Brontës. Clement Shorter also suggested that Wright's information came from his 'many visits' to County Down, and adds that Wright 'probably' made his researches with the Brontë novels in mind.[2] It is hard to understand why Harrison and other commentators such as Angus MacKay and J.D. Ramsden who attacked Wright did not check out his background. There are indeed problems with Wright's work, but these attacks strike one as being biased and ill-informed.

William Wright was born on 15 January 1837 at Finard or Finnards, about $3\frac{1}{2}$ miles (two intervening townlands) from Patrick Brontë's birthplace. His later relative, Uel Wright, gives details of his descent and life in his 1986 lecture to the Presbyterian Historical Society.[3] The Wrights were emigrants from Scotland in the seventeenth century, among others who settled in the neighbourhood of Finard. Uel Wright quotes William as saying 'No people on earth slaved so hard as the Irish tenant farmers. They worked early and late. Their wives and daughters and little children rose with the sun and laboured the live-long day'. Wright was still a child when the Irish famine broke out and did not forget it; we shall see later that it affected even the relatively well positioned Brontës. Wright started school at Ballykeel local school in the next townland and parish of Drumgath, and was a quick and voracious reader. It is thought that he attended the Belfast Royal Academical Institution, though so far no record has surfaced. Before this he was tutored by Revd William McAllister and Revd William McCracken, both of whom are important in providing evidence about the Brontë background. Wright went on to Queen's College and, after obtaining his BA, to Belfast Presbyterian College. Licensed by the Belfast Presbytery, he was directed to Damascus and spent ten years as a missionary in the Middle East. One thing he learned there was that oral evidence of past times is not necessarily invalid. His surviving letters show a forceful, perhaps authoritarian, character. His hand was firm and his phrasing polite but determined. As has been said, he did embroider his material, but not misrepresent it. Of course he did not employ modern historical methods to check his facts, but he did not invent.

Wright was involved in translating some Hittite inscriptions, and in 1882 he was suggested for an honorary Doctorate of Divinity at Glasgow University. His sponsor was James Robertson, Professor of Oriental Languages there. Robertson quoted Professor E.H. Palmer of Cambridge regarding Wright's quick mastery of Arabic, and his facility in preaching. He had constantly been cited for his aid by the Palestine Exploration Fund. Samuel Davidson had written, 'If I was asked to recommend any English scholar to the attention of the Senators of your University, I should at once mention Mr Wright as one on whom the degree of D.D. might worthily be conferred.' He is also said to have used 'ingenious arguments' and to have been 'fearless and searching' in the cause of Bible publication.[4] Early in his book, Wright said, 'When I was a child I came into contact with the Irish Brontës, and even then I was startled by their genius, before any literary work had made their name famous in England'. Could this be true?

My insistence on probing the character and antecedents of Wright might seem fussy, if it were not for the fact that in 2015 there are still sceptics about his information. It needs to be stressed that he provides much detail that is simply unavailable elsewhere, some of which can be confirmed from documents but a good deal of which cannot. Andrew MacKay accused Wright of partisanship, referring to the prominence given to the theory of Tenant Right in his book. Wright did present Hugh Prunty as a reformer but not a revolutionary. We shall discuss whether this could be accurate in view of the attitudes and actions of some of the family and Hugh's known associates. Missionary zeal is part of the make-up of nineteenth-century Presbyterianism, and this shows itself in Wright's determination to inform the world about Brontë origins, and to gain for Ulster and Ireland credit for nurturing the Brontë genius.

The next stage in our hunt for Brontë antecedents is to try to trace those who informed Wright and interested him in the Brontës in the first place. Wright's father was a farmer in the townland of Finnards, part of the large parish of Newry. It is likely, but not certain, that the family worshipped at Ryans Presbyterian Church, a record of which existed from 1826, but which was rebuilt in 1840. Wright's father seems to have been prosperous enough to employ a nurse, whom Wright describes as 'a close relative of Kaly Nesbit'; she had lived 'within a quarter of a mile' of the Pruntys (Wright anachronistically called them 'Brontës' throughout). We can suppose this nurse looked after William when he was 3 or 4. 'Kaly Nesbit' can be identified as Caleb Nesbit, who married a woman named Jane McKee on 13 July 1802 at Rathfriland. The Nesbits had a large holding in Imdel townland, their farm being in the same lane as the corn kiln where Patrick was born. It stretched to a point almost opposite the kiln. A girl, Margaret Nesbit, was born to Caleb and baptised at Glascar Presbyterian church on 22 May 1803; she is surely Wright's nurse. Wright had substantiated his point: his nurse was brought up across the fields from the old Prunty home, though they had moved a small distance away by the time she was born. Miss Nesbit gave Wright 'much Brontë lore', but he does not specify what she told him. For a small child, she will perhaps have tempered Hugh Prunty's stories. The point is, however, that Hugh and his exploits are shown to be well known in the locality and worth telling.[5]

Another of Wright's acquaintances while he still lived at Finnards was the Revd William McAllister (various spellings of the surname). He was the minister at Ryans from 1851. This was McAllister's second appointment after twenty-four years at Clarkesbridge, but he was coming home, since he had been born at Derrydrummuck, the next townland to Glascar, and baptised at Glascar Presbyterian church on 5 July 1801. When Wright was fourteen his parents appointed McAllister as his tutor. It is especially important to examine the McAllister family, since they provide some of the most detailed accounts of Hugh Prunty's stories. Fortunately, a study of the family in the Glascar area was carried out by Mr Henry McMaster of Holywood, County Down, one of William's descendants, who kindly sent me details of his genealogical research.[6]

William was the second son and third child of Samuel McAllister who died in 1849, his will being proved by William and his older brother, Samuel, who was of 'Derrydrummuck' and had presumably inherited the mill. According to McMaster's evidence, the elder Samuel (died 1849) mentioned here, had a brother Joseph, who had eight known children, the youngest of whom was John, baptised at Glascar in 1798. However, Glascar registers seem to give a Samuel as his father. Joseph's eldest son, Hugh, was ordained and became minister at Loughbrickland in 1804. Both John and Joseph would therefore have been cousins of William, Wright's teacher at Finnards. I am glad to update the information given in my earlier book. Tracing the McAllisters is, however, fraught with difficulties because of the constant recurrence of Christian names.

William McAllister gained a splendid reputation. He was said to be 'a little dark man of indomitable energy and a tender heart … original and good humoured and jovial … pious without being straight-laced or sanctimonious'. He was educated at the Royal Belfast Academical Institution, obtaining the Institution's General Certificate in 1824. At Ryans he was a lively controversialist, being greatly opposed to the disestablishment of the Church of Ireland. He had a lively wit; on one occasion he was seen filling a tobacco pipe by a brother minister who said, 'Mr McAllister, that tobacco is the devil's weed'. 'Then the sooner we set fire to it the better' was the reply, and William lit the pipe. One feels he would have been a lively and interesting teacher for William Wright, whom he clearly inspired with enthusiasm. His birth in 1801 may have been too late for him to hear Hugh Prunty first hand, but his father, Samuel, was an accurate source of information.

Wright mentioned as one of his sources the brothers Todd; James and John. The Todd family proliferated in Ballynaskeagh and Glascar. They had large holdings in both townlands and their Ballynaskeagh farm lay opposite that of the Nesbits. The family were Presbyterians, attending Glascar church. They had been in the parish of Aghaderg at least since 1745, when a deed provides evidence of their landholding in Ballynaskeagh. Wright did not say which of his details came from the Todds, though he mentioned them as customers of Mount Pleasant limekilns at Ballymascanlan, a parish which we shall explore as part of Hugh Prunty's life story. We can take it as certain that they heard him narrating in the kiln cottage in the 1780s.

Another informant was Hugh Norton, who was a member of Glascar congregation, born about 1803. His daughter Jane is recorded as marrying on 12 January 1856, though it is not certain that she was baptised at Glascar, since there is no record of it. His other children were baptised there in the 1830s. Hugh occupied a small house near the sluice, on land held by the later minister of the church, David McKee. He also had a part to play in describing the Prunty/Brontë family, but he did not meet Hugh and his testimony mainly concerns the younger generation.

Another informant who knew about the character of the young Patrick was William John McCracken, a contemporary of Wright's, who was baptised at Glascar in 1836. We shall need to consult his memories at a later stage, when we consider the early life of Patrick. So far we have been concentrating on explaining the sources of Wright's information about the life and narratives of Hugh Prunty.

Much is made in *The Brontës in Ireland* of information given to Wright by Revd David McKee, minister of First Annaghlone Presbyterian church, who lived and held land at Ballynaskeagh. He was another energetic resident, who impressed his neighbours and many others with his character. He was sympathetic to the cause of the 1798 uprising, and was living at the time near Ballynahinch, the site of a well-known battle, at which we shall also find a member of the Prunty family. The Revd W. Dobbin wrote of him:

> David McKee was the friend of liberty, the stern foe of oppression and injustice. He believed that God made the earth for the children of men, and not exclusively for feudal absolutism. His sympathies were accordingly with the people. We find him visiting the insurgent camp the night before the Ballynahinch fight, and looking with interest on the stern men who were ready to risk their lives for what they considered to be the welfare of their native land …[7]

McKee arrived in Ballynaskeagh in 1804. It is not certain that he knew Hugh or Patrick Prunty personally, and Wright did not allege this. He farmed as well as held his post at Annaghlone, saying to one of his neighbours, 'If you would thrash a little and dig a little it would do you good'. He was on good terms with the local Catholic priest. He was a subscriber to the novels of Sir Walter Scott as they came out. Very aware of the Classical tradition, he produced vigorous oral versions of Homer's *Iliad* and taught a Classical curriculum to pupils at his manse across the fields from the Prunty residences. We can be quite sure Wright reported him accurately, as he married McKee's daughter Annie. Patrick's brothers would visit him at times, and certainly consulted him about a copy of *Jane Eyre* sent to them from Haworth. After her husband's death, Mrs McKee emigrated to New Zealand, but Wright was in touch with his mother-in-law when he wrote *The Brontës in Ireland*, and we shall examine a letter which she sent confirming her late husband's knowledge of the Brontës and of Hugh Prunty's 'yarns'.

As we shall see, criticism of Wright's work began almost as soon as it was published. It was not only that critics wished to relocate Charlotte in particular to England, as she herself would have wished, but also that they discerned what they saw as a political bias in the sections where Wright discussed Hugh Prunty's alleged political philosophy. This political view also surfaced in his accounts of the Harshaws and their relations with the Martin family, and perhaps also Samuel Barber. J.D. Ramsden, for example, dislikes Presbyterianism itself as anti-establishment and therefore deals with it in the context of bitter controversy over the issue of Home Rule. Later commentators had no idea how closely Wright was bound up with the 'Brontë Homeland' and didn't wish to find out. They followed the lead of Patrick and Charlotte in disregarding the Irish connection, regarding it as toxic. More recently Banbridge Council and other Northern Irish authorities have advertised this connection, but unfortunately sources of evidence were lost in the early days, perhaps sometimes due to the local feeling that any interviews given would be misconstrued.

But Wright's book cannot be sidelined. He had faults which undermine his narrative. One is his insistence in the first edition that the name of the family was always 'Brontë'. In later editions he retreated from this but not very firmly. Another error was to believe too literally Patrick's assertion that Hugh had come from 'the south'. Again, Wright realised too late that as a little boy Hugh had probably had a home in the north. He relied quite properly on his informants at Glascar, Ballynaskeagh and elsewhere near the Pruntys' home, but didn't search enough for dates to enable us to check his work. During his research in the Boyne Valley, undertaken about 1860, he seems to have confined his survey too tightly to the banks of the river.

All these points are to be taken into consideration, and they are unfortunate. But they do not undermine Wright's extremely valuable work, which has never been given the credit it deserves.

PUBLICATION AND CONTROVERSY

Wright was living in Norwood as he completed his work on the Irish Brontës. He first published an account in *McClure's Magazine* for 1893, then turned it into book form. It is not clear how often he visited Ireland but he did return to Ballynaskeagh in 1870-1 to visit his father-in-law at the manse.[1] By this time he would have known about the fame of the Brontë sisters, and would surely have recognised that he had unusual quali-fications for adding to the story of their background. It is odd that he didn't collect more material at this time, but it may be that some of the details he gave in his book actually came from that visit. Wright's wife, Annie McKee, died in 1877, leaving him with five children, by which time the family lived in London. He married again, and seems to have spent much time attending to business connected with the Presbyterian Church. We do not know what stimulated him to begin writing down his account of the Brontës, but he made contact with several clergyman in County Down, and they seem to have been the suppliers of information during the 1880s. In particular he acknowledged the help of Revd H.W. Lett, rector of Aghaderg, and Revd J.B. Lusk, min-ister at Glascar. Wright claimed that he had written down Brontë details in his youth. There is no reason to dispute this, but we do not know how far he still had access to these writings when he came to write more formally about the family.

The Revd John Brown Lusk was ordained in 1889 and was minister at Glascar for fifty years. His memorial tablet in the church records his humor-ous talk, his charity and loving kindness. He was able to talk confidingly to many of the residents of Glascar, Ballynaskeagh and Imdel. He confirmed much of what Wright had to say, though he was a little hampered by the reserve of the Brontë descendants, perhaps including Alice Brontë herself, the only one of Patrick's siblings still alive when Wright was finalising his book. The fame of Charlotte and the other sisters exercised an influence on the picture they wished to paint of the Brontë family in the late eighteenth and early nineteenth centuries, though these were very different ages. There was no such reserve in other residents. Lusk made notes which have been lost, but much of their substance passed into Wright's account and subsequent minor contributions.

An important addition to their publication was made in 1918, when an anonymous writer calling himself 'Shebna the Scribe' wrote to the *Irish Churchman* and this letter was reprinted in the *Banbridge Chronicle,* adding to Lusk's previous comments.[2] 'Shebna's' letter is addressed from Slieve Croob, the high hill north of Castlewellan, overlooking the plain where the Brontës lived. 'Shebna' wished to modify the poor view of Wright's book which had by then become prevalent, following the interventions of MacKay, Ramsden, Horsfall Turner and others, including Sir Robertson Nicoll, who dismissed Wright's account as 'legendary'. 'Shebna' was still in contact with Lusk, who summarised matters by saying 'I have no doubt that old Hugh … told the story of his life and family history – if not with the completeness which Dr Wright has given – at any rate in its main features'. 'Shebna' was a pseudonym for the Revd William Shaw Kerr, a committed Unionist, who was incumbent at Seapatrick (Banbridge) from 1915 to 1932. Elements of his evidence will be given, with acknowledgement, in this book. There is no doubt that both Lett and Lusk worked hard at a matter that interested them, but Alice was the only Brontë sibling left, and even she died on 15 January 1891, aged 95. It also has to be remembered that she was more than fifteen years Patrick's junior, and could not have known first-hand about his early experiences. She had not been alive during the days when he had lived in the 'Brontë kiln' and heard his father's lively presentations of his life story.

Alice's evidence told to Lusk, and recorded in note form in his lost notebook went as follows:

Her father [was] from Drogheda. Stout, not very tall. [Her brothers] Welsh and Hugh [were] great fighters. Neighbours drew them into quarrels.
Her father['s?] slave, followed making ditches. [Her father] Hugh built all the house. Patrick born in Emdale. The rest in Lisnacreevy. Alice born in Ballynaskeagh. One sister died[;] a day's illness.
Father very fond of family. Mad about his 'own childer'. Wrought to the last for them. Mother died after father. Counted very purty [pretty]. Minister of Magnally [*sic*] said when they were going out Prettiest couple ever married.
Father had but one girl.
Father sandy haired. Mother fair haired. At her best before her father died.
Patrick kept school at Glasker Hill. In Meeting House she thinks. (Alice at a wee sod school house. School master has to get meat and lodgings in the houses).

In very young days went to Drumballyroney Church. All christened & all
buried there.

Patrick taught school in old John Rogers['] time. Andy Harshaw taught in
Ballynafern. Jamie [one of Hugh's sons] saw Charlotte [Brontë] said she
was terrible sharp and inquisitive. 'That she was for nothing but ornamenting a parlour.' Charlotte asked about the Knock Hill and Lough Neagh.
(Patrick tallest[;] Hughy & Welsh nearly the same height.)

Ann [Brontë], the youngest, wanted to come home with Jamie. Jamie thought
it queer that she called Ireland home. Charlotte fainted in the theatre.
Terrible troubled with a sore head.

Alice lived in Ballynaskeagh till they were all dead & left her (marching
Lisnacreevy: only river between her house and Lisna).

Mother's maiden name Alice McClory[;] born about Ballynaskeagh.
An uncle (of her father) took her father when he was 8 years old to make
him his heir. But after he went his wife had a child then her father 'left'
and never saw them or his mother again. His sister however came to see
him. 'Tarrible purty she was.' Shop keeper in Rathfriland courted her but
she would not have him.

Miss Gregg from Lisburn (a gentlewoman) came to see Miss Alice Brontë and
wanted to push on her nephew Nelus. 'Wanted him for a man.'

Brothers had a great fight with the bully of Warrenpoint; Bab Wilson raised
fight. Welsh took his part. Hughey away and when he came back he vaun-
tered any man (Barney Ker the bully. Mother's name Ker in Warrenpoint).

Hughey very stout hearted. Rose up at 12 or 1 o'clock to haunted place. Took
gun or sword in one hand & the Bible.

(First published in Christopher Heywood's 'A Brontë Narrative: Hugh Brontë's Tale
of Welsh', *Durham University Journal*, July 1995)

All this evidence is of course priceless, but some of it is only fleshed out in the
stories Hugh told in the corn kiln or perhaps at other later gatherings where Alice
was not present. No one else of Alice's generation survived to be interviewed,
and other traditions replace 'eight' by 'six'. Fixing Hugh's date of birth is in any
case problematic. There is a reference in the article by Christopher Heywood to
an alleged note by Colin Johnston Robb (now lost) which refers to a record of him
in an 1821 census. This census for Ballynaskeagh was destroyed in the 1922 fire at
the Public Records Office in Dublin, but there are some indications that Johnston
Robb had seen a copy before this, giving Hugh's age as 71. This is a not unlikely
date, and I am prepared to accept it.[3] We can be fairly certain therefore that he
was born in 1750. Alice is not recorded as having said much about her other siblings, though this may be due to her evidence having disappeared. Her brothers,

apart from Patrick, were William, Hugh, James and Walsh or Welsh, and the sisters Jane, Mary, Rose, Sarah and Alice.

Before examining testimony which became public after Wright's book was published, we need to look at two attacks which were made on it. These were by Angus MacKay and J.D. Ramsden.

Angus MacKay was an important contributor to the *Westminster Review*, a paper which had begun as an anti-Whig radical medium, but was perhaps losing the radical stance by this time.

We do, however, have to remember the political situation in Ireland and the rest of the United Kingdom in the 1890s. In the General Election of 1892 Gladstone's Home Rulers, 274 British and 81 Irish were elected, against 269 Conservatives and 46 Liberal Unionists. MacKay and Ramsden, both anti-Home Rule, found very distasteful attitudes in Wright's book and this coloured their opinions of the rest of Wright's work, meaning that neither would examine the book dispassionately.

MacKay began his attack in a *Westminster Review* article, 'A Crop of Brontë Myths'. His attack was fierce and generalised: 'Surely nothing but the improbabilities are necessary to expose the falsity of this so-called history' (p. 427); 'To read Wright's book is like being in a dream, nothing surprises' (p. 429). These comments and others are supported by chronological calculations which are hazardous. To some extent Wright had only himself to blame because of his wish to fill out imaginatively some of the material he gathered, but MacKay was a partisan critic who saw a Presbyterian background as hostile to the establishment of the Church of England and Ireland (which indeed it often was) and widened his disfavour to include Wright's romanticised but essentially truthful account. MacKay later wrote an enlarged critique in *The Brontës: Fact and Fiction*.

J.D. Ramsden is a slightly different critic, since he actually went to County Down to explore. He crossed the Irish Sea in a stormy passage and made his way to Loughbrickland, then along what is now the B3 to Ballynaskeagh and Imdel. He talked to a Patrick McClory in Loughbrickland, who claimed some kinship with the McClorys of Ballynaskeagh but added nothing to the Brontë story. Entering Ballynaskeagh, Wright discovered two sisters related to the Brontës, one of whom, though he did not name her, was presumably Maggie Shannon, a grandniece of Patrick brothers. Ramsden saw similarities to the Brontë sisters in her looks. In Imdel he explored the surroundings of the Brontës and heard stories of the brothers and their exploits. He found a resident to tell him that Wright's account was 'nearly all lies'. The story of Hugh's upbringing by 'Welsh', and his escape, which we shall soon examine in detail, was dismissed as '[P]ure assumption, repudiated with indignation by the surviving race and other reliable authorities'.[4] Ramsden did not give any names. His view was echoed by later commentators and has persisted. In Chapter VI he widened the attack, moving to

Hugh Prunty's alleged tenant-right sympathies. A specimen of his rhetoric will give a flavour of his own stance:

> [Wright] introduces his extreme Nationalist views about the Land Question, and from these extreme and imaginative cases, holds up all the Irish landlords, without a single exception, as being *fac-similes* of this chapter, [Wright's Chapter 4] which is nothing else than a bit of a novel, written for the express purpose of vomiting forth his own low ideas concerning the Irish protestant land-proprietor.

Wright did not do this. He praised the Sharman Crawford Estate particularly, but did not anywhere suggest that all landlords 'without exception' behaved like 'Welsh' and the absentee landlord he served. We shall see later that the Prunty/Brontë family lived mainly on Sharman Crawford land.

Maggie Shannon agreed that Hugh had been living in Drogheda with his sister and 'an uncle, a brother of their mother's, both parents being dead'. She also said that Hugh 'afterwards came down to the neighbourhood of Hilltown to some relatives of his mother'.[5] Her evidence is important, and needs thought. Drogheda is an important town, but the word can also include the nearby territory of the Earl of Drogheda, which stretched along the Boyne Valley to the west of the city. There is nothing inconsistent between Maggie Shannon's 'Drogheda' and Wright's Boyne Valley. She was the only witness to mention Hilltown, a clue that needs to be followed up. She stated that the 'uncle' [i.e 'Welsh'] who brought Hugh up was his 'mother's brother'. This also needs analysis, since it seems to clash with Wright's account.

Maggie Shannon had clearly heard a good deal about Hugh Prunty. A silver pencil case, which seems to have been given to Walsh by Patrick, was exhibited to Ramsden, and Wright recorded having seen it or one given to another brother. Presumably it was this souvenir which had caused Maggie to ask about Hugh's story: a family heirloom. It was seen as evidence of the visit of Hugh, Patrick's brother, to England. The precise date of this visit is hard to pin down.

Confirmation of it came from an older relative, Rose Ann Heslip, whose family had moved to Yorkshire. She had been born in 1821, the product of an alleged 'runaway marriage' between Simon Collins and Sarah Brunty (one of Patrick's sisters), and remembered that her Uncle Hugh had visited England when she was working for him.[6] She did not give a date, but confused the matter by saying it was when Hugh was 'a boy'. Since he was born in 1781 this disagrees with her statement that she was working for him at the time. We cannot unravel the matter, but linking it with Maggie Shannon's statement, we might put 1827-37 as likely parameters for the visit; the matter will be addressed again in Part II. She said Hugh had gone to help with corn-threshing and been shown Robin Hood's grave and tried on his helmet. He had also been to London and seen the queen. Which 'queen' was meant? *The* queen in 1837 is likely to have meant Queen Victoria, so we might put the visit mentioned by these two women as happening after 1837 when Victoria came to the throne. Both women gave more details about the family in the nineteenth century, which we shall examine later. Neither had heard the story of Welsh the 'wicked uncle'.

An article on Rose Anne Heslip was published by Imelda Marsden in *Brontë Studies* in 2010.[7] This was useful in two ways: it brought together magazine interviews with Rose Ann from the 1890s, and added material which had not been previously known. Her own mother, Sarah, had married 'early in life', having had seven children before Rose Ann, all of whom died young. The likely date for Sarah's marriage is about 1802, when she would have been 19. Four of these early-dying children were named after Brontë aunts (Patrick's sisters), but not in order of age, Alice being the first named. Rose Ann was the fifth to be so named, after Rose Brontë, of whom very little is known. Strangely, Rose Ann Heslip did not mention anything about her mother being Rose's twin. Rose Ann Heslip had lived with the other Brontës at or near Ballynaskeagh until about 1838. It was known in the family that Patrick had been the ambitious one, keen to get away from Ulster.

There were other small points added by Rose Ann and mentioned in local or national media at the time. Patrick had sent money each year to the family in Ballynaskeagh; we need not doubt this, as Rose Ann would have been old enough to remember these sums arriving. She also remembered stories being told about an 'aunt' of old Hugh Prunty coming to visit in County Down, bringing with her a young daughter. A Rathfriland (Rose Ann, said 'local', while Wright named the town) trader fell in love with her, but she declined his offer. There was no question of a second visit to England by Hugh, though Rose Ann added that he became ill *during*, rather than after his visit. She repeated to two reporters that Charlotte also had sent 'a present' to the Ballynaskeagh Brontës. This nowhere appears in Charlotte's correspondence.

A final point unearthed by Imelda Marsden was that 'Hugh' 'declared his intention of breaking the will of Revd Patrick Brontë, who did not leave [Ireland] in accordance with his wishes'. This appears to be a statement by Hugh, Patrick's brother, though it was to him that Patrick seems to have turned as a representative of the Irish Brontës when he wrote to them. One wonders if this tradition possibly refers to Hugh Prunty, Patrick's father, and not his brother.

A third descendant to contribute was John Brontë, a New Zealand pharmacist. He was the grandson of William Prunty, Patrick's next brother, two years younger than Patrick. John Brontë did not try to refute Wright as the two women did. He gave general assent to Wright 'on the treatment of the history of my ancestors'. This suggests that he, as a descendant of an older brother, may have heard the 'Uncle Welsh' story, whereas perhaps Alice Brontë, Maggie

Shannon and Rose Heslip had not. We cannot put much weight on this point, but at least John Brontë did not deny Wright. He had much to say about his grandfather's escapade in the 1798 rebellion, which we shall examine later. He was concerned to refute any notion that the Brontës of Ballynaskeagh were superstitious: they were 'a peculiar family ... quite different from the ordinary folk in intellectual grasp'. James, for example, had denied the existence of fairies, saying 'Fairies Hell! There's no such thing as fairies. All lies and superstition'. The Brontë brothers, as roadmen, took on the completion of a road through a 'forth' after a previous contractor had died on the job supposedly through supernatural agency. While none of the exploits of the later nineteenth-century Brontës, as opposed to the information the Brontë sisters received from their father about the Prunty past, could affect the sisters' work, we shall look at some of this material as illustrating the character of some of the Brontë relatives.

In 1897, a Yorkshire writer, J. Horsfall Turner, collected Patrick Brontë's work under the title *Brontëana* and published this corpus with an account of the Brontë family based on a journey to Ballynaskeagh and talks with Rose Heslip. This was a rather more balanced contribution than those of Ramsden and MacKay, providing us with a little more background data, and it was well presented. Details based on his interviews will be given in the appropriate pages below.

4

THE FAMILY HISTORY
ACCORDING TO WRIGHT

It will be important to try to discover how the Brontë sisters at Haworth learned anything about their Irish background. For the moment we shall try to establish what there was to know. This material divides into two parts: their own father's life after he was born in Imdel, and their grandfather's life before that. The current chapter begins to describe and discuss the second matter. First we need to look at what Wright said, stripping away probable embroideries.

He said of William McAllister, '[H]e had often heard … Hugh, the grandfather of Charlotte, narrate to a spellbound audience the incidents which formed the groundwork of *Wuthering Heights.*'

There are again two parts to Hugh Prunty's story, both of which rely on his veracity. One of these parts deals with Hugh's own life, the other with what he heard about events which occurred before he was born or when he was too young to be aware of them. We shall look first at Wright's account of Hugh's story of his own life, avoiding for the moment ways of checking on its accuracy.

Hugh apparently said that he had grown up with a 'large' family of brothers and sisters. His home was many miles from the Boyne Valley, where he later lived. Since Wright gave details of his journey away from his original home to the Boyne, it should be possible to work out how far this was, but not very accurately. For a long while, Wright thought the original home was in the 'south', but he later changed his mind and decided it was in the north. Hugh said that at about the age of 8, he was visited by an uncle and an aunt, who proposed to take him back with them to the Boyne, where they lived. They promised he could then 'spend his life among ponies and dogs, and ramble through orchards and among flowers, and fish for trout in the River Boyne and be a great scholar'. These promises are not quite so generalised as may appear. We might particularly note the last; to be 'a great scholar' (a point to which I shall refer later on a number of occasions). The picture painted here of ponies, etc., implies that

Welsh was promising a life on an 'Ascendancy' estate (an estate leased or owned by members of the Anglo-Irish hierarchy).

Hugh agreed to go with them, and the journey began, in a cart, on an evening in early autumn (this can be deduced from the blooming heather and rising sun). It was to take four days. Assuming the cart was moving at about 2 to 2½ miles per hour, this would mean that distance between this northern home and the Boyne was about 100 miles, very roughly.

No sooner had they left Hugh's home than the demeanour of the uncle changed; he now acted roughly to Hugh, knocking him about and shouting at him. This attitude continued all the way. Hugh's 'fearful journey' is detailed. The cart travelled all night. Hugh woke early and looked over the side of the cart:

> On the west rose a mountain abloom with heather. The rising sun shone upon it, and gave a golden tint to the ruby heath. On the east, bordered by the sea, stretched a level plain: Crows flew overhead, wheatears on the rocks flashed their white-ringed tails … but the land was desolate. Even the track … could scarcely be called a road. (p. 41)

Wheatears are migratory, leaving Ireland for the winter. (Of course, this may be an addition by Wright.) Most Irish roads in 1758 were 'tracks'.

Hugh fell asleep again. He woke again when the sun was 'hot'. The cart was drawn up near a cottage which sold apples but was also a 'public house'. A blacksmith's forge was opposite, and the smith lifted him from the cart. They were about to talk together when the aunt came out of the shop and led Hugh into it. He was allowed to buy some food with money his family had given him. He then went to sleep by the kitchen fire until late in the afternoon. As evening fell, bringing rain, they all went back to the cart and spent the night in the rain, splashing through muddy puddles. Next morning they arrived at a 'large village'. Here was an inn of considerable importance. So ended the second night.

Hugh was given some bread and milk, and put to bed in a small room at the inn. Interestingly, his new clothes were taken off him and he was given 'a suit of green corduroy with shining brass buttons'. After another night's travel, they reached another 'large town' with an inn. Thus ended the third night. Here Hugh tried to tell the innkeeper his story, but 'the man could not comprehend what he said, and he could not understand what the man said *owing to the brogue'* (my italics). A crowd gathered and Hugh was beginning to make himself understood when the uncle appeared and whisked him into the cart again. Here he stayed until nightfall, when the next part of the journey began. After the night passed, they arrived at Drogheda. Wright named this town, but we do not know whether this was Hugh's own information. There was a short pause before the cart went on to the Boyne 'home' 'on the banks of the Boyne'.

There is a great deal to consider here, since this is the major contribution to the solution of the location of Hugh's real home. We need to ask whether this journey can be put into geographical context. To begin with, there is little doubt that the near town must be Drogheda. It is possible that Hugh named it, but even if he didn't, there are no other likely candidates. If the journey was from the 'south' the cart would have passed Dublin on the way to Drogheda. The previous town with the inn and the 'crowd' must be Dundalk. The third night, then, was from a 'large village' with an inn to Dundalk. I propose Ballybay as this 'large village', though this is not a certainty. The first stop is much harder to locate: perhaps Belturbet, possibly Ballyhaise.

Could Wright have made all this up? We shall soon follow him into an account of what happened to Hugh after he arrived at the Boyne Valley, and discover an independent account confirming and adding to what he had to report. The detail in this is no more complex than the account of the journey, so we may accept that Hugh did tell this story, and that he had a number of attentive listeners. If we accept that day three ended at Dundalk, could the geography of the first three days lead us anywhere else but towards Monaghan and Fermanagh? This is where we need to turn to demographic evidence concerning the distribution of the name Prunty.

Why couldn't Hugh make himself understood in front of the inn at Dundalk? What did Wright mean by his comment on 'the brogue'? Wright, living in the second part of the nineteenth century, is unlikely to have thought much about the Irish language. He sought a reason why Hugh's language was unintelligible and used the word 'brogue'. But in 1758, there would have been a range of speakers of either Irish or English. My suggestion is that the Dundalk innkeeper was an English speaker and Hugh spoke only Irish at that time of his life. There will be more to say about the language issue, but for now I think we can be sure that the problem of understanding indicates more than a difference of accent between the north of County Louth and somewhere in mid-Ulster.

We now need to examine other matters which arise from the description of the journey given by Wright. I have already suggested that any journey from the south would have meant passing or going through Dublin. Perhaps a more cogent argument arises from the distribution of the name Prunty. Evidence comes from Hearth Tax rolls, cited by Edward McLysaght in *More Irish Families*.[1] He traces the name in County Monaghan (O'Prounty) and Armagh (O'Prunty). This is supported by the Armagh historian T.G.F. Paterson. In Armagh manor Hugh Ó Prunty appears on a court roll in 1625. Donell Ó Prenty appears as a witness at Hockley, Armagh, in 1641-2. Paterson also finds Thomas Ó Pronty in Armagh in 1664. Also on the Hearth Money rolls are Teage Ó Pronty and Edmund Ó Pronty of Lurghaboy. Torlagh Ó Pronty was a tenant of Armagh manor in 1714. Paterson also finds Pruntys in Tyrone and one in Dungannon. He confirms McLysaght's record of

O'Prountys in Monaghan with Patrick and Philip of Carrickanare, Tullycorbet, in 1663. An Irish poet, Pádraig Ó Pronnntaigh, gave his origin in the eighteenth century as 'the Erne' (we shall look at the original Irish version later). No records of Pruntys south of this are mentioned.

Many Irish records have been lost over the years. For this reason two nineteenth-century documents are important. These are the Tithe Applotment following the Composition Act of 1823, and Griffith's 'Valuation', published between 1847 and 1864.[2] These two registered virtually all holders of land, including houses, mills, schools, churches, etc. They do not constitute a census, since they exclude people who hold no land at all, and do not give family relations. Nevertheless, they give a generally accurate picture of the population in the nineteenth century, so that we can see where people with the name Prunty/Brunty lived at that time. Incidences of the name almost all occur in a band from the north of County Cavan, along the Erne Valley in Fermanagh, through Monaghan and Armagh. There are some examples in Longford and Roscommon, but here the name begins to change towards Printy and Prenty. It is clear that the name is not native to County Down, nor to anywhere south of wider Ulster.

Scattered fragments of the 1821 and later censuses do exist, partly because they were copied by scholars or by chance. Such is the Forkhill census of 1821, which survives in what seems to be a copy made before it was submitted. These fragments are enough to give us some demographic help in discovering, for example, Christian names given to children from different religious backgrounds. We shall be examining the name 'Hugh' to support the conclusion that he was born in Fermanagh. Even by the 1860s, Pruntys were found in Loughgall, Armagh. Young Hugh's journey, however, cannot have been from Loughgall, since it would not have taken four days from there to Drogheda, in the way Hugh's account records. It is hard to see how the journey can have been from another area where Pruntys survived through the nineteenth century into the twentieth, to appear both in Griffith's 'Valuation' and the 1901 census; the neighbourhood of Rosslea in the east of County Fermanagh. This district has its attractions, especially since the name Hugh is also recorded there, but I cannot square a journey from Rosslea with the sight of the 'sea' (surely a lake) on the first morning. We must, therefore, look more closely at the Erne Valley itself.

5

SEARCHING THE ERNE DISTRICT OF FERMANAGH

L et us first summarise the reasons why the search for Brontë (Prunty) origins is concentrated on the Erne Valley.

(A) There are no Pruntys recorded outside wider Ulster (a few in Longford/ Roscommon). There are no Pruntys in Antrim, Derry or Donegal.

(B) Hugh's journey was of four days, on the last of which he arrived at the Boyne via Drogheda, and the day before almost certainly ended in Dundalk.

(C) After the first night he awoke and thought the sun was rising over the sea. It could not have been the sea, and must have been a large lake.

(D) Large lakes could include Lough Neagh, but from here it would not have taken two days to Dundalk. It must have been Lough Erne. From Lower Lough Erne it would probably have taken more than two days to Dundalk. We cannot rule out Lower Lough Erne, but probability is against it; Upper Lough Erne is more likely.

Seeking information for the mid-eighteenth century in Fermanagh is difficult since very few documents from that time still survive. In particular, references to the native Irish population, most of whom were Catholics, simply do not exist except sometimes for statistical purposes. The Pruntys seem to fall into this category. In 1796 the government, wishing to encourage flax growing, provided subsidies for small farmers who would plant flax in an area of their farms. No Pruntys appear on these lists. The British Government wished to rationalise the system of tithes, or Church taxes, in the 1820s. In Ireland, records kept are called the Tithe Applotment. Here the Pruntys of Fermanagh appear for the first time, sixty years or more after Hugh Prunty was taken from his 'comfortable home'. The likelihood that his family would still be occupying exactly the same land as in 1758 is possible if dubious, though Irish tenants were very tenacious of their farms and localities.

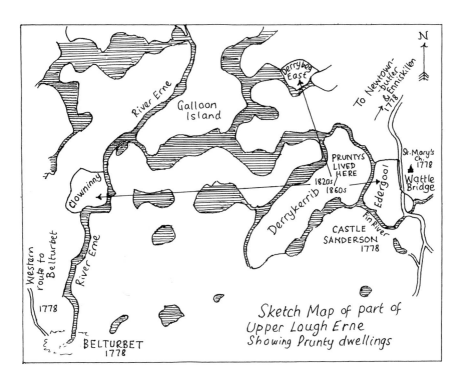

Sketch map of Upper Lough Erne (authorial, including information from Taylor & Skinner and later OS maps).

Griffith's 'Valuation' gives further information, locating Prunty land in the 1860s. We may compare these two lists, expecting that the more detailed Griffith list will supplement the Tithe Applotment. First and second names are given in both lists, and there should be some carry-over.

If there is continuity between the lists, possibly the land held in the 1820s was also held in the 1750s. Nothing can make this certain, but we can regard this as a hypothesis. We may start then, with the Tithe Applotment, concentrating on the parishes in the Erne Valley. Any other Pruntys in Fermanagh but outside the Erne Valley may or may not be connected.

The Tithe Applotment reveals three Pruntys. They are Thomas Pruntey, in Lisseneal, parish of Aghalurcher (1833); Charles Prunty, Derrybeg East, parish of Galloon (1834); Thomas Prunty, Nulfield (an error for Nutfield), parish of Aghavea (1832). On the island townland of Derrykerrib lived a Prunty Maguire (1828). We can follow some of these to Griffith.

Griffith's 'Valuation' provides us with six Pruntys: Edward, in Drumbrughas North, perhaps a descendant of Thomas of Lisseneal; James in Derrybeg East, probably a son of Charles; Thomas in Rockfield, Galloon parish, near Donagh; Hugh (interestingly) at Drumad near Lisbellaw and (again interestingly) John and

Patrick respectively at Edergool and Derrykerrib (adjacent townlands). A John also farmed land in Derrykerrib; he is perhaps the same John as in Edergool.

Exactly how all these Pruntys were related is impossible to tell; in fact their connection may be several generations back. One other small point is that Derrybeg East is very near Derrykerrib, and James farmed the whole town-land and even leased property to his next-door neighbour. The Derrykerrib/Derrybeg East/Edergool neighbourhood is worth a closer look.

Adjacent to the Prunty land in Griffith's 'Valuation' was land farmed by Margaret Maguire. This strengthens the evidence to suggest that Pruntys and Maguires are related, and we may think Prunty Maguire was so named after his mother or an ancestor. Use of a surname as a Christian name is very rare in these lists. Of 1,579 names I have examined on the Census, Tithe and Griffith's lists in Fermanagh, Cavan and Louth there are only nine with this type of name. They all seem to be Scots or English: Prunty Maguire is the only native Irish example in the whole number.[1] Both John and Patrick, perhaps also James, may have been his in-laws. There was clearly a family of Pruntys not rich, but well enough off to be renting farmland, including the whole townland of Derrybeg East; they were a family which wished to preserve the family name. There are several strange matters to be linked to this small area of the Upper Erne, but before we look at them, we have to face a problem: Hugh's early home cannot have been at Derrykerrib, since apparently he did not recognise the Erne as a lake, but as 'the sea'. Added to which, a journey from Derrykerrib would not have produced the profile of the journey detailed by Wright.

We need to look here at one of the 'strange circumstances' I have just men-tioned. In 1894, a Mr Henry Barcroft of the Glen, Newry, wrote to William Wright supporting his view that the Brontë (Prunty) origin was in the north.[2] Mr Barcroft had been at Wattle Bridge, in the townland of Edergool, looking for a river pilot. He was helped to hail a likely man on the nearby island of Derrykerrib. The man soon appeared and proved to be a certain Frank Prunty. We can follow out his tenancy of the same farm which John and Patrick had occupied on the island through the Griffith's continuation books and discover more about him from the 1901 and 1911 censuses.[3] He was born in 1865, mar-ried a woman named Ellen from County Cavan, and had no children. He said his father had died a few years before, aged about 89. His father was surely either John or Patrick Prunty, mentioned above. Pressed by Mr Barcroft as to where his father had come from, he is alleged to have said 'Galway', but it might more likely have been 'Galloon', the next parish. There were certainly no Pruntys in Galway. Barcroft felt Frank Prunty was a Brontë relation, as his probable father. And it is certainly worth noting the Christian name Patrick, though this was a popular name for people of native Irish descent, as might be expected.

Turning to another issue, we ask, why Prunty Maguire, the only native Irishman to have one, was given a surname as a Christian name? Was the name 'Prunty' worth preserving? We have no idea of the age of Prunty Maguire, but to appear on the Tithe list he would probably have been in his thirties or forties. Prunty is either the name of his mother or another older relation, and it seems reasonable to suppose that the memorable Prunty he was named for was Pádraig Ó Pronntaigh the celebrated poet and scribe. Ó Pronntaigh stated in a colophon to one of his 1759 manuscripts that he came from the Erne Valley.[4] The latest date of an Ó Pronntaigh manuscript that I am aware of, other than his work recopied by another scribe, is 1772. He was alive, then, while Hugh was growing up. I have previously considered whether Hugh Prunty was Ó Pronntaigh's son. There is much circumstantial evidence to suggest so, but it is impossible so far to clinch this question. In passing, we note the antiquity of the Maguire name in Fermanagh.

Even if it cannot be shown that the relationship between Hugh and Ó Pronntaigh was as close as that, it seems impossible that they were not related at all. It is therefore worth considering the contents of Ó Pronntaigh's manuscript known today as Egerton 172 as an example of his interests. He wrote equivocal verses in English which may be taken either as a support for the Jacobites or the Hanoverians. The whole is quoted in Constable, p. 29. The first two lines read:

I love with all my heart   The Tory part as here
The Hanoverian part   Most hateful doth appear

The next item is his welcome to the Catholic archbishop of Armagh, on his arrival at Ballymascanlan. There is then a variant of the 'Connspoid' between a farmer and a harper, regretting how low the harper's vocation has fallen; this has interesting implications for the geographical placing of Ó Pronntaigh, to which we shall return later. The content of the Hanoverian/Jacobean poem underlines both the political views of Pádraig Ó Pronntaigh, and the subterfuge needed to express them. Later, we find Hugh Prunty expressing anti-government views, though not anti-royalist.

In conclusion, it is worth mentioning that the border between Fermanagh and County Cavan is very circuitous and a Patrick Prunty is recorded by Griffith in Clowninny townland, almost opposite Derrykerrib, in the parish of Drumlane in that county. There are also Pruntys recorded as living at Ballyhaise, County Cavan, with the head of the family, John.

6

THE BOYNE
VALLEY

We have followed Wright's account up to the point where Hugh Prunty, travelling with his aunt and cruel uncle, reached a place described by Wright as in the Boyne Valley, between Oldbridge and Navan. Wright carried out a strange expedition dressed in peasant clothes to try to find it, but without success. As he was looking for a farm once occupied by Brontës (since at the time he believed that this was the form of the name used) his search was doomed to failure. But working from maps and documents, we may be able to improve on his efforts. It is here, also, that our new evidence will fit into the picture, but for the moment, we shall follow Wright.

Up to this point we have been relying on Hugh's own narrative, as told to Wright by William McAllister and confirmed to a degree by the Todds, Hugh Norton and others. But the story of the Brontë heritage goes back further, reaching an earlier generation and concerning the origins of 'Welsh' the cruel uncle, and his wife, Hugh's aunt, Mary.

Hugh was to remain in the 'Boyne' farmhouse for about eight years. He mentioned no other members of the 'Brontë' family still living nearby. He did talk of a man named Gallagher, who was privy to the previous history, who became his enemy and tormentor. Hugh also became close to his aunt, Mary, and formed a friendship with a neighbour on the next farm. According to Wright, when Hugh was ill, 'Aunt Mary became communicative, and then, and in after years, told him secretly the tragic story of the Brontë family.'[1] Aunt Mary was therefore the main source of Hugh's knowledge of his family history, though it was perhaps enhanced by others.

At this point we need to discount Wright's certainty that he was dealing with a 'Brontë' family. The tragic family were not called 'Brontë' but were instead the Walshes. This part of the north bank of the Boyne was owned by two old noble families, the Earls of Drogheda (the Moore family), and the Nettervilles. They were absentee landlords, as was common in Ireland at the time. Wright

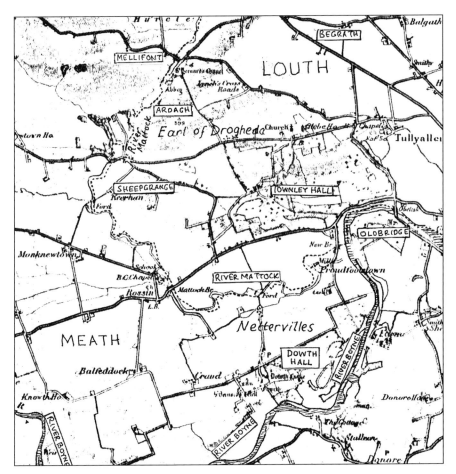

Rivers Boyne and Mattock, Townley Hall and Dowth, based on the 1899 OS map with authorial additions.

said (p. 25) 'the landlord of Brontë's farm was an absentee'. Instead of the Earl himself administering his land, this was done by an agent, in the 1720s and 30s, one Anthony Walsh or Welsh. Anthony and his family lived in a farmhouse in the townland of Ardagh, in the far south of County Louth, on the edge of a river, a tributary of the Boyne, called the Mattock. I believe that these prosperous Walshes were the family that Wright thought were the eighteenth-century Brontës. There would certainly have been ponies and orchards on the farm, which was not far from the old abbey of Mellifont.

Hugh's narrative, going back from about 1758, when he arrived at the Boyne Valley, was, we can suppose, that told by Aunt Mary. She had originally been one of the Walsh sisters (if my suggestion is accepted) and Wright suggested she was the youngest. She was in a position to give accurate details of anything which happened in her lifetime, but was relying on

Baptistery at Mellifont Abbey, first published in *Irish Pictures*, 1888.

hearsay for anything further back. These details come to us via the filter of Hugh, McAllister and Wright. For the moment, we shall follow their narrative, before introducing in Chapter 8 the new evidence from a clearer source. The farm where they all lived was a part-demolished ruin. Mary was able to tell Hugh of the fights one or more of her brothers had with 'Welsh' when they were young.[2] She could tell of the way in which her father favoured 'Welsh' and took him to cattle fairs, finally sailing overseas with him, as she believed, to Liverpool to sell cattle. Her brothers did not experience the same trust. There is a problem with the suggestion that Liverpool was involved in the sale of cattle, since it was not until 1759 that the embargo on Irish cattle being exported to Liverpool was ended. Cattle products, such as tallow, could be imported into England, but not live cattle. The Liverpool connection is dealt with in Appendix 2.

Mary believed that her father had died on a boat coming back from Liverpool. 'Welsh' had been on the boat, but did not return. The brothers were 'well educated', but knew nothing about farm management. (We might note here that 'well educated' must mean that they were of a higher social standing.) Finally

'Welsh' did come back, well dressed and demanding that he would run the farm if he could marry Mary. The brothers refused. 'Welsh' said he would marry Mary nevertheless, and they would all 'be scattered'. Nothing is here said about Mary's mother. The brothers, of whom Wright mentioned that there were three, went away to secure employment. Now Wright mentioned the mother, in whose name the farm was presumably held, stating that he and the 'sisters' were supported by money sent home by the brothers. The date of all this is hard to establish, but the 1740s seems likely.

Mary could tell from first-hand how 'Welsh' fulfilled his prophecy. She was courted by him, being given small gifts. Through the intervention of a woman called Meg – given a terrible reputation in Wright's account, but surely this was not from Mary – she agreed to meet 'Welsh' in a local 'plantation'. Whatever happened in the plantation, Mary felt herself bound to 'Welsh' and they were married by a 'buckle-beggar', as Wright described the travelling clergyman. Meanwhile 'Welsh' had become the sub-agent and the farm was transferred to him. Nothing further is said about Mary's mother. Throughout this part of his narrative, relaying Hugh's narrative, relaying that of Mary in turn, Wright was happy to call the family the Brontës. They were not; they seem almost certainly to have been called Welsh or Walsh. The only other name we have from Wright is that of 'Gallagher', a depraved ally of 'Welsh'.

The next step is to try to discover from external sources anything we can about the Walsh family of the Boyne Valley. As has been said, all the land on the north side of the Boyne, as far as Mellifont, was owned in the 1730s by the Earl of Drogheda, whose family name was Moore, or by the Nettervilles, whose residence was Dowth Hall. In 1714 Anthony Walsh was the 'steward' (agent) for the Earl of Drogheda. Leaving the house that year Mary, Countess of Drogheda, gave instructions to Walsh concerning the administration of the estate. They show that he had liberty to employ servants, to grow corn and oats, and to supervise the mowing of a meadow called Bograth, to be identified with the hamlet of Begrath, north-east of Townley Hall. In 1736, Anthony was in possession of 570 acres 'at Mellifont', which was part of the Earl of Drogheda's estate.[3] A series of letters discovered in the 1990s by C.E.F. Trench gives us names and details of other family members (see Appendix 2).[4] Meanwhile we can note that a corn census of 1740 listing 'wo'[widow] Walsh of Ardagh credited her with a large quantity of oat production.

Reviewing this evidence, as well as points to be discussed in Appendix 2, we can see that the Walshes were major landlords, under the Earls of Drogheda, from at least 1714 to 1740, but about that time the father died and a son, Thomas, joined the navy. Wright's account of the Boyne Valley 'Brontës' indicates a sub-nobility family whose father died and caused the sons to leave. We cannot tie the Walshes more closely to Hugh Prunty than that, but there are

Drogheda from the railway bridge in the nineteenth century.

really no other candidates for the position, and there is the name 'Welsh' to take into account. On the matter of the name for 'Welsh' there are three points to be made. First names would not be used by wives at the time, and Mary might well have called her husband 'Mr Walsh'. That he was allegedly called 'Welsh' because he looked Welsh is interesting, but it is possibly worth noting that the Irish for Welsh is '*Breathnach*', while the Irish for cunning or deceitful is '*bréagach*'. The character of 'Welsh' is certainly that. I am not putting any weight on this suggestion; we remember that the story of 'Welsh's' naming comes via disillusioned Mary.

It may be that the location of the Ardagh farm can be discerned from the first-edition Ordnance Survey map, which shows a road through the Townley Hall demesne, then carrying on to Mellifont. On the west side of the old road is an enclosure by that time without a house, but clearly a destroyed or abandoned farm: this may well have been the Walshes' property.[5] Another un-authenticated issue is the assertion that 'Welsh' was found by chance on a Liverpool boat. As has been said, there was an embargo on cattle being exported from Ireland to Liverpool, though cattle products such as candles and skins could be sent.[6] Remembering that this story comes through Mary, a child when she would have heard it, and remembering that the father of the family favoured 'Welsh', we may wonder whether he was this man's (perhaps Anthony Walsh's) illegitimate son. At one point Wright maintained that Hugh said 'Welsh' was not an Irishman and 'no Brontë'.

Before moving on, we can note an implication of the previous deductions. In Wright's account, Hugh, while in his early home, which we have suggested is Fermanagh, was a Brontë (i.e. a Prunty). Wright had no difficulty in thinking that Mary too was a 'Brontë'. She would have been Hugh's aunt because she was Hugh's father's sister. But in the revised scenario, she became Hugh's mother's niece, and thus we might deduce that a Fermanagh Prunty married a County Louth Walsh.

However, at this point the reference to Hilltown comes into the picture: we need to follow this up in chapter 35.

A FIGHT
LEADING TO A FLIGHT

T he end of Hugh's residence at the 'Brontë' farm seems to have come quite quickly. According to Wright it was due to a violent quarrel between 'Welsh' and his neighbour concerning disputed land, described by Wright as a bog. This was the culmination of a long-term feud which was perhaps the cause of the 'Brontë' farm being burnt down. However, Wright seemed confused about this: his lack of dates makes it hard to pin down the sequence of events. The death of the head of the Walsh household, perhaps in 1738, as we have seen, precipitated changes. Wright said on p. 68 that the then agent was 'murdered' and the 'Brontë' (Walsh) farmhouse burnt. It was in this half-destroyed condition that Hugh found it when he came back with 'Welsh' about 1758. A murder did take place, in 1742-3, when a member of the Nettterville family apparently killed a Michael Walsh. The trial was to happen at the Irish House of Lords, but for various reasons it did not occur.[1] It has been said that the Nettervilles owned property neighbouring on that of the Earl of Drogheda, and at one time some of their land was certainly tenanted by the Walshes. It looks as if this murder was the one Wright referred to.

By about 1766, when Hugh was about 16, there was still no resolution. Wright quoted Hugh as asserting that there was a physical fight between 'Welsh' and a 'neighbour' - we suppose a Netterville or one of their employees – and 'Welsh' was injured. He took to his bed. Hugh had witnessed this altercation but took no part in it. He reminded 'Welsh', in bed, of the promises that he had made of lordly living, and that the outcome had been far from the promise. According to Wright, two other matters helped Hugh make up his mind to run away; he had the support of 'a neighbour' and there was a new child in the family, a son and heir, according to Wright, but perhaps actually a daughter.[2] The neighbour helped in the escape by providing clothes and a little money. Wright claimed this flight included swimming down the river, but we have no corroboration of this. Hugh was on his way towards Drogheda.

According to Wright, Hugh's flight took him through Castlebellingham towards the north of the county. It is impossible to tell whether this was part of Hugh's narrative or not, but he did, without question, end up in the parish of Ballymascanlan (variously spelt). Wright stated that Hugh did not choose this destination, but was attracted to a site in the parish, Swift McNeill's lime kilns, because he saw steam while he was travelling in an easterly direction, which would have taken him to Carlingford. There are many considerations, however, connected with this account and with the parish of Ballymascanlan, which might throw doubt on Wright's claim. It may be that the route and destination of Hugh's escape did not much interest Wright, but Ballymascanlan needs study: perhaps Hugh had reasons for going there.

Once again I have to return to the evidence quoted by Angus MacKay in *The Brontës: Fact and Fiction* (p.121), that Hugh 'afterwards' (after his escape) came down to Hilltown, to some relations of his mother. The origin of this information is Maggie Shannon. MacKay placed this immediately after Hugh's flight from Drogheda, but I prefer to locate it a little later, when we shall discuss the implications of the remark about relations of his mother. Before we reach this, there is a good deal to say about Ballymascanlan. One surprise is that Ballymascanlan was for many years part of the estate of the Earls of Drogheda, administered by the Walsh family. Part at least was originally part of Mellifont Abbey land, which appears in the instructions left to Anthony Walsh by the Countess of Drogheda in 1714. She did not, however, mention Ballymascanlan. The Earls of Drogheda, the Moores, were left bankrupt by the behaviour of one of their number, and sold the Ballymascanlan lands to Thomas Fortescue in 1735. It is not impossible (but we have no evidence) that the parish and landowner were the subject of conversations between Hugh and Aunt Mary in the 1760s. Hugh may perhaps have known where he was running to.

Even if we do not think it possible that Hugh had heard of Ballymascanlan, we may ask why Hugh instinctively ran north when he left the Boyne. It was seven or eight years since he had come from that direction as a child. Was he trying to go back home? He may have recognised Dundalk, knew that he needed to leave the main road just north of there, and chosen the right instead of the left direction: this is, of course, speculation. There is also the matter of Hugh's long acquaintance with his Aunt Mary. It seems very unlikely that he would not at some stage have asked her where his origins were. She might have prevaricated for years because of her fear of 'Welsh', but in the end have capitulated, or at least given hints. Wright had apparently heard that Hugh wandered rather aimlessly along the edge of Carlingford Lough until the sight of steam from the Mount Pleasant kilns caught his eye. Possibly the name of Ballymascanlan attracted his attention; perhaps he had an idea that he had relations not far away. We need to be quite clear that this is all speculation, but there will be coincidences in that area, other than the land ownership, which could indicate intention.

A major question hangs over the possible relationship of Hugh Prunty with the Irish scholar and poet, Pádraig Ó Pronntaigh (variously spelt) whom we introduced above. Many years ago Douglas Hyde wrote that 'Patrick O Pronty was (I think) an ancestor of Charlotte Brontë'.[3] There are two strong points in favour of this hypothesis and several other supporting indications. Pádraig Ó Pronntaigh remarked in a colophon to a work in one of his manuscripts, that he was '*Pádruig Uá Pronntaigh mhic Néill mhic Seadhain &c anfaír o Loch Eírne*'(son of Neil, son of John from Loch Erne in the West).[4] We have offered evidence that Hugh Prunty was also from Loch Erne. The name Sean (John), as we have seen, occurs in the Derrykerrib family. In the same area we find Pruntys called Patrick.

It is hard to discover much about Pádraig Ó Pronntaigh, but authorities such as L.P. Murray say that he was living in Ballymascanlan in 1738, when he wrote the poem welcoming a new Catholic archbishop to the parish, Bryan McMahon, who was to live there under the name of Ennis to escape detection and prosecution under the penal laws. Ó Pronntaigh was a versatile poet and copyist, able to write in English as well as Irish in writings other than the one already mentioned.[5] He might fairly qualify as a 'great scholar', a future which Hugh Prunty desired as a small boy, and which was promised to him by 'Uncle Welsh' (see above, p. 28). Pádraig was in Ballymascanlan at the end of the 1730s, and he is also said to have taught in a school (presumably a 'hedge school') in Forkhill. We shall discuss evidence that he was actually Hugh's father in Part II.

As we shall see, Hugh grew up to be a compelling raconteur, an Irish *seanchaí* who told the story of his own life but also many traditional stories which were compared to the Classical Greek legends. There are at least three places where he could have encountered these old stories. He could have heard them, told in Irish, by his father in the Erne Valley, and retained them. He might have encountered them in the Boyne Valley, though the Walsh family must have been Anglo-Irish or Anglicised. Drogheda was a strongly Irish-speaking town, indeed a German visitor, J.C. Kohl, called Drogheda in 1843 'the last genuine Irish town', where he encountered many fluent Irish speakers. Unfortunately we do not know much about the contacts Hugh had in the Drogheda area between the ages of 8 and 16. He could have learned these stories at Ballymascanlan, where there were Irish speakers among the Presbyterians and even collectors of Irish manuscripts, such as the Coulter family of Carnbeg. When he died in 1803, Samuel Coulter had in his library eight printed books in Irish and some bound and unbound Irish manuscripts.[6] One of Pádraig's manuscripts was added to by Edward Carolan of Dundalk, the next parish to Ballymascanlan.[7]

Dundalk, Ballymascanlan and the neighbouring areas were certainly places where Hugh could have heard and learned Irish hero tales. If he knew his father (or possibly some other relative) had been active there, he might have been all the more determined to find them out; indeed perhaps he could meet people who knew Pádraig Ó Pronntaigh, whose dates are doubtful, but who was still writing in 1773, while Hugh was in Ballymascanlan. Hard evidence, unfortunately, is sparse.

My own view is that Hugh Prunty, grandfather of the Haworth Brontës, was the son of the Irish scribe and poet, Pádraig Ó Pronntaigh. It is most unlikely that any written record of this will be found, but the following are the circumstantial arguments supporting this conclusion, though we must recognise that it is not watertight.

(A) Pádraig Ó Pronntaigh was a native of the Erne Valley. Hugh Prunty probably grew up there.

(B) Pádraig was in Ballymascanlan by 1738. Hugh probably passed through it in 1758 and worked there about 1767.

(C) Hugh's ambition was to be 'a great scholar'. Pádraig was perhaps his role model.

(D) One of Pádraig's manuscripts involved a dialogue; one of the speakers was named MacLabhraidh, the Irish form of McClory.[8] The name is centred on South Down. Hugh later married a woman named McClory.

(E) The Irish traditional naming system. This was adopted by Hugh and Eilís. They named their third son Hugh after his father as protocol suggested. We can therefore reasonably suppose that Patrick, the name of their first son, was also the name of his grandfather.

None of these facts proves anything about Hugh's relationship with Pádraig Ó Pronntaigh, but it seems impossible to find another hypothesis which explains them.

All sources are agreed that Hugh easily found employment at Mount Pleasant lime kilns, known as Swift McNeill's. He became a labourer in charge of making sure the kilns were lit so that customers could buy slaked lime in the mornings. Limestone was plentiful in the hills round Ballymascanlan, and customers travelled from a wide area, including South Down. It is not clear where Hugh lived during this time, or what contacts he made. He was later to adapt the process of lime burning to that of 'beeking' corn. The McNeill mansion house was across a field from the kilns, approached, according to Taylor and Skinner's map, by a straight road from the north. The house was rebuilt in the nineteenth century and no idea can be gained of its eighteenth-century appearance from the map mentioned above. The McNeill family had originated in Argyll, the earliest known name being that of Torquil McNeill, whose descendant in the eighteenth-century carried the same first name.

8

ASTONISHING SUPPORT FOR THE BOYNE VALLEY NARRATIVE

(In this chapter I italicise direct quotations from the Poyntzpass article.)

So far we have been following the narrative told by Hugh (so it is alleged) based on the witness of Wright, following the McAllisters, Todds and Nesbits. This evidence has been filtered through the prism of Wright's understanding. As I was writing this book, my attention was called to a version of Hugh's story which avoids Wright entirely. The pursuit of this version was exciting and frustrating. Readers will not be surprised to know that, as so often in the Prunty story, some primary material has been lost or destroyed. However, we can cautiously reconstruct much of it.

The story begins with an article in *Before I Forget*, the magazine of the Poyntzpass Local History Society, issue 7, 1994, pp. 87ff, under the title 'The Pruntys'. This was written by Mr Griffith Wylie, then a prominent amateur member of the society. Before proceeding to give details of what he wrote, I must acknowledge the very valuable help in assessing the value of his contribution by Mr Frank Watters, who was a colleague of Mr Wylie, and I talked with him about his memories of the article before and during its writing. Mr Watters has been enormously helpful in giving me the background to the article, and in trying to trace its sources in the archives of the *Banbridge Chronicle* and The Irish and Local Studies Library in Armagh. Mr Watters emphasised that Mr Wylie was not an experienced historian and was not likely to have read any other material about the Prunty background, nor would he have been particularly able to evaluate what he had discovered.

The article begins:

The following narrative is based on some papers in the archives of 'The Banbridge Chronicle'.
These papers are records of the recollections of Rev. John McAllister of conversations he had with Hugh Prunty from about 1770 onwards. They also include similar records of the recollections of Samuel McAllister and another John McAllister.

In the following pages, I hope to analyse the Poyntzpass version of Hugh's story, showing that it was put together in an unsophisticated way, and includes some direct quotes from the original. Specific links to *Wuthering Heights* will be dealt with in Part II.[1] One major difference between this version and the version retold by Wright is the absence of detail about the four-day journey taken by 'Welsh', Mary and Hugh to reach the Boyne Valley.

The Poyntzpass version has some elements of direct narrative. The connective 'Now' is used on several occasions: *'Now, the more the children were antagonistic towards the brat, the more Hugh Brontë* [sic] *protected him'*. On one occasion, a first person plural appears; after describing the final journey of the adopted father of 'Welsh', there follows the phrase *'that much we know'*. The 'we' here must mean the three McAllisters of the introduction. Hugh Prunty is on one occasion just 'he' without the grammatical subject being mentioned: *'Welsh was not a good man, no better than ever he was, and he wondered why Mary didn't speak out'*. This second 'he' looks like a report by the McAllisters of something told them by Hugh. At one point we get the remark, *'He is recorded in Hugh's notes as "Red Paddy"'*. Hugh was illiterate and could make no notes; the Poyntzpass version means, 'the notes of Hugh's narrative made by the McAllisters'.

When I found this account I contacted Mr Watters to see if the original could be found. What were these 'papers'? Mr Wylie had unfortunately died. His widow kindly looked through his remaining papers, but could not find his notes of the *Banbridge Chronicle* material, which Mr Watters had seen during preparation of the article. The editor of the *Chronicle* gave Mr Watters permission to search among their remaining archives to see if the script could be discovered, but the newspaper had moved premises and unwanted material had been destroyed, with microfilm of the newspapers themselves being sent to Armagh. We are therefore in the unhappy position of trying to reconstruct the 'papers' from the article, on the lines mentioned above.

The first matter to settle was the question of the authors of the 'papers'. As has been shown above, they called themselves 'we' and 'Hugh's notes' means notes they took down from his narration.

The claim that this was in the 1770s may not mean that all three listened to Hugh at that time.

Samuel McAllister is presumably William McAllister's father, from whom, via William, Wright also got his account. The two Johns mentioned may be (**A**) a contemporary John – there are several – from the 1770s, one dying in 1792, and (**B**) Revd John McAllister, a controversialist who came to prominence in the nineteenth century, and who must have been from a younger generation. He was an Armagh Presbyterian, involved in a dispute with the Catholic priest Revd Charles Quin. No other 'Revd' John was traceable in Armagh library.

These 'papers' found by Mr Griffith Wylie are therefore likely to have been drawn up by the Revd John.

One other point needs thought. Could Mr Wylie have read other relevant material and incorporated it in the article? Mr Watters thinks not; Mr Wylie and he visited the Brontë Interpretative Centre at Drumballyroney, but did not ask questions, and came away with a pamphlet which does not add to common knowledge. Any alleged influence from Hugh's story to *Wuthering Heights* could not have been 'read back' from the novel into the article.

Despite the difficulty of interpretation, we can now proceed to look at the differences or additions to the narrative given by Wright, though in general the narrative confirms Wright's. Some incidents given here are not in Wright's account at all. Another interesting difference is the view of Mary (Hugh's 'aunt') given in this version. In Wright's, she was tricked into marriage, while in this version she had taken to 'Welsh' even from the first. This issue will be explored below. Hugh's courtship and marriage to Eilís are also rather divergent in each account.

The Poyntzpass article begins *'According to Rev. John McAllister, Hugh Prunty told him that his grandfather, – also Hugh Prunty – farmed on the banks of the River Boyne at about the beginning of the 18th century'*. We can discount this as a precisely true account on two grounds; Mr Wylie had said he would use the version 'Prunty' throughout, but on two occasions wrote 'Brontë'. We have allocated Revd John McAllister to the nineteenth century, and it would therefore probably be more accurate to say that Samuel McAllister was the recipient of the information, and passed it down to Revd John.

Added to Wright's account is the suggestion that the Boyne farm specialised in fattening cattle and exporting them to Liverpool. As has been said, the export of live cattle was prohibited until 1759, so this seems improbable. There is more detail on the behaviour of the farm children towards Welsh: he was given *'the odd thump'*. On one occasion he was buried under a haystack to try to kill him. The more this kind of thing happened, the fonder of him Mr 'Prunty' grew. This account agrees with Wright in comparing the relationship between Welsh and the farmer to that of dog and master. Welsh became a good judge of cattle. When the old man died on board a boat returning from Liverpool, Welsh was nowhere to be found. The money received from the sale of a large number of cattle was gone.

Poyntzpass omitted Wright's gloss on the children's education that they had 'been a good deal in England'. The farm did not prosper, and when Welsh returned looking like a gentleman, the brothers agreed to his help, but his stipulation was that he should marry Mary. Poyntzpass treated this issue very differently from Wright, who put a 'vile harpy', Meg, in the forefront of Welsh's wooing of Mary. Poyntzpass said of the arrival of Welsh from the Liverpool ship, *'The rest of the family did not accept him with the exception of one little girl called Mary'*, and said later, *'Now Mary liked Welsh'*. Later still: *'Mary seemed to be pleased with the attention* [given by Welsh] *and was quite agreeable to talk to this woman Meg'*. This divergence is remarkable. It reminds us that there is no possibility that the Poyntzpass version could have come from Wright, but what does it mean? Wright's version comes via William McAllister, while Poyntzpass comes, it seems, from Samuel.

Hugh is the prime purveyor of most of this information, but one wonders whether an additional informant, knowing more about Mary, could have contributed. Alternatively, William could have been trying to clear Mary's reputation. There is a little more in Poyntzpass about the state of the 'Brontë' farm in the Boyne Valley. It was a *'long, low, thatched farmhouse … the land was excellent grazing'*. When little Hugh arrived with his wicked uncle, *'some of the local people around the Drogheda-Boyne area [had] burned Welsh's house. He was hated by all the local farmers as he was still the sub-agent'*. This is not in Wright's version.

There is another 'we' in the later narrative, discussing the first visit of Hugh to the McClorys: *'Hugh for the first few years of his life would have been brought up to go to Church, we never knew what church exactly, possibly Anglican (it wasn't Roman Catholic), but from he was 6 years old* [sic] *until he left Welsh there was no going to church, there was nothing to do with religion at all.'* This adds to our impression that Hugh may have himself been the product of a mixed marriage.

Some other small divergences or additions are worth mention, as well as material to be discussed in Part II. On the journey back from Hugh's birthplace, *'in some of the pubs they were stopping overnight'*. This may be a guesswork addition by one of the McAllisters, as it contradicts Wright's fuller version. Poyntzpass, considering, as does Wright, that the farm on the Boyne was a 'Brontë/Prunty' farm, accounted for the location of Hugh's birth as *'this son with whom Mrs Prunty lived, moved. There is some doubt about where he moved to but it was about 120 miles from Drogheda and it is thought it was somewhere near Enniskillen. It was certainly "mid-Ulster" and there was a lake near but the precise area is just not known'*. This is one of the most tantalising comments in Mr Wylie's article. The 'lake' may come from a revised version of Hugh's story, as he thought he could not have seen 'the sea' on his journey. If he did say this, 'Enniskillen' as shorthand for County Fermanagh, has added weight. There is unfortunately a slight feeling that this comes from a modern source, though Mr Watters is adamant that Mr Wylie would not have encountered such a source.

Revd John McAllister had more to say about Hugh's own life in County Down. Surprisingly, the article states that the Harshaws, with whom Hugh got work before his marriage, were driven to 'Donaghmore parish church' by Hugh. We have seen firm evidence that the Harshaws were very determined Presbyterians. Confirming the 'messages in a hollow tree' story (see p. 57), the article goes on to confirm Eilís' confiding her love to her parish priest, and his toleration of it, though Wright's timing had changed. Poyntzpass deals with Hugh's wedding, and the events leading up to it. We shall look at Wright's version on p. 60. Eilís was to marry a neighbour of the McClory family, farmer Burns, but Eilís *'couldn't bear the thought of marrying him'*. Here Poyntzpass claimed that she actually wrote a letter to Hugh and gave a text, which in my view is highly contentious, containing for example the clause *'They have been getting at me…'* In this version, on the wedding morning the neighbours were not competing for 'the broth' but simply going 'for a ride round the country'. The eloping pair still travelled via Banbridge to be married at Magherally.

A little more detail is added to the settling of Hugh in the kiln cottage after the wedding, *'They had nothing, money didn't just enter into their way of living at that stage. Alice had a spinning wheel, Paddy gave them a couple of sheep, some hens and a rood of ground to grow potatoes … Hugh made a kiln and from the local mill, which probably could have been Glascar Mill, he subcontracted drying of grain and did this at his own house cutting timber and drying the grain and he got a portion of the grain as wages'*. Later, Paddy [McClory] lent the Pruntys a horse and cart. The comment about Glascar is interesting. Samuel McAllister, the father of William, worked Derrydrummuck mill. Another Samuel McAllister is recorded in Griffith as tenant of a mill in Glaskermore. *'Which probably could have been …'* is a strange way to record primary speech by the Samuel McAllister who is supposed to be one of the contributors to this piece, but this 'aside' is presumably included because it relates to one of the principals.

9

HUGH PRUNTY MEETS THE MCCLORYS

We saw that Pádraig Ó Pronnntaigh wrote a work about a controversy between a farmer and a harper. The farmer's name was O(Uá) Labhraidh, which would be turned into English spelling as 'O (or Mac) Lory', in other words, McLory or McClory.[1] In some ways this is startling, because McClory is a highly localised name in Ireland, though there are some records also in Scotland. In Griffith's 'Valuation' members of the McClory family are heavily concentrated on the three parishes of Aghaderg, Annaclone and Drumballyroney. Though all the sources I can find link Pádraig with Ballymascanlan and Forkhill after leaving the Erne Valley, it seems he was in some way also connected with these three County Down parishes. Now we find Hugh Prunty, who may have been his son, meeting McClorys in real life. One wonders if this is what Patrick meant in telling Mrs Gaskell that he might be 'of Ancient Family', though there are other possibilities to be examined on p. 128 and in Appendix II.

Tracing the earlier history of the Imdel McClorys is likely to be impossible, but a Felix McClory was buried at Donaghmore in 1786.[2] A James McClory was a freeholder at Imdel in 1781. This seems to indicate that he was not a Catholic, as most of the Imdel branch appears to have been (Catholics were eligible for this status only after 1793). There is absolutely no question that the 'Red' Paddy McClory, whom Hugh Prunty was about to meet at Mount Pleasant limekilns, was a Catholic, and it is possible that James misstated his religious affiliation. At this point we need to remind ourselves that though the genealogical focus may naturally be on the Pruntys, the McClorys are just as much Brontë ancestors as Pruntys. Eilís (Ayles, Alice) McClory was the grandmother of the three sisters and Branwell.

We have already wondered whether Hugh Prunty, as he ran away from Ardagh and went north to Dundalk, knew or hoped he would find relations in the neighbourhood. Possibly he knew he was looking for a McClory family. There is absolutely no evidence for this, but if Pádraig was his father, or even an uncle (we remember that Hugh wanted to become 'a great scholar'), he may have been aware that Pádraig had written about an Uá Labhraidh. According to Wright, he took to Red Paddy immediately. They 'resembled each other', said Wright, 'in the fiery colour of their hair'. I stress that this is going far beyond our evidence, but so little is known of the people and relations in South Down at the time that we are justified in making conjectures. There will be one more supposition to be built on these shaky foundations later.

We are now on to material supplied directly by Hugh in his corn kiln story sessions to his listeners, including the McAllisters, the Todds and Fletchers. Wright did not mention the Fletchers, but we can reasonably add them; they were in the same farming 'industry' as the McClorys and had the same need for processed lime from Mount Pleasant and later roasted corn from Imdel. Red Paddy McClory was about the same age as Hugh and they quickly formed a friendship. This led to an invitation to spend Christmas at Imdel. It was on this occasion that Hugh first met Eilís McClory. Wright gave a description of Eilís presumably obtained from his many acquaintances who had known her in her youth. He mentioned her golden hair and hazel eyes, the latter perhaps the only physical characteristic she passed on to her granddaughters.

One difficult issue concerning these events is the matter of dating them. This may not appear important, but it has to be remembered that with so little evidence context is useful. If we can't date the context, we can't assess the likelihood of a tradition being true or not. Patrick told Mrs Gaskell that Hugh had 'made an early but suitable marriage'.[3] We should like to know what he meant by 'early'; we know that it took place in 1776. Hugh would then have been 26. He had left Ardagh, we think, in 1766; this leaves ten years before he married Eilís McClory, and indeed Wright did give the impression of a long wait. During the first part of this interval Hugh lost his position at Mount Pleasant, apparently because he became indifferent to his work.[4] How long he was working at the lime-kilns is pure guesswork; we might suppose about two or three years.

A most interesting piece of information then comes from Maggie Shannon, told to Angus MacKay and quoted in *The Brontës: Fact and Fiction*. Maggie, Walsh Brontë's daughter, told him in a letter, 'Hugh afterwards came down to the neighbourhood of Hilltown, to some relatives of his mother'.[5] This gives us a definite location, but not a date. Maggie had missed out the Mount Pleasant period, but our impression is that on arrival in the Dundalk area, Hugh went first to the lime-kilns. Therefore we can suppose that this move to Hilltown followed his departure from the kilns. The mention of relatives of his mother near Hilltown opens up further questions, or clues to his family background. We need to summarise the somewhat cloudy genealogical situation.

Hugh was brought up in Fermanagh. He was surely related to Pádraig Ó Pronntaigh, perhaps he was his son. He wanted to follow in his footsteps and become a 'great scholar'. His Aunt Mary (Welsh or Walsh) seems likely have been the daughter of his mother's sister. On this theory, she had married a Walsh and gone to live in the Boyne Valley. Now we have the information that a third sister lived or had relations near Hilltown. This is all the more interesting because Hilltown didn't exist until the later 1760s. The area was formerly well known for the betrayal and death of the outlaw Redmond O'Hanlon whose head was cut off after his death in April 1681 to stop the head falling into the hands of his enemies.[6] Hilltown itself was planted by the Hill family who apparently wanted a linen producing village and attracted or transferred a number of Catholic families into houses which they built there. It is this new building of Hilltown which makes the dating of Hugh's arrival there important.

Hilltown church, a new church for the parish of Clonduff, was being built by 1766 and was apparently finished by 1767. It is questionable whether houses in the new village could become habitable until two or three years later, by which time Hugh might have left Mount Pleasant. However, it is certain that the Walshes were from a higher social class than the linen producers, which implies that Hugh's Aunt Mary, his mother and this unnamed sister were also higher up the social scale. There is also a religious implication which will be examined later. We are probably looking for a family living at or near the site of Hilltown before it existed as a village, and before the name Hilltown was conferred on this site, a crossroads in the townland of Carcullion 8 miles from Newry and 3 from Rathfriland. Here we invoke the 1777 survey by Taylor and Skinner, which still shows no village at Hilltown, though it shows the new church.[7]

At the east end of the road where Hilltown was built or being built was 'Eight-Mile Bridge', near to an old (now ruined) church called 'Eight mile church'. A house on the west side of the road was later inhabited by a Lindsay family. One other house is shown, on the east. In 1836 the Ordnance Survey team interviewed 'John Morgan, an old man who has lived in the parish for 85 years or thereabouts', who put the new church building at 1764 and said 'there were only two houses in Hilltown and there was only a bridle road to the place. The lime used for building was brought on the horses' backs'. One possibility is that John Morgan was a relation of Mary Walsh, another is that the Lindsays of Eight-Mile Bridge were relations. This matter will be further explored in Part II. There is a further surprising possibility.

Just across the River Bann lived a family called O'Neill (variously spelt) at an old house called Bannvale (sometimes 'Banville'). These were some of the last members of an ancient Ulster family, represented until 1744 by a John O'Neill and after that until 1809 by his son, another John, and by a second son, Felix. They were descended from a Hugh (Aodh) O'Neill. The family is sometimes thought to have died out after the death at Bannvale of Frances O'Neill, sister of the younger John. *If* (it is a speculative 'if') Hugh's mother was an O'Neill, this may tie up with Pádraig Ó Pronntaigh's claim that he was 'Mhic' (Mac) Neill, and also that of Patrick that he was 'of ancient family'. The 'family' could be the highly prestigious native Irish O'Neill family. A further speculation: could Hugh's Christian name be a reflection of this? Seamus Ó Casaide says that the O'Neills died out in Bannvale but Griffith's 'Valuation' shows an O'Neill still on traditional territory, as well as what appear to be descendants of the Magennis family with the Christian name Felix, an O'Neill name. Ó Casaide says that John O'Neill, during his lifetime, was 'looked up to by the Catholics of the county as their natural leader.[8]

It was perhaps from Hilltown that Hugh travelled the 8 miles to Newry to present himself at the hiring fair. Before leaving the account of the visit of Mary Welsh/Walsh, we can record details, of which surely she was the only informant, given by Wright in a letter to *The Academy*, Vol.45, 6 January 1894, p. 15. He wrote:

> Welsh's end was one of the many tragic matters that I left out of my book. He returned home one night drunk, turned his wife [Mary] out of the house and was found burnt to a cinder on his own hearth. The Celtic heart does not hate the dead, and it is possible that Hugh's wrath may have given place to pity and kindly feeling.

Thus Wright tried to explain why Hugh named one of his sons after the alleged wicked uncle.

10

HIRED OUT TO PRESBYTERIANS

Now out of work and having formed an attachment to Eilís McClory, Hugh would have been anxious to begin earning again. We have no information about early steps he may have taken to do so, but his skills were agricultural and he was a sturdy young man by all accounts.[1] Wright and others say he was still illiterate. There was little option but to hire himself out at the hiring fair at Newry, where those looking for work would stand, hoping to be selected by potential employers. Hugh must have known Newry well, having passed through it on various occasions on his way to or from Imdel. Though I have not found any record of it, the fair would probably have been held in the Market Square. Here came James Harshaw, farmer and landowner of Donaghmore, seeking a general servant. Harshaw was an enthusiastic Presbyterian. He hired Hugh and thus changed his life. Though it is possible that he had already encountered Presbyterianism at Ballymascanlan, in the shape perhaps of Samuel Coulter or one of his family, we certainly have no evidence of this, and must date the beginning of Hugh's allegiance to Protestantism, and thus that of his son Patrick, to this pivotal moment when Hugh rode with his new employer (we can reasonably suppose) to his new home at Ringbane.

The Harshaw family were extraordinary, and Donaghmore Presbyterian church held distinctly radical strands. Wright said Hugh Prunty drove the Harshaws to this church on Sundays and 'sat with them in their pew'.[2] Because we cannot fix the date of Hugh's employment precisely, we cannot be sure whether he heard Revd George Richie (variously spelt) preach. He died in December 1771 and was replaced by Revd Joseph Hay. It seems quite likely, but by no means certain, that Hugh would have heard the funeral sermon for George Richie, preached by Samuel Barber of Rathfriland, an important radical, whom we shall meet later. Even if he did not hear the sermon personally, it would have been fresh in the minds of the Harshaws as they explained Presbyterianism to their new employee. By this time he was in his early twenties.

Donaghmore Presbyterian church had existed on the site, just in Newry parish, since at least 1705. When Hugh Prunty was there the building was comparatively new, having been rebuilt in 1762.[3] There is more to be said about Hugh's religious affiliation, but we may say with certainty that the meetings at Donaghmore would have been a revelation to him, as was the family he served. There were many Harshaws in the area, in Newry, Aghaderg and other local parishes. Head of the household at Ringbane was James Harshaw, born in 1744. He had at least three children, not very old at the time of Hugh's residence. Wright said confidently that it was these children who taught their coachman to read, and there is nothing unlikely in this. The whole family seems to have taught him much more than simply reading; they taught him a Presbyterian outlook. Ringbane was Scottish by tradition, much different in make-up from the population of either the Boyne Valley or Imdel. The Presbyterians took their religion very seriously, deriving from it a social gospel near to the political. This acutely political interest passed down in due course to Patrick Brontë at Haworth.

Wright's birthplace was little more than 2 miles away from Ringbane, and he tried to check with the nineteenth-century occupant there whether there were any details of Hugh's residence. Unfortunately John Harshaw, his contact, had no information. We therefore have only Hugh's word for the Harshaws' attitude, which seems to have been encouraging and most influential. Wright suggested, I feel wrongly, that Hugh was the originator of the Harshaws' and their relatives' interest in 'tenant right', a theory which sought to reform the manner in which Irish tenants held their property. With such influences as Samuel Barber, it is most likely that the members at Donaghmore were radical before Hugh's advent. However, when Hugh told his story to them, it would only illustrate what they thought, that absentee landlordism and the traditional ways of letting out land were pernicious. It was this 'tone' in Wright's book which led MacKay and Ramsden to vilify Wright, an attack from which his reputation has never really recovered.

It may appear a side issue, but is not quite irrelevant, that one of James Harshaw's children, Jane, married one of the Martins of the next townland, Loughorne. Her second son was John Martin, associate of John Mitchel, an important Irish 'Young Irelander', whom Martin met at school in Newry. Hugh did not know Mitchel, but this family link between the Harshaws and the Martins shows the character of the politics they espoused. Jane Harshaw's son, John Martin, was eventually sent to Tasmania for anti-British journalism.[4]

What other kinds of work Hugh Prunty did at Ringbane is unclear. Quite probably he would have helped in the fields round the house which was no mansion, but a solidly built two-storey home, different from the single-storey house at the Boyne Valley and a little larger than the contemporary farmhouses. Whether or not he worked in the fields, he will have taken walks across them to the lake after which the next townland, Loughorne, is named. He had evidently kept in touch with Eilís, and perhaps met her sometimes near the lake. Wright alleged that messages were left by both of them in a hollow tree: possibly this is Wright's romanticism speaking, but he was in a position to know, his childhood home being near to Loughorne. The story is confirmed in the Poyntzpass article.

If messages were left, this implies that Hugh had now learned to write. His previous lack of literacy may seem strange but he had left Fermanagh aged 8, before he could have read much – and we do not know the literacy level of his mother, though she may possibly have been English-speaking. 'Welsh' ill-treated Hugh, and would probably have had low literacy himself; there would not have been much reading in the Boyne Valley. Lime kilns do not require a high standard of literacy to operate successfully. If Hugh could read and write at all before Ringbane it would have been at a very low level. We can therefore agree that the Harshaw children may well have taught him to read, surely on the Bible, so often used as an aid to learning to read in those days. This lack of literacy should not be taken to mean lack of culture; Hugh must already have been the possessor of orally transmitted stories. Wright suggested that he would tell the children some of these in exchange for his reading tuition.[5]

We can see that the sojourn with the Harshaws was life-changing for Hugh Prunty. Here he became engaged for the first time in the kind of religion which led to practical action. This was an Anglo-Scottish environment (the original Harshaws were supposed to be from England, but Presbyterianism was overwhelmingly Scottish). Hugh had fretted about his status at Ardagh, but at Ringbane he learned that the whole system of landlord and tenant was deeply flawed as it was practised in his country. His attitude passed down to his sons, including Patrick, who in turn passed on some aspects of this radicalism to his daughters.

11

RETURN
TO IMDEL

The Harshaw employment took place in the mid-1770s. We know that Patrick Prunty (Brontë) was born in 1777, but most written evidence before this is destroyed or never existed. As we shall see, tradition is consistent with a runaway marriage in 1776, but no contemporary records, such as a marriage certificate, confirm the tradition. We have the evidence of Wright, quoting William McAllister, and the Poyntzpass version from other members of the McAllister family. We have to weigh up these accounts, trying to check where we can, and taking into account contemporary conditions. In this period, religious affiliations were important, and we shall therefore discuss first whether Hugh Prunty had any.

In the Erne Valley, especially in Upper Lough Erne, there was a great deal of native Irish and Catholic tradition. This is shown by the 1901 census, which is specific about the religion of each person, and goes beyond statistics. Though we could not locate Hugh Prunty in Derrykerrib, his early home seems almost certain to have been somewhere to the south of Enniskillen. Pádraig Ó Pronntaigh wrote a poem welcoming the Catholic archbishop to Ballymascanlan, and we have found much circumstantial evidence to suggest that he was at least a close relation of Hugh. There is one caveat here: even if Hugh's father was a Roman Catholic, we note the relationship between Aunt Mary, a Walsh from the Boyne, and Hugh's mother. If Aunt Mary was a non-Catholic, so possibly was Hugh's mother, though she had allegedly taught Hugh some prayers.[1]

In the Boyne Valley it seems that Hugh attended no church. Gallagher, 'Welsh's' hated accomplice, was allegedly a Catholic, but it is not sure what is meant by that label. 'Meg', the witchy fortune-teller, was perhaps a nominal Catholic but actually a pagan. Hugh then ran away to Ballymascanlan, where he may have encountered Presbyterians, but the majority of the workers would surely have been Catholics. Then he went to Hilltown, to an unknown family. Finally he arrived at Ringbane, with a deeply committed Presbyterian family, where he began to read the Bible

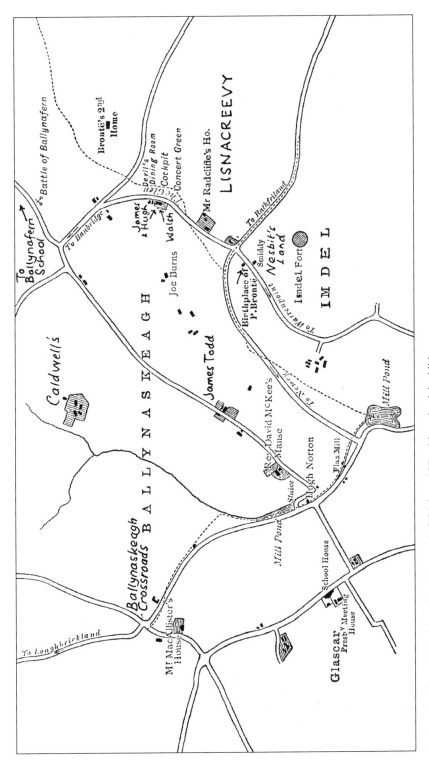

Ballynaskeagh and Imdel, based on the map in Wright, p.107, with authorial additions.

and frequently attended Donaghmore Presbyterian church. Our conclusion may be that he was from a Catholic background in Fermanagh, no religion in the Boyne Valley, but now inclined to Presbyterianism. He was at the time in love with Catholic Eilís. This situation will lead us to try to examine the state of Catholicism in Imdel (Drumballyroney) and Ballynaskeagh (Aghaderg) in the 1770s.

The penal laws were still operating, but beginning to fray. The McClory family, or some of them, had perhaps avoided them by nominally adopting Protestantism, but it is absolutely certain from our authorities that this was not the case with the family of Red Paddy and Eilís.[2] They adhered to Catholicism. Where and how did they worship? We have some help from accounts produced by the Catholic diocese of Dromore.[3] On the whole Catholic parish boundaries had followed those which had been in existence before the Reformation and Plantation. Thus there was a parish of Aghaderg, while Drumballyroney had been amalgamated with Annaclone (variously spelt). (The Church of Ireland parish had been amalgamated with Drumgooland.) There seem to have been no dedicated buildings in which the local Catholics could worship, and mass was celebrated at various 'stations' or on dedicated rocks. A 'mass house' was in existence in Aghaderg in 1768, possibly at Lisnagade, a considerable distance from Ballynaskeagh. In Annaclone there were four mass rocks, including one at Ballynafoy and one on land owned by McClorys at 'Poland's Bridge'. It seems probable that Red Paddy's family worshipped at one of these, but there is absolutely no proof.[4] These McClorys were not nominal Catholics, but practising. A further Catholic mass station, a little further away, was the O'Neill's mill at Bannvale.

Hugh had kept in touch with Eilís, perhaps, as previously stated, through the system of exchanging notes via the hollow tree at Loughorne. The Poyntzpass source, however, quoted Red Paddy as saying 'No sister of mine is going to marry a Protestant'. Instead, a marriage was arranged between Eilís and a Catholic neighbour called Burns, possibly with the first name Joseph.[5] Accounts suggest that he was an honourable man but much older than Eilís. His descendants lived in a farm adjoining the McClory holding. Wright was vague about how this marriage would take place. Catholic marriages were not legal, as such, in 1776. We also have in Wright's account the story of an early morning horse ride. This was a traditional competition at weddings for a prize which Wright called 'the broth'. In Scotland it was called 'bruize' and 'brace'.[6] Possibly it replaced a competition to win the woman as bride.

Tradition, as detailed by Wright, says that the proposed wedding ceremony with Joe Burns was circumvented by the elopement of Hugh and Eilís along the Banbridge road and so to Magherally, where they were married at the Church of Ireland church. Some early records, which might perhaps have recorded the marriage, were destroyed in the Dublin fire of 1922, so there is nothing left from 1776. The 'old' church had been built on a traditional site in 1770, and has been replaced by a newer one, leaving only a shell of the church in which the runa-ways were apparently married. Visiting it, one can be forgiven for wondering how much of the 1770 building was really new.

There are still some old graves in the churchyard, but nothing related to the Pruntys. It is not at all clear why Hugh and Eilís chose this church, at some distance from Ballynaskeagh. Possibly it was that very distance which influenced their choice, but there must have been some negotiation with the clergyman beforehand. No serious theory has yet been offered to explain all this.

It is not sure whether the pair returned to Ballynaskeagh but the local Catholic priest, who had agreed with the marriage to Burns, apparently acquiesced in the new arrangement. Wright credited him with calming the consternation, calling on the assembly to drink the bride's health.

Wright did not name him, simply calling him 'the kind and courteous old priest'. He may have been Revd Edmund Derry, later Bishop of Dromore, though he was not particularly 'old' at that time. In 1778 Derry is recorded as being 'Pastor of Annaclone and Drumballyroney', but there does not seem to be specific information about the clergy at Aghaderg.[7] This tolerant attitude was not always passed down to religious adherents in general. Party strife in South Down at the time is an issue which will have to be explored, since there will be direct implications for Patrick Brontë and his daughters. For now, we can record that this 'mixed' marriage between two people with a native Irish back-ground had not been the cause of dissension. Hugh and Eilís would bring up their family making use of both Scots-Irish and native Irish cultures.

PATRICK PRUNTY AND HIS EARLY UPBRINGING

Hugh Prunty was the stranger in Imdel, while the McClorys, though certainly not wealthy, were well established there. It seems sure that the McClorys gave Hugh support in setting up his family home, the small cottage just beyond the crossroads and opposite land belonging to the Nesbit family. Also on the other side of the road was the local blacksmith's smithy. Doubts have been expressed as to how a family could be brought up in such a small building, but these have by now long been laid to rest. It has to be remembered that though Patrick was born there, the family moved to Lisnacreevy before it was much enlarged. Their old home became known as 'the Brontë kiln'.

Hugh Prunty's first married home was, then, a small 'cabin', built of local stone. It had surrounding fields but they were not in Hugh's holding. In Griffith's 'Valuation' the plot was regarded as too small to measure, and by then was rated at 15 shillings a year. It faced south-east and the morning sun would presumably have come in during summer. The lane in front was important but not very busy. The remains currently pointed out to the public are the bottom five courses of stone, rising in places much higher. The bottom courses of the doorway are still visible, but they do not seem quite to tally with what can be seen from nineteenth-century illustrations. However, there is no doubt that the door was in that exact place. The building was divided by a transverse wall. The front, south-east, portion was used as a living room but also contained a kiln, while the rear was used for sleeping. There would not have been much privacy in the front, since it was here that Hugh carried on his trade. A window in the rear portion is shown in old pictures. The roof was certainly thatch, and figures in one of the episodes mentioned by Wright. Old pictures show a wooden beam holding up the roof of the front room and another over the door between the rooms. Part of the south gable end still stands. The whole building is tiny, and it is not surprising that Hugh and Eilís decided to move when the second child was expected or arrived. It is not clear whether Hugh continued his corn 'beeking' in the kiln after their move or whether the move was the catalyst for him to take up other work. However, as we shall see, Patrick was later recorded as helping a blacksmith, surely the one whose forge was opposite the kiln. It seems likely that Hugh continued to use the kiln even after their move.

In 1778 Revd Thomas Tighe was appointed to the living of Drumballyroney, then linked with Drumgooland. He was much later asked to testify to Patrick's age when Patrick applied for holy orders. He had to reply by citing the christening of the second child, William, who was baptized on 16 March 1779. Before that no register had been kept. This entry reads, '[Ma]rch 16 Bap^d William son of Hugh & Elenor Brunty Ballyrony'. None of the register entries on the page gives townlands. The entry 'Elenor' has led some commentators to think Eilís could have been called Eleanor or Elinor. I think, as has been said, that Tighe heard 'Ayles' and rationalised this. William was perhaps named after his mother's father. The name was certainly in the McClory family, an apparent close relative being recorded on adjacent property by Griffith. We also note that the surname has been spelt with B rather than P. This indicates a softening of the 'plosive' sound, and means that sometimes the Prunty family's name was spelt 'Brunty'. There can be little doubt that Hugh and Eilís were living in Lisnacreevy by this time.

There is very little information about the second Prunty/Brunty home. The best imaginative interpretation is perhaps that of W. Haughton Crowe in *The Brontës of Ballynaskeagh*.[1] He suggests that it may have been now that Hugh began his additional work at mending fences and digging ditches, as well as keeping on the kiln. The Lisnacreevy house is about half a mile from the kiln; there

Patrick Brontë's birthplace in the nineteenth century. (From Wright, *The Brontës in Ireland*)

would have been no difficulty keeping it up. The only record of Patrick during his childhood is from the 'diary' of John Greenwood, the Haworth stationer, who was told by Patrick of an occasion when he was assisting the blacksmith, when he was about six or seven years old. After theorising about the meaning of the word 'gentleman', it seems a client noticed Patrick and described him as 'a gentleman by nature'. There was indeed always something about the Irish Brontës which led to this kind of observation, just as in the 1890s Henry Barcroft noted the 'fine features' of Frank Prunty, the Fermanagh boatman.[2]

To keep the house warm, peat was used. There were no usable bogs in the neighbourhood of Imdel, or those parts of Ballynaskeagh or Lisnacreevy. The later evidence of Griffith's 'Valuation' shows that the Pruntys rented land at Lackan, including bog in a large area of Sharman Crawford's estate. It seems likely that Patrick would have gone with his siblings to collect peat, which would have had to be dug out and then transported by pack-animal to their home. The townland of Lackan is in Drumballyroney, beyond the church and school where Patrick eventually taught. Later, some descendants would live at Lackan, and we shall explore them in due course.

There were altogether ten Prunty/Brunty siblings. They were William, baptized at Drumballyroney on 16 March 1779, as already mentioned; Hugh, named after his grandfather and baptized on 27 May 1781; James, baptized 3 November 1783; Welsh (or 'Walsh') about whose name we shall comment later, baptized on 19 February 1786; Jane, baptized on 1 February 1789; Mary,

The author at Patrick Brontë`s birthplace in 1998. (Photo: Helena Haffield)

Drumballyroney church. (Photo: Alex Flanigan)

baptized on 1 May 1791; Rose (sometimes 'Rose Ann') and Sarah, twins, baptism date unsure; and Alice, born about 1796. The reason for the doubt about the dates of the younger children is the move to the other side of the brook, which moved the family into Aghaderg, and thus removed them from the jurisdiction and recording energy of Thomas Tighe. (Baptisms and burials for Aghaderg parish survive only from 1814.) However, this does prove that the 'Better House' was built after the birth of Mary; we can therefore estimate 1792, when Patrick was 15.

This new house still stands, retaining all its Georgian features. It is not exactly a gentleman's residence, but still superior to many in the area. It surely represents a considerable lift in the fortunes of the Pruntys, though it may well have been partly financed by McClory money. Alice later told J.B. Lusk that Hugh had built it all himself. At the rear a small field probably allowed chickens and pigs to roam, with perhaps a cow; our only evidence for these matters comes from the much later will of Welsh/Walsh Brontë ('Bruntie'). The aspect was across fields towards the house of farmer Burns and beyond that, 'Caldwells Fields', a much larger holding. We can assume that the smaller children would have played in these fields, as well as across the road in the stream bottom and the grass plot beyond it. This 'plot' was not level and included small trees. It was divided later into land rented by

Welsh and that rented by Hugh and James. The elder children, including Patrick, would certainly have been working by this time. We have no direct mention of flax spinning by Eilís, though this was mentioned several times by Patrick in his early work, and the sisters spun during the 'Brontë' dancing in the glen, which we shall encounter in a later chapter. We can be sure that Eilís would have been working at this and its associated skills. The whole economy of much of Ulster worked on spinning linen. Hugh was presumably still mending fences and digging ditches, though later the work of road mending became a permanent source of sound income to the brothers Hugh and James.

It is quite probable that Patrick would have been helping the blacksmith at least to the age of 10 or 11. Wright said he worked there until about 14, blowing the bellows and welding scrap iron.

The Widow Flanagan's party. (From Samuel Lover's *Handy Andy*, 1842)

Banbridge Brown linen market in 1783. (T.W. Dennis, Scarborough)

A registered apprenticeship was the normal way to learn a trade, and an obvious trade would be linen weaving. The Pruntys turned to Robert Donald in Drumballyroney parish. He was a Presbyterian, but not attached to Glascar, though a Joseph Donald did attend. He appears on the flax-growers' list of 1796, a fact which implies that he had enough land as a small farmer to allocate at least an acre to flax growing. I have not been able to place his residence in the parish any more accurately. Looms were cumbersome and the work was thought to be suitable for men. Wright quoted an elderly Mr Frazer (whom we shall discuss later) as saying that Patrick became interested in Presbyterianism during his period of working for Donald, who conducted prayers every morning and night. On this basis, it seems that Patrick lived in at Donald's house.[3] Frazer thought that, like his mother, Patrick had previously been a Catholic. Wright emphasised Patrick's skill as a weaver, but said that he was often to be found reading at the same time as weaving.

Patrick soon became an expert weaver and gained a contract from James Clibborn at Banbridge. Later writers give the impression that he actually worked at Banbridge, but Wright thought he took yarn back home from Clibborn's establishment to work on a loom in Ballynaskeagh.[4] This would imply a loom in one of the upper rooms in the 'Better House'. The Clibborn family became large cloth producers at the site near where the Crozier memorial now stands by the River Bann at the bottom of Bridge Street. Patrick's contact with Banbridge would have been important; the Clibborns were also Presbyterians. His weaving career did not last; before long he became a school teacher.

Since one of my aims is to show how Hugh Prunty's narratives influenced the three Brontë novelists, we need to explore exactly what he said, and reserve to a later chapter the question of transmission. We have already dealt with Hugh's story of his own life, and will need to return to it later. Unfortunately little information is given by Wright about other stories Hugh told. 'Many of Hugh's stories were far removed from the region of romance', said Wright on p. 133. We shall look in more detail at the types of stories Hugh might have told in Appendix 1. Perhaps here a summary of the contents is all that is necessary, followed by an analogy with the style and methods of the best known storyteller of all, Peig Sayers. Wright said (p. 133):

> [H]e had the literary art of giving an artistic touch to everything he said, which added a charm to the narration independent of what he narrated. The story of his early life … was delivered in the rhapsodic style of the ancient bards, but simple enough to be understood by the most unlettered ploughboy.

The stories 'though sometimes rough in texture, and interspersed with emphatic expletives, after the manner of the time, had always a healthy, moral bearing' (pp. 131-2).

Peig Sayers lived for most of her life on the Great Blasket Island, far from County Down, but Hugh's method of delivery might be expected to be similar. She produced almost 400 tales for the collectors. She could 'switch from gravity to gaiety… and her changes of mood and face were like the changes of running water. As she talked her hands would be working too; a little clap of the hands to cap a phrase, a flash of the thumb over her shoulder to mark a mystery…'.[5]

While he was being tutored by William McAllister, Wright was told 'some of [Hugh's] other stories, which he assured me were just as striking and worthy to be recounted as the wrath of Achilles or the wanderings of Pius Aeneas. These stories I would reproduce, sometimes in writing, but oftener *viva voce*, with as much spirit as possible …' (pp. 7-8). Wright thus clearly associated Hugh's stories with Classical Greek legend or literature. We shall see later that Irish hero legends are in some ways comparable. Unfortunately, this is all Wright had to say about the Classical Irish hero stories which Hugh apparently knew, though he had been taught to reproduce them himself.

We shall later try to discover the reaction of the Brontë children and their friends to stories told by Patrick, which surely derived from these stories of Hugh. Mary Robinson says that Emily was 'nursed on grisly Irish horrors'.[6]

Patrick learned these stories from an early age. Later, as an orthodox clergyman, he disliked 'superstition', and transmitted that attitude to his family, though a sense of the otherworldly breaks through from time to time. There are signs, which we shall explore, that the other Brontë brothers took a sceptical view of 'fairy stories'. For the moment we can note that Patrick heard and absorbed these stories: Hugh's life, the hero tales, the oral folk tales, from his father, first while listening in the kiln cottage and then (perhaps, but we have no precise evidence) at evening firesides at Lisnacreevy and in 'The Better House'.

'The Better House', or 'The Glen', built by Hugh about 1792. (From Wright, p. 121)

GLASCAR AND PRESBYTERIANISM

Hugh Prunty had been brought up in a mixture of religious traditions: native Irish and therefore presumably Catholic in Fermanagh (though his mother may perhaps have been from a Protestant background); nothing much in the Boyne Valley; Presbyterian influence in Mount Pleasant leading to keen Presbyterianism at Ringbane; the Catholic McClorys and Church of Ireland at Magherally.

Patrick had worked for Robert Donald, perhaps living in with him and experiencing a return to the Harshaws' Presbyterian discipline. Though Hugh and Eilís do not seem to have been involved, Patrick made a connection with Glascar Presbyterian church, the main Nonconformist church in the Imdel and Ballynaskeagh district, though itself in the townland of Glaskermore.

It is likely that William Wright was correct in his information as to how this happened. He put it down to the intervention of another Presbyterian, Andrew Harshaw. He was a fascinating and unorthodox scholar, who had been trained for the Presbyterian ministry but rejected on grounds which Wright did not quite explain. He was probably related to the Harshaws who had employed Hugh, but quite distantly. Andrew's branch of the Harshaws were tenants of land in Ballynafern, to the north of Lisnacreevy. According to Wright, Revd Andrew Harshaw first met Patrick on the top of Imdel 'fort', where Patrick was reading *Paradise Lost* and saying the poetry over to himself, lost in the magic of the verse and narrative. Harshaw was a schoolmaster, running his own school on a small piece of land carved out of the Harshaw farm. It seems most probable that he introduced Patrick at Glascar. Glascar congregation had been established about 1756, a lease for their meeting house being issued on 10 August.[1] During Patrick's time, the meeting house was a small oblong building, with ecclesiastical windows, but this probably replaced an earlier building. It was a 'seceding' congregation, a group which had split from the Scottish-based Church early in the eighteenth century. All churches in Ireland, especially in the north, had been affected by John Wesley's visits and preaching. During Patrick's alliance with Presbyterians there were two ministers at Glascar: first Revd John Moore (1778-1796) (Wright called him 'Alexander'), then Revd John Rogers, appointed in 1798.[2] Moore seems to have been happy to accept 'mongrel' Pat as a teacher in the school, while John Rogers may not have been.

Patrick made a strong impression throughout his life on everyone he met. In Imdel, Ballynaskeagh and Glascar he must have become known for his determination but also his scholarship: he was always reading the few books he could get hold of. Uncorroborated stories tell of him journeying as far as Belfast to find books. He certainly did read the Bible, *Pilgrim's Progress* and *Paradise Lost*.[3] Members of the chief local families in the area, the Todds and McAllisters, would have been well aware of this. Both families were adherents of Glascar, their names occurring frequently in the registers from 1780 on. The McAllisters seem to have owned the freehold, or a long lease, on the site of the meeting house.[4] It was not surprising that Patrick was appointed teacher at the school, although he was only 16 (the year was 1793). Wright, the only authority here, suggested that it was due in part to the influence of the Harshaws and that Patrick was a second choice teacher, the original contender having withdrawn.

Wright had many contacts who could tell him about Patrick's methods of teaching. One was his contemporary, Revd William McCracken, who had been baptized at Glascar on 6 January 1836, and was a native of the townland. His mother (whom I think I wrongly identified as Elizabeth Wilson in 1986) had

The Revd William McAllister's manse. (From *Ryans Presbyterian Church, 1835-1985*)

been taught by Patrick and would have had every opportunity to tell William about her experience and Patrick's teaching. We have no option here but to trust Wright's memory, recalling that in his youth he lived in the area and, under the influence of William McAllister, was fascinated by the Prunty/Brontë family. He seems to have understood that Patrick was already an enthusiast for education, an attitude which comes out strongly in the determination with which he tried to have his six children educated.

The school where Patrick taught was not the one generally depicted, which stands by the road, and is understandably pointed out to visitors in the Banbridge area. This school was certainly Patrick's school's successor. His building was much smaller, a room not much bigger than a parlour, standing in front of the church. Comments made to Ramsden by Henry McFaddon locate this old schoolroom in front of the church, at right-angles to the road.[5] Here this young man taught many pupils. Wright stressed the unusual nature of his curriculum and his methods; this was not the era of any nationally laid-down strategy for education. There were no certified exams to trouble these children, and Patrick was able to use *Paradise Lost* and other classics as class books. He must have had to teach reading itself, surely not by any 'synthetic phonic' method, but apparently by getting children to copy out passages and learning them, then reciting them the following day. Patrick practised what would now be called 'differentiation', finding out children's abilities and allocating appropriate work at each level. He would surely have had to do this in a class of mixed ages and ability.

In this rural situation, with farming, spinning and home duties to consider, it is not surprising that some parents would withdraw their children at times. The Ordnance Surveyor, Lieutenant G.A. Bennet, noted in Aghaderg parish, as late as 1834:

> The people are generally very anxious to send their children to school, and frequently lament their inability to do so. The causes which prevent them are… the want of means and the utility of the services the children can perform for their parents at the earliest ages. They very soon become useful, particularly when the linen trade is thriving.[6]

Patrick was very keen for them to come back to school, visiting their parents and talking persuasively. McCracken's mother told of a time when she had been withdrawn for work at home, and Patrick had come to the cottage and insisted that she should return, substituting a sister who was not so promising. It seems that though he understood 'slow learners' he wished particularly to encourage the abler children. Nevertheless, he began a special night school for the less able, with gymnastics included, and hymn singing in which the children could lead the singing as they wished.[7] Wright suggested that he abandoned the habit of

Glascar Meeting in Prunty days. (From Wright, *The Brontës in Ireland*)

corporal punishment, common in schools at the time. The co-operation offered by his pupils contrasted, unfortunately, with the opposition Charlotte and Anne Brontë suffered from theirs.

Sadly, there are no independent records confirming Wright's account of some of Patrick's methods at Glascar school. Wright was not a first-hand witness, and must have heard of these from McCracken's mother, or the McAllisters, or other inhabitants such as the Todds, but he did not give chapter and verse. One example for which we should like confirmation is the expedition he guided to Slieve Donard, the highest point of the Mourne Mountains. It took place in the summer. Slieve Donard is more than 20 miles from Glascar, but it is highly likely that the boys, led by Patrick, would have walked all the way. However, a mist descended and the party lost its way. It took three days to return home. In later years at Haworth, Patrick walked many miles round his parish in harsh conditions; it was in County Down that he had learned the tricks weather could play and how to judge them.[8]

Despite this teaching at a Presbyterian-run school, there was always doubt about the religious affiliation of the Prunty (possibly by this time 'Brunty') family. Patrick himself was apparently assailed by non-Catholics calling him 'Mongrel' and 'Papish Pat'. Eilís McClory, now Prunty or Brunty, in her well-remembered

red cloak, ran the gauntlet of neighbours. The parents at Glascar do not seem to have worried about this, but we have the impression that at this time Hugh and his family were regarded by some with suspicion. Wright records the attitude of one person who believed Hugh was 'in league with the devil'. Many remarks suggest that they were thought of as slightly alien, superior and clannish.[9] Patrick was bookish, unconventional, disregarding of religious difference. He seems to have inherited Hugh's intelligence and flexibility, as well as his narrative capacity. Wright said 'he made the acquaintance of the Rev. David Barber, Presbyterian minister of Rathfriland, and from him he was able to borrow such books as Spenser's *Fairie Queen*, *The Spectator*, Hume's *History of England*, and above all Shakespeare's works'.[10] Barber's first name was Samuel, and there is much more to say about him; for now we note that he was a source of books for Patrick Prunty.

We are still in Wright's hands when we examine poetry Patrick is alleged to have written at this time. That he was a poet there can be no doubt, since he later published collections of poetry. Wright considered that some of the *Cottage Poems* were written about 1798, and we have no way of knowing if this is true. However, he did print a poem much different in style and content, called 'Vision of Hell'. Evaluating this poem is tricky, but it is worth trying. Two questions arise: **(A)** Is it by Patrick? and **(B)** What does it say and imply? The poem begins 'At midnight, alone, in the lonely dell/ Through a rent I beheld the court of hell.' This recalls the famous Irish language poem by Brian Merriman called 'The Midnight Court' suggesting the possibility that Hugh had memorised some eighteenth-century Irish poetry. He may well have encountered this as early as his childhood in Fermanagh, but it would also have been known in the hotbeds of Irish language culture in Drogheda and around Dundalk. (We remember the proximity of Coulter's Carnbeg library to the lime works at Mount Pleasant.) It is my personal view that Patrick heard and understood this poem in Irish; at the very least Hugh told him about it and gave an outline. The content of the alleged Brontë poem is very different, but the first line is indubitably reminiscent. Why does this dreamer imagine the 'rent' in a 'lonely dell'? Possibly because Patrick Prunty/Brunty lived opposite to such a dell (as well as for the rhyme scheme).

Wright picked up the *tradition* that this poem is by Patrick: obviously unreliable, but not necessarily wrong. Without putting much weight on this, we shall discuss the poem's content.

Through the crack in the earth the observer sees the devil holding court. What is interesting is those who appear before him in his court: not the common thieves and adulterers, but:

> Ye clergy, who fed the fires of hate,
> Neglected the poor, and cringed to the great,
> Ye shall roast in honour within my gate.

These are said to have flouted Christ's commands and they 'drove the poor from their native sod'. The next stanza deals with 'landlords', while the third runs:

> Attorneys and agents, I love you well,
> But you throng with your numbers the courts of hell;
> Bastard-bearers and bailiffs need place as well
> For their hellish deeds no tongue can tell.

This stanza takes us back to the Boyne Valley, where 'Welsh' was threatened with being taken to Dublin to a foundling hospital, but unclaimed babies were often handed over to these 'bastard-bearers', who claimed money for doing that, but actually dumped the newborn children in a nearby bog. Wright added in a footnote that 'the remains of infants were often dug up in bogs by turf-cutters'.[11]

The tone of this poem accords well with Hugh Prunty's known attitudes, exemplified by a series of propositions he has been credited with. These were set out with comment by Wright, but are briefly summarised here. They are (1) The Church is not Christ's; (2) The world is not God's; (3) Ireland is not the king's; (4) Irish law is not justice; (5) Obedience to law is not a duty; (6) Patriotism is not a virtue. In the next chapter we shall look at the causes and results of rebellion in Ireland during the time when Patrick was a young man. For now we note the similarity of these alleged propositions of Hugh to the poem attributed to Patrick. The 'bastard-bearers' do not figure in Hugh's words, but the mention of them does point back to the Boyne Valley experience.[12]

The impression we get from Wright's account, deriving we may suppose from William McCracken's mother as well as the McAllisters, is that Patrick was an inspiring and indefatigable teacher at Glascar, and that the parents were well satisfied with his work. Yet sometime between 1796 and 1798 he lost his job. Wright gave one clear reason, but there may have been others too.

In 1796 Patrick was 19. He was an intelligent, handsome young man who seemed to be approaching a stable career, having left behind both blacksmithing and weaving. His boy and girl pupils went up to the age of 16. He even attracted at least one from a distance, as witnessed by a payment entry in a missing account book belonging to John Lindsay of Bangrove, a farmhouse on the other side of Rathfriland near a landmark over the River Bann called McComb's bridge. The entry reads 'Paid Pat Prunty, one pound, David's school bill'. The date is November 1793. Since McComb's bridge is not far from Hilltown, where Hugh had been before coming to Imdel, it is worth asking the difficult question, whether David Lindsay was actually a relative. This matter will be dealt with next, but the dismissal of Patrick from Glascar had nothing to do with the Lindsays.

The following points are more in the nature of speculation than evidenced proposals. Since Hilltown was the place where Hugh Prunty had allegedly come after his dismissal from the Mount Pleasant lime kilns, and according to Maggie Shannon 'to some relatives of his mother', and since the Lindsays occupied land where Hilltown would be built in the 1760s, taking into account David Lindsay's travel to Glascar to be taught by Patrick, we might pursue the issue of the Lindsays' possible relevance. Bangrove was about 2½ miles from Eight-Mile Bridge at Hilltown, on a different road, though both holdings are by the side of the River Bann.

Unfortunately there is no evidence so far discovered about these particular Lindsays in the later eighteenth century (the name is a common one). We have to make the most of much later material, from the tithe award and Griffith. The *Newry Commercial Telegraph* for 22 February 1828 records the death of what appears to be the last Lindsay of Bangrove, a maiden lady. David and John Lindsay are on the flax growers' list of 1796, which does not give townlands, but states that they lived in the parish of Clonduff, where Eight-Mile Bridge is situated. Two flax mills are recorded by the Ordnance Surveyors as belonging to David Lindsay in the townland of Ballyaughian, near Hilltown in 1836.[13] Griffith's 'Valuation' shows territory in Ballyaughian split between David Lindsay and William Lindsay. Much of this land was based on the old Lindsay property to the east of Hilltown, called Hilltown Lodge. The thought arises, were the Lindsays the 'relatives' Maggie Shannon referred to? If so, and if Pádraig Ó Pronntaigh was Hugh's father, there must have been some marital link between Pádraig and a Lindsay, despite the fact that this would imply another mixed marriage. It would, however, account for Hugh's uncertain religious affiliation, stressed by Wright.[14] We have, in any event, to account for the relation between the Walshes/Welshes of Ardagh and the Pruntys of County Fermanagh. However, this is only a speculative theory; the O'Neill family, mentioned previously, and living just the other side of the river near Eight-Mile Bridge are also possible candidates.

There appear to be two events which could have caused Patrick Prunty's exit from his Glascar post. One is personal, while the other may be theological. For the first, we have only the evidence of Wright. It concerns a young student with whom Patrick is said to have been in love. One day when he called at her parents' farm, the pair kissed each other near the corn-stacks, and thus the liaison was discovered by her brothers. According to Wright, the words 'mongrel' and 'papish brat' were used, and the farmers, who were influential at a Glascar Meeting, instigated Patrick's dismissal. Wright mentioned a number of versions of the episode, but did not give any variants; all we can say is that there must be some foundation to these stories. I have tried hard to identify the family and the pupil, but have not been able to do so conclusively. Here is what we may deduce.

Wright said this family had 'aristocratic tendencies ... more acres and more cattle than most of [the] neighbours'.[14] In the Glascar, Imdel, Ballynaskeagh context this points to another branch of the McAllisters, or the Todds. Other influential families, such as the Caldwells, do not seem to have had any connection with Glascar Meeting. Thus we are on doubtful territory for our identification. Is it possible to find a 'Helen' in Glascar registers? The short answer is 'No'; the name seems absent from the Scottish derived names. 'Helen' could be a pseudonym: we may therefore look for a girl baptized in Glascar about 1782 (16 in 1798) whatever the name. The only candidate is Jean, daughter of Andrew Mc...(here the microfilm transcriber found the rest illegible or missing). She was baptized on 6 October 1782, and was almost certainly a McAllister. After searching many years' register entries without finding a Helen I finally discovered that a Helen McAllister of Imdel died and had a will proved in 1792. Of course she could not herself have been Patrick's Helen, and this proves little except that this rare name did exist in Imdel and that it was used in a branch of the McAllister family. A further clue, which I have not been able to follow up, is that according to Wright 'Helen' married a farmer and 'Her descendants are among the most respected people of the neighbourhood'. We need more evidence to clinch this matter. Sadly, none has emerged.

There is another reason why Patrick might no longer have been welcome at Glascar, despite his excellent record as a teacher. In 1796 Alexander (John?) Moore left Glascar to emigrate. There was a gap in the ministerial appointments, but by 1798 Revd John Rogers was in charge. He seems to have been more anti-Catholic than Moore had been, as may be shown by his father's voting against the repeal of the penal laws at a 'volunteer' meeting in 1782.[15] Ramsden vehemently denied this, but one recalls the allegation that the words 'mongrel' and 'papish' had been used by Patrick's accusers, and thoughts turn to quasi-theological causes. It is also interesting to a suspicious mind that the session book has disappeared while the registers remain; the book would presumably have given more detail about the issue. Much later, Revd J.B. Lusk, then the minister, helped Wright with his investigation. He did not mention this book, and we can presume it had gone before his arrival. Once again we note the influence of sectarianism among the County Down residents at this time.

14

THE PRUNTY FAMILY
IN 1798

In my previous book, I believe I failed to probe sufficiently the political situation in Ireland in the later years of the eighteenth century, and in particular
the involvement of the Prunty family in the 1798 rebellion and matters surrounding it. A strong lead was provided by the recorded participation in the
battle at Ballynahinch of William Prunty, Patrick's second brother, but I had
not looked closely enough at the influence of Revd Samuel Barber or wondered
enough about Patrick's attitude to the whole matter. This was despite the alleged
prospectus of Hugh Prunty, briefly delineated in the previous chapter, which at
the time I could not evaluate. Let us return to it now, examining two aspects of it.

Wright devoted a whole chapter to the Prunty thesis, providing later critics
with ammunition to suggest that he was bending Hugh Prunty to his own political viewpoint as a supporter of the Tenants' Rights movement.[1] Commenting
on these theses of Hugh's, he accepted that he was noted for 'disloyalty' and
wondered how Hugh escaped being personally involved, noting the way in
which William played an active part. He said nothing about Patrick in these
pages, leaving us to speculate on how this affected the eldest son of the family.
To some extent Wright contradicted himself, recording an alleged occasion
when the 'Welsh Horse', a cavalry regiment, came to Ballynaskeagh and tried
to burn down the house. He said that Hugh talked to the Welsh in Irish, which
they could understand as a cognate language to their own. In passing, we register the fact that Hugh knew the native language, but we also feel that he had
been, to some extent involved. Why else should the Welsh Horse arrive at
Ballynaskeagh and decide which house to burn down?

The political situation in Ireland during the 1780s and 1790s, when Patrick
was a child and a young man, was extremely complex and volatile; it is
impossible to give full details here, and Irish readers will know this already.
For non-Irish readers, a few social and political points need to be explained.
These decades constitute the time when the events of the American War

of Independence and the French Revolution dominated western attitudes. It was very unlikely that they would have had no effect on Ireland, where there were contrasting and mutually intolerant attitudes in different sections of society. At the top of Irish power were English nobles, exercising power with varying degrees of legitimacy. The English parliament was seen by many as the source of all Ireland's problems, and as having no right to this power. On the other hand, there was King George III, the ruler by 'the divine right of kings', a constitutional view which in his alleged theses Hugh Prunty did not challenge.

Presbyterianism was originally a Scottish export to Ireland, and its whole ethos was not favourable to autocratic power. Presbyterians, as we have seen in the case of the Harshaws and John Martin, were totally out of sympathy with the political structure. They wanted change by democratic means, and their numbers included influential Belfast merchants. They were prepared to go beyond unarmed protest if circumstances arose. Then there were the Catholics, the majority of the people of Ireland in most areas, just emerging from the worst repression of the penal laws. Among this section were a large number of Irish patriots whose motivation was to see the country as a free and Catholic-orientated country. As can be seen, sometimes the interests of these dissident groups coincided and sometimes not. In Aghaderg and Drumballyroney there were elements of all three, but chiefly the last two groups, living with a degree of tension which erupted at times. Patrick Prunty grew up in this atmosphere, in which two things were clear; the current autocratic quasi-English system had to go, and similar polities in America and France had been changed by force.

The Irish parliament reluctantly passed bills in the 1780s and 1790s giving more power to these dissidents. In 1793 a bill gave voting rights and some civil rights to certain Catholics. Thus they appear on the 1796 lists of 'flax growers', who could benefit from subsidy if they grew some flax in their fields. Presbyterian marriages are recorded in Glascar Meeting registers from 1781, having become legal just as Church of Ireland marriages were. But these tinkerings with law did not satisfy the dissidents, amongst whom were the Pruntys. Patrick would have grown up noting injustice and fighting it; an attitude strongly seen in Charlotte Brontë. Like his father, Patrick was a thinker, becoming more interested in reading and developing judgement. This brings us to his friendship with Revd Samuel Barber of Rathfriland.

Samuel Barber, born in Antrim, had been educated at Glasgow College from 1757, where he gained an MA degree. He was studious and sober, having a love of Latin books, especially Tacitus, the Roman historian who bitterly criticised the imperial power of the first and second centuries AD. Tacitus expressed himself in the tersest Latin, which is full of pithy sayings and also at times, paradox. Barber seems to have gained some of his understanding of political issues and his ideas of what should be done from this highly expressive writer.[2] He was ordained at Rathfriland in 1763, where he took charge of an historic, flourishing Meeting. He had the Meeting rebuilt in 1775 with the support of Rathfriland residents describing themselves as 'merchants'.[3] In 1779 he became head of the new Volunteer Corps at Rathfriland, devising rules for the members. They were preceded by a statement of aims (it might now be called a 'mission statement'): they were established 'for the purpose of learning the military art … to defend our civil and relig[ious] liberty and to keep the peace in our town and neighbourhood … we hereby promise to be obeydient to our superior officers, and to march and do military duty where they command us within the county of Down.' Patrick Brontë was always interested in military matters; here was where that interest began.

Revd Samuel Barber.

Quotations from a 1780 resolution passed by Volunteer officers meeting at Newry will give the tone of the organisation. '[W]e have heard with concern and astonishment that the house of commons in Ireland has adopted an alteration made by the privy council of England in the bill for the better regulation of the army of this kingdom, an alteration of the most alarming tendency', which would take away the control of the army in Ireland from the Irish parliament. Further, 'That we are firmly convinced that the influence of the crown has increased, is increasing, and ought to be diminished, and that the freedom of this country can only be preserved by the spirit of the people and the virtue of the house of commons.' It is easy to see how the Volunteers, intending to be loyal to the constitution, in fact slipped into perceived treachery because of their democratic outlook.

Wright recorded that Patrick Prunty 'borrowed books' from Barber. What does this statement imply? One does not borrow books from a stranger so we can conclude that Patrick knew Barber well. Perhaps through Revd Andrew Harshaw, a Presbyterian who had met Patrick and knew how he thirsted for knowledge and had perhaps been influenced by his father's political stance, Patrick must have been introduced to Barber and perhaps attended the Rathfriland Meeting (this, however, is guesswork). Samuel Barber lived about 2 miles away at Tullyquilly. It seems likely that Patrick went there to collect the books and probably to listen to Barber's ideas. It is interesting also that by far the largest donor to an appeal for money for arms for the army volunteers at Rathfriland was the Church of Ireland clergyman, Thomas Tighe. So far, however, there was no hint of armed rebellion against the (British) state. This was not yet a movement which involved Catholics.

However, factional discontent among both Presbyterians and Catholics broke out into scuffles and fighting throughout County Down. We can imagine how the 'mongrel' Patrick Prunty felt.

Barber was an active politician, who helped in the election of 1790 to return a Presbyterian, the Hon. Robert Stewart, who later became Lord Castlereagh. This was when Patrick was 13, and surely interested by now in politics as well as weaving. The following year, what started out as a debating club and ended as a force for rebellion was formed in Dublin: the 'United Irishmen'.

This organisation tried to link the interests of the Presbyterians with those of the Catholics. Here, surely, the Prunty family would feel some relief; they could now be on the same side as the majority of their relatives and neighbours. The Irish parliament passed a bill in 1793 to suppress both organisations, but without success. By this time Patrick was 16 and beginning his work at Glascar. The threat of war with France had hung over the British Isles; King Louis was beheaded on 21 January 1793, and war broke out on 1 February. Despite their interest (especially that of Charlotte) in the French language, the Brontë family had no love for the French.

One of the most important episodes in the 1798 rising was the Battle of Ballynahinch. William Prunty, Patrick's next brother, was present. It is not clear how far the local Catholics and Presbyterians in Imdel and Ballynaskeagh really united under the United Irishmen banner. Most reports suggest that the rising in County Down was heavily dominated by Presbyterians, democratic and even republican in outlook, while in Wexford and Waterford Catholics played a major part, their uprising culminating in defeat at Vinegar Hill near Enniscorthy. We do not know whether William, then 19, joined the rebels through Catholic or Presbyterian sympathy. The Volunteers had hardened their stance and become convinced that only rebellion could solve Ireland's problems, and we may therefore be fairly certain that in 1798 Patrick would have been of this opinion. Is it possible that he too went to Ballynahinch? The United Irishmen were led by Henry Munro, reputed to have been less than an adequate leader. They were not well trained and were eventually defeated by the English forces. William escaped, threading his way through bogs and swimming the canal until he reached County Armagh. He told his family that the cavalry had followed him; since it is unlikely that they had focused particularly on this ordinary fighter, it seems that there were enough men who had escaped together to excite the interest of the cavalry. Nothing is said of Patrick in his account. Meanwhile an interested spectator at the battle was David McKee, a future Presbyterian minister at Annaclone, who was to live in Ballynanskeagh and play a part in the Brontë story.

It is quite certain that on his return to Ballynaskeagh William would tell the story in detail, perhaps again and again. His son John remembered it and told it in the 1890s. William had lain in a gorse patch on an Armagh hill, while the cavalry tested the site with their swords, but found nothing in the gathering dusk (we cannot identify the hill in question). When they had disappeared towards Newry William trudged wearily home. The uprising had been defeated and the ringleaders would be savagely punished. It would be very surprising if Patrick had not heard the story his brother told, and indeed repeated it to the children at Haworth. It is, however, tantalising that we do not know precisely how Patrick, the friend of Samuel Barber, reacted to these events. Barber was now arrested, taken to Downpatrick prison and charged with high treason. At his trial he convinced the court-martial that he was not a United Irishman and was released. In this he was surely very fortunate, as many of those involved in the rebellion were executed.

15

THOMAS TIGHE
EMPLOYS PATRICK

Patrick Prunty was now unemployed, and we can suppose some discussion would have taken place at Ballynaskeagh about what the future held. He had been a teacher, while the family as a whole were engaged in manual tasks, though these were providing a fair income. But Hugh had wanted to be 'a great scholar' and his eldest son had shown signs of developing in this direction. However, there was no doubt that already the failure to belong to one or other clear party was not helping the family socially. Patrick had taught at Glascar, and according to Wright his brothers had also attended the Meeting there. The marriage of the parents had been in a Church of Ireland church and the children had been baptized at Drumballyroney parish church. Eilís' family were Catholics. Which religious group would own Patrick? The answer, as we all know, was a strange one: the Church of Ireland and England, initially in the person of Thomas Tighe, friend of John Wesley.

The steps leading up to this development appear to have been (A) Patrick's friendship with Samuel Barber; (B) Wesley's influence on Barber's thinking, and (C) the fact that Samuel Barber and Thomas Tighe had both entertained John Wesley during his tours of Ireland. Wesley had visited Barber in 1787. Elsie Harrison quotes Wesley as praising members of his group drawn from the three sectional interests, Anglican, Presbyterian and Papist for having no 'striving' between them.[1] It has to be remembered that Wesleyanism did not yet constitute a church, but was still more a 'society' influencing all denominations. This situation is reflected in Patrick's later novelette *The Maid of Killarney*. Wesley wrote in June 1787 of the area round Rathfriland, 'The country was uncommon pleasant, running between two high ridges of mountains; but it was uphill and down all the way so that we did not reach Rathfryland [*sic*] till near noon. Mr Barber the Presbyterian Minister (a princely personage I believe six feet and a half high) offering me his new spacious preaching house the congregation quickly gathered together'.

Later members of the Brontë family thought that perhaps Walsh Brontë, Patrick's youngest brother, was named after Thomas Walsh, a Methodist preacher. He was a Limerick man who had been active in the 1750s, preaching in Irish. It is certainly possible that Walsh was named after him, but Hugh's system up to that point had been to use family names. Possibly Hugh had originally given Walsh his name based on family history, but later learnt about Thomas Walsh and changed his 'reasons' for the name. No firm judgement can be made. What is certain is that Samuel Barber was a friend to the Methodist outlook and so was Thomas Tighe.

With Tighe we are moving into a different stratum of society, though he will turn out to be a very homely man. He was the son of William Tighe of Rosanna (also spelt Rossana and Rossanagh) in County Wicklow. William Tighe was married twice; Thomas was a son of his second wife, but he had a half-brother (also William) who lived at Rosanna and entertained John Wesley, who made his base there when he visited Ireland. Here we can be sure Thomas met and was influenced by him. His half-brother William became MP for Wicklow and married Sarah Fownes, a baronet's daughter from Woodstock, Inistioge, near Kilkenny. His son, another William, was MP for Wicklow in the British parliament from 1806. Thomas Tighe himself was educated at Harrow and then St John's College, Cambridge, following this by becoming a fellow of Peterhouse. He returned to Ireland and became a clergyman in County Down in 1778.

Ballyroney Glebe. (From Horsfall Turner's *Brontëana*, 1898)

The two parishes of Drumballyroney and Drumgooland were united and in 1778 Thomas became vicar of both. He then took up residence in a house at Parson's Hill, near to Ballyward and some way from Drumballyroney church. A nephew wrote to *Notes and Queries* in 1879 to give details of the house: 'My uncle lived in a cottage not as good as the residence of a gentleman's steward. A parlour and two bedrooms, a kitchen and servants' room, and a housekeeper's room formed the whole house'.[2] The writer said he was entertained at Parson's Hill with his father and mother, his father being presumably the William mentioned above who represented Wicklow in the British parliament. Thomas had at least two sons, born in 1787 and 1788 after his marriage to Eliza Beers of Ballygorian.

At this time, Thomas 'used to have clerical meetings at his house, and lay down mattresses for his guests, as on board ship'.[3] Eventually the house at Parson's Hill must have become too small for growing boys, and negotiations began for a better dwelling. Twenty Irish acres 'Plantation measure' were allocated for this in 1795, being roughly the land still recognised as glebe in Griffith's 'Valuation'.[4] Thomas Tighe 'bought the property intending to build, but his wife died young and he continued to live in the cottage [Parson's Hill]'.[5] It seems probable that Patrick Prunty would also have lived at Parson's Hill while in Tighe's employ.

When Tighe died in 1821, a memorial tablet was put up. Though couched in conventional terms, it is rather more emotive than we find on some memorials. He 'discharged the duties of the pastoral office with zeal unabating, diligence unwearied and love unfeigned. Affectionately desirous of the temporal and eternal welfare of his parishioners, they are his witnesses how holily justly and unblamably he walked before them.' He had died on 25 August after laying the foundation stone of the church personally on 18 June.

There is some suggestion that Thomas Tighe's library passed on to his successor, Revd John Dubordieu and that these would be books which Patrick read.[6] Dubordieu was a literary figure, though apt to be abrasive in conversation. He had written *A Statistical Survey of County Down* and might have wished to keep Tighe's books. On the other hand, there have also been suggestions that Tighe's library was dispersed at his death. There are in any case two main results from Patrick's association with Tighe: (i) He was introduced to a world of clerics, some of whom were linked to the aristocracy; (ii) In the school he refined his pedagogic skills and developed his enthusiasm for education, which he satisfied in Tighe's library. We know that Samuel Barber read Tacitus, but we don't know whether there were any other Latin or Greek authors whose works he recommended to Patrick. Patrick later found Homer's *Iliad* a valuable work, and presumably saw it as a military epic. In Latin, he was particularly fond of Horace and Virgil, and he introduced Branwell and Emily to both of them. These are not mentioned in comments on Barber's influences, and perhaps therefore belong to the Tighe period.

The letter quoted above from 'H', the relative of Thomas Tighe, denied that Patrick Prunty had ever been tutor to Tighe's two sons. This seems very likely on two grounds: 'H' was a close relative who might well have been in full possession of the facts, and 'Patrick Prunty' is not likely to have been thought learned enough to teach the sons of a gentleman. What is certain is that Tighe considered him well qualified to teach the local children at the school in Aughnavallog (Drumballyroney), having regard no doubt to his recent success at Glascar. (Thomas Tighe may well have also taught Patrick to fire a pistol; the use of weapons is a feature of *The Maid of Killarney*. In later years, Patrick taught his feisty daughter Emily to fire as well.) The Ordnance Surveyors in 1836 did not ascertain the age of the school then existing, which accommodated 30 pupils. It seems quite likely that this was about the number Patrick taught at the turn of the century. The schoolhouse is still shown to visitors on the 'Brontë Homeland Drive'. It is currently slated, but would almost certainly have been thatched in 1798. Adjacent to the church, it is approached by a separate pathway. Older illustrations show a single-storey building with three windows on each side, and the early Ordnance Survey maps show it in its current position. It has been fitted out as an early nineteenth-century schoolroom, though we cannot be quite sure what it looked like when Patrick taught there. Nevertheless, the school and church are well worth a visit to feel the atmosphere of the place where Patrick honed his skills.

Even in Patrick's day the church at Aughnavallog was only one of Tighe's parish churches. It had been built by Thomas Tighe in 1780, and substantially stands today as it was then. In the tradition of the new wave of Church of Ireland churches from the late eighteenth and early nineteenth centuries, it is a rectangular building with an entrance porch, set in a plot of land which was then used as a burial ground. Set on a hill, the churchyard gives a fine view of the Mourne Mountains, and we can imagine Patrick looking out of the schoolhouse windows across to this splendid view. The modern visitor will once again be reminded how rural this area is, with the life of the people in the late eighteenth century secured by agriculture and the home linen industry. The step Patrick Prunty was about to take from these green acres to the close-built town of Cambridge, in a different country, was enormous.

The decision to try for a place at one of the chief seats of learning in England must have been made with Thomas Tighe's active intervention and encouragement. We recall the phrase that rang in Hugh Prunty's ears during his childhood and exile: 'to be a great scholar'. Though Hugh himself could never attain it, Patrick, through the patronage of Tighe, was about to do so. He needed support both from home and the Wesley-taught clergyman. However, the question needs to be asked, why did Patrick not choose to go to Dublin or Glasgow? Samuel Barber chose Glasgow, we may suppose, because it was a clear choice for many Presbyterians. Despite his close association with Presbyterianism, Patrick was

Revd William John McCracken (taken in Ballyeaston days).

not a member. He had taught at Glascar, but had been removed from his post in circumstances which might have made it difficult to give a clearly approving reference. Trinity College Dublin was a venerable institution, but the question arises whether Patrick's Catholic background would be a bar. The ecumenism of the Prunty family counted severely against them, since they could declare no partisan allegiance. It would be difficult for Patrick to progress against the prejudice of various Irish groups. One wonders, too, how far any sympathy the family may have shown to the 1798 rebellion, and the association with Samuel Barber, might have counted against him. It must have been Thomas Tighe who decided that Patrick must leave his native land and cross to England. There is a rather enigmatic note in Edith M. Clarke's *City Set on a Hill*, in which she said that:

> To study at a university had long been the ambition of Patrick. In this he had hitherto been thwarted by a set-back in the family fortunes, through the dishonesty of one whom his father had trusted. [7]

This cannot, surely, have been Thomas Tighe; it was someone Hugh, not Patrick, had trusted. I cannot unravel this mystery.

In a letter of 12 November 1808, Patrick wrote to an American colleague about the 'voluntary exile' from their 'Dear Homes'. However, he went on, 'literally speaking it is not voluntary'. In the context he was talking about a call from God, but one wonders whether the family participation in the 1798 rebellion, and also Thomas Tighe's association with the Rathfriland Volunteers, might have made him nervous about staying in Ireland; did he perhaps think he was in some ways a 'wanted man'? In the same letter he mentioned that he had heard from the Irish relatives and that 'they are all well'.[8]

16

THE BRONTËS
IN IRELAND

In 1808, Patrick was still receiving letters from Ireland, but the evidence for his continued links with his family is hard to find. We shall be examining some clear examples, some of which are within the lifetimes of the three Brontë novelists, but despite his aim of concealing such links, secondary sources often say he maintained them well and even regularly sent home money.

Wright and others have had a lot to say about the family in general, and some of the actions and events they report relate to times before Patrick went to England. We shall therefore look at these, bearing in mind that dating precise events is difficult.

We have seen that the aspect and demeanour of the Prunty family were thought unusual. Patrick was characterised by the visitor to the forge as a natural gentleman. On the other hand, Wright reported the view of a local resident that Hugh was 'in league with the devil'.[1] He had been told, when he first began to take an interest in the Prunty/Brontë family to keep out of their way 'lest I should hear their odious language'. 'Shebna the Scribe' had met one of the Brontës' close neighbours. She 'lived beside the last surviving uncles and aunts of Charlotte Brontë' and 'She reflected the awe felt by the people of Ballynaskeagh for the strange family'. An account of the impressive appearance of the Pruntys comes from William McAllister reported by Wright in his Chapter 18. Here he quoted 'almost in the same words' a cousin of McAllister who saw the Prunty brothers in 1812. They 'marched in step across a field towards a level road'. Here they began to play a traditional Irish game called 'long bullets'. During the game, they 'gave utterance to their thoughts with a pent-up and concentrated energy never equalled in rugged force by the novelists'. McAllister's cousin noted their 'quaint conceptions, glowing thoughts and ferocious epithets'. He added that from the Pruntys there was heard 'a profusion of strong language that literally made our flesh creep and our hair stand on end'.

The game being played by the Prunty brothers, perhaps joined by McClorys, has been formalised as 'Irish road bowling' and has a regular players' association. A large steel ball weighing about six pounds, according to McAllister's friend, is thrown along the road and bets are placed on aspects of its progress. The Armagh historian T.G.F. Paterson quotes a reference in a poem written in 1728 by Jonathan Swift at Markethill in County Armagh.[2] The game was apparently widespread but later localised to areas including County Louth and Armagh; we cannot therefore be sure where the Pruntys learned it, but it seems likely that this was part of the Armagh locality, and not necessarily imported by Hugh. Though Wright quoted the incident and others following in inverted commas, we cannot be sure whether he was quoting from a document he had before him or how far he was using his own version of the event, heard orally from McAllister. If so, this does not necessarily invalidate the stories, since we accept his assertion that McAllister interested him in the Pruntys when he was being coached in the 1850s. It is quite possible that he was using an old notebook or papers.

The cousin watched these strange players go back to work in the fields. Here they cut the hay with sickles, and snatches of songs could be heard, which 'we afterwards found to be from Robert Burns'. The cousin then made enquiries about them, hearing that they had a clergyman brother who was visiting them from England (Patrick). He found that they would spend some part of their evenings in the 'glen' opposite the 'Better House' in Ballynaskeagh holding what he describes as a 'concert'. He could not return to his own home until later, so pretended to be collecting blackberries while surreptitiously watching what the Pruntys did. The blackberry collecting places this event in August or September 1812. There is an echo here of the 'in league with the devil' remark, since this reporter was told it would be dangerous to watch the Pruntys, because they practised 'the black art'. Nevertheless, he watched. A horn was blown at six o'clock. The brothers left their harvest work and were joined in the glen by three sisters, one with a spinning wheel, another with a fiddle in a bag and another with food. After their meal, a brother struck up a tune on the fiddle and the sisters began to dance. It appeared that all the brothers could play the fiddle, since they took it in turn.

It seems that the men did not dance; this was a female perquisite. The dances are described as 'country dances' and 'eight point reels', social dances, but not clearly danced by the men. McAllister's friend (as reported by Wright) gave a romantic account of the appearance of the Prunty sisters; they were handsome and graceful, had pink cheeks and long hair which hung in ringlets. Their dancing had nothing of 'the rough peasant or the country clown' about it, but was graceful. Part of his description stressed the beauty of the 'glen' with its overhanging trees, wild roses and honeysuckle. Though this was a romantic picture, ending with a note about the declining sun shining on this late summer evening on Slieve

Donard and other heights of the Mourne Mountains, there is no reason to doubt its general accuracy, though the vocabulary and tone may be Wright's.

What evidence can we rescue from Wright's colourful version of the Prunty family at work and play? The site of their evening entertainment is still to be seen. It is opposite the Pruntys' one-time residence, bordered on the east side by the brook, and is a more or less level field, down from the road. There can be no doubt that this event happened, and that it happened where it is alleged to have happened. The horn blown as a signal can be identified as a horn from an aurochs, dug up from a bog. A number of these finds have been recorded from the area. All the brothers seem to have played the violin. This indicates a musical tradition in the family which passed in good measure to the Brontës of Haworth. We also note the songs, 'from Robert Burns'. Burns was a favourite with the Haworth Brontës, Anne, for example, including three Burns songs in her music manuscript book. However, Burns used traditional melodies for his poems, and often adapted existing lyrics. What McAllister's cousin heard may have been the original folk-songs rather than the Burns versions. It is a matter of conjecture whether the Prunty brothers could read music. It seems much more likely that they had learned the songs from oral tradition. Among a number of authors who have examined Ulster folk song is Hugh Shields, who gave a number of examples from the whole province, though many of his versions come from County Derry.

The McAllisters came from the Scots Presbyterian tradition. When the 'cousin' heard the violin playing and watched the dancing, he will have had little concept of Irish dancing. That it was very much alive throughout Ulster is witnessed by the notes of the Ordnance Survey reporters. Arthur Young, travelling in the late 1770s, noted how frequent a pastime dancing was, and commented on the dancing masters who taught these dances. I have not found a reference to dancing in South Down from this period, but a reference from Holywood in the north of the county is worth quoting:

> The young people of both sexes are fond of dancing, and have frequent meetings in the village, or in the farm-houses, where, in imitation of their superiors, they keep up the revel from eight or nine in the evening until day-break.[3]

Some of McAllister's description of the dances is vague, though he did say the performance ended with 'Scotch jigs'. It is just as likely that these were Irish jigs, known to the Presbyterian McAllisters from their Scottish versions. On the whole, the céili described seems to have been an Irish traditional entertainment seen through Scots-Irish eyes.

It is an interesting point, mentioned above, that the English clergyman brother was visiting the family at this time in 1812. Patrick was currently incumbent at Hartshead in Yorkshire, but there is a lack of clarity in the register during late July and early August 1812, confirming the possibility of Patrick being in Ballynaskeagh at that time. I have examined microfilm of the Hartshead register, and find that only weddings are signed by the officiating clergyman before 1813. There is a gap in the weddings between 19 July and 5 October and in baptisms between 12 July and 9 August. There are burials, but no note of who took the service. This leaves us with no evidence *against* Patrick's absence, but no conclusive evidence for it. The 'cousin's' account, however, concludes with the remark that 'the clergyman brother … walked to and fro in solemn black, apparently in meditation, and taking no notice of the gleeful recreation of his brother and sisters'. This point is hardly likely to have been invented in the 1850s, and it does suggest the distancing attitude of Patrick to the whole of his Irish background. Only three sisters are mentioned out of the five. Jane was to die early; perhaps her health was not up to dancing. Perhaps Alice, 17, was thought too young: these are mere speculations. In the next chapter we shall discuss the question of whether Patrick paid any more visits to Ireland.

Though Wright romanticised this account, we might notice some unchallenged aspects which point forward to the Brontës of Haworth. This is open-air entertainment. 'My sister Emily loved the moors', wrote Charlotte much later. In this she was following in the tracks of the Pruntys of Ballynaskeagh. The musical content of this scene is very high. Music was perhaps the main entertainment of the native Irish during the years of repression; it takes no money at all to sing, especially when songs have been handed down without the aid of print. Emily especially, but the other Brontës too, were very musical. They had an acute sense of rhythm, as we see in the poetry of all of them, including Branwell. Emily and Anne played the piano, while Branwell played the flute. In Belgium, Emily was tutored by a first-class pianist. This musical capacity depends on aural sensitivity, which they all had, most clearly Emily, with her lively verbal exchanges in *Wuthering Heights*, which leap from the page. The songs of the Prunty brothers and sisters would have been worth hearing. Wright claimed that no one else was ever involved in these outdoor events except Joe Burns.

Two other points might be made. The Irish Pruntys were unselfconscious. They got on with their dancing and singing without regard to the hidden McAllisters. They were absorbed in the art form, expressing and creating in their own way. It was also a family affair. In the 'long bullets' game there must have been some McClorys involved, and we don't know if there were any on the dance floor in the evening. McClorys and Pruntys lived in their own society, having no need for others. The family milieu in which Patrick Brontë grew up was to some extent inward-looking, content with the society of other family members. This was likely in Ballynaskeagh, where different political and religious opinions made external liaisons more difficult. To the Presbyterians, the whole performance was strange. We shall find other examples of the way in which the Prunty family were thought unusual.

17

AFTER PATRICK
WENT TO ENGLAND

We know from some letters of Patrick's which survived that he kept in contact with the Irish Bruntys (later 'Brontës). We do not know how far this contact went. A letter from Ballynaskeagh is mentioned in the 1808 reply which I have quoted, showing that some members of the family had enough literacy to communicate. Not all the family were literate, and it is a matter of great regret that we do not possess this letter, which would have thrown light on their literacy status. An unconfirmed rumour states that Patrick sent money back home on a regular basis. We shall note later two confirmed visits of Brontë uncles to Haworth, and ponder over another. Through these visits, and perhaps through letters, the younger generation could keep abreast of developments in County Down. It is therefore fruitful to probe the lives of the rest of the family after Patrick left for England. There is some documentary evidence to help, as well as memories of the direct descendants tapped by Wright and others in the 1890s.

The principal evidence which appears in official records consists of the already mentioned tithe award, the early Ordnance Survey maps, Griffith's 'Valuation' and Sharman Crawford's rent roll.

Patrick's next brother, William, married Jane Shaw and lived until he was 83. He had seven children, at least one of whom emigrated to Australia. James and Hugh never married, but Walsh married Elizabeth Campbell and had at least three children, one of whom fathered Maggie Shannon, already mentioned. Walsh himself lived to the age of 82. Of the sisters, only Sarah married and was mentioned by Charlotte as 'Aunt Collins'. The Lackan group lived on land which was part of the Sharman Crawford estate, just as the Ballynaskeagh property was. William's second son, Patrick, married Catherine Murphy and predeceased her. In her will, made in 1857, she referred to disagreements among the legatees to Sharman Crawford, or the rector, Revd Garstin. We may deduce, both from her spelling of her name 'Brontë' and by her use of the rector as mediator, that she followed Patrick Brontë into the Church of England and Ireland. In Sharman Crawford's rent roll of 1851ff, the name is spelt 'Bronty'.[1] How far Patrick knew these relatives, or kept in contact with them, we do not know.

For the Ballynaskeagh properties, Sharman Crawford's official usually wrote 'Hu & Jas Brunty', 'Alice Brunty' and 'Welsh Brunty', though his writing is so appalling that it is not always possible to guess what exactly he was writing. It is interesting, however, that even in the 1850s Patrick's way of spelling his name had not been adopted by these siblings, or at least not taken up by officials. Griffith did indeed choose the 'Brontë' spelling. Catherine Brontë was illiterate when her will was made, and signed with an X. It is not clear that spelling was of any concern whatsoever to the Irish Brontës, many of whom may have been as illiterate as Catherine. (We have to be careful here; 'illiterate' does not mean uncultured or unintelligent, merely that they could not write.) Wright's assertion that the name had always been Brontë may make sense in the light of Ulster pronunciation. The small Brontë holdings in Lackan are bounded by the bog already mentioned. Among neighbours in the fields detailed in Griffith's 'Valuation' are some McClorys and 'Murphy Brontë'. Murphy was the eldest son of Pat and Catherine Brontë. Though this Christian name is evidence of native Irish ancestry, we cannot assume that Catherine or her children were Catholics, especially in view of the involvement of the local rector of the Church of Ireland in the disposal of her will.

It may be worth noting the ages of the Brontë brothers on death. Patrick himself lived to be 84, an age well in line with those of the other brothers. Evidently the Brontë family were sometimes long-lived, raising the question why this was not true of Branwell or the three sisters. Many suggestions have been made about this, including the idea that Patrick was a carrier of tuberculosis. Even Patrick's sisters, except for Jane, lived long lives. This incursion into family health does not seem to help in working out why the Haworth family were so ill. The Brontës in Ireland do not appear to have been buried in Aghaderg churchyard; there is no record of them in the register. Legend says they were all interred at Drumballyroney. Though Drumballyroney church burials are extant for this period, the only Brontë officially buried there is James Brontë of Lackan, third son of William Brontë, and thus Patrick's nephew, who was buried on 13 January 1873. Were the Aghaderg Brontës avoiding registration on the grounds that they should have been buried in their own parish?

We have already found that Patrick visited Ireland, almost certainly in 1812. Wright said there were several visits, and he indicated a likely one in 1824. In one passage he actually claimed to have seen Patrick himself.[2] We cannot place too much credence on this claim, but it is not impossible that Patrick could have made a journey to Ireland in the 1840s, when Wright was still a child. Alice Brontë said he had returned after his ordination and preached in

Drumballyroney church 'and never had anything in his han' the whole time', a tribute to a clergyman who was thought to be speaking from the heart and not merely following out a schedule he had arranged beforehand on paper (itself slightly suspect). She may have been referring to the occasion we have dealt with before, when he paced up and down the far side of the glen while his brothers and sisters danced, sang, and ate their evening meal. Possibly 'after his ordination' means soon afterwards, when another visit is implied. It is doubtful whether Patrick had many opportunities to visit Ireland, once he was busy at Haworth. In a letter to his sister Mary, dated 1 February 1859, he said, 'Ireland must in many respects be greatly changed from what it was when I resided in it'.[3] This seems to indicate that he had not kept up with changes in the land, and suggests that he had not visited it recently. In the same letter he said he had heard that Sarah, another sister, was not well, and sent her a £1 postal order, which Mary was to redeem at Loughbrickland post office.

As Hugh and James grew up they apparently did not require any outside companionship. They shared the 'Better House', though it is in the name of James only in Griffith, while in the Crawford rent roll it is in the names of both. Since James was the younger brother, one might have expected Hugh to be recorded as the tenant of the land in Ballynaskeagh. Like their father before them, they evidently worked at a number of trades. They were the main road menders of the district, tarring roads as the technique became available, but also mending fences and carrying out other minor repairs; as we have seen they also cultivated their farmland. Wright continually stressed their difference from other inhabitants of the area, and that they were looked upon as strange. He wrote:

> When I first began to take an interest in the Brontës, I was admonished in
> a mysterious manner to have nothing to do with such people. I was advised
> to keep out of their way, lest I should hear their odious language; and it was
> even hinted that they might, in some satanic way, do me some bodily harm …
> [E]ven educated people … have sometimes felt called on to remind me that
> I was taking much pains with regard to a dangerous and outlandish family.[4]

Whether or not the language was 'odious' it was certainly strange, as will be shown. We shall also look briefly at this charge of being somehow 'satanic'. John Brontë, the New Zealand pharmacist son of William, agreed that the family were unusual ('a peculiar family') because they were quite different from the ordinary folk in intellectual grasp.

What emerges from these comments is that the Irish Brontës were indeed different from the other local people, but we have to remember party differences of all sorts, which might influence local judgements. Not all the Brontë brothers were successful. Walsh, though 'gentlemanly' according to Wright, had two sons, one of whom, also Walsh, died while fording the River Bann when only 22, and his brother, Cornelius, married to Margaret Todd, was the father of an illegitimate daughter, Margaret Barr, born on 11 May 1851 and christened at Aghaderg, the father's name being spelt Brontee ('labourer').[5] 'Neelus' was characterised in John Brontë's letter from New Zealand as being 'saturated with drink, and became a confirmed drunkard, to fill a premature grave'.

Walsh/Welsh, Patrick's brother 'of Ballynaskeagh', died in 1865, leaving his farm and cows for three years to his sisters, Mary, Rosann [*sic*] and 'Eleanor'[Alice]. After that they were to go to 'Curnelous Bruntie' Walsh's son, and Margaret 'Shennan' was to have £16. A small legacy went to Thomas, Maggie's son. The executor was Christopher Radcliff junior of Lisnacreevy.

UNCONVENTIONAL FEATURES OF THE IRISH BRONTËS

W e shall discuss later visits of the Irish family to England. One such visit relates to the Irish potato famine and was timed just as the three sisters were working on their famous novels. The next step, therefore, is to explore the way in which the Irish potato famine affected County Down, and in particular the Brontë family in South Down. This can be done in part with evidence provided by Ros Davies on her Family History Research Site.[1] Other material comes direct from Wright, who was 7 or 8 when the famine took place. Though he did not formally state this, he will have had first-hand experience of the famine in the Brontë area.

First, we need to look very briefly at what caused the famine, and how it affected Ireland in general. This is, of course, a well-known matter for Irish readers, but much less known in other countries.

The famine was a major factor in Irish disenchantment with the British government, coinciding as it did with Robert Peel's Corn Law Importation Bill. This was a measure to repeal the levy on the importation of foreign corn to Britain and after much controversy it was passed in 1846. The furious argument over it eclipsed the necessary attention to the Irish famine, and made very difficult situations worse. We are not concerned here with the impact of the Bill in the rest of the British Isles, but in Ireland it highlighted wretched agricultural practices and worsened responses to the potato famine both directly and indirectly.[2] The one redeeming feature for Ulster was the linen trade, which mitigated to some extent the effect of the famine, since many Ulster homes had a part in the production of linen.

Diet in the Irish rural communities was based on potatoes. In the Ordnance Survey Memoirs, mainly concerned with Ulster, we read again and again of a diet of buttermilk, potatoes, herrings where possible, and oats. (The importance of oats had been recognised long before, hence the Louth 'corn census' which we quoted before). This was not necessarily an unhealthy diet, and indeed potatoes had much to offer by way of vitamins and carbohydrates. In South Down, herrings were brought in via Dundalk and Newry and for many people added useful nutrition. In his poem, 'The Irish Cabin', Patrick later wrote of a supper of 'The mealy potato and herring' with spring water. The potato famine in the west of Ireland struck more forcibly than in Ulster, but this does not mean that Ulster was immune. Ulster residents shared their outrage with their even worse placed neighbours in the west. Belfast workhouse deaths rose from an average of 300 per year to 1,500 in 1847.[3]

The first signs of the potato disease were found in America, then continental Europe, spreading to Ireland in the late summer of 1845. Crop failure was caused by a fungus called *Phytophthora Infestans*, which began by attacking the leaves and stems of potato plants but then spread below ground to devastate the tubers. Botanists were not clear about the nature of the fungus and didn't foresee its virulence. By November 1845 the disease had made its appearance in South Down, and was causing notices in local papers.[4] Various local landlords held meetings to try to work out possible solutions to its effects, and to the poverty caused by unemployment, which added to the potato problem.

It was in 1846 that a really major disaster succeeded the famine of the previous year. There had been a movement to introduce a programme of public works in Ireland, thus providing income for the previously unemployed, but in August 1846 this was discontinued. In the same month 'blackened and withered stems' were appearing on potato plants in County Derry/Londonderry and during this autumn there was potato failure on a grand scale. The London government had no clear policy, and indeed the catastrophe overtook them, whether men of goodwill struggling against circumstances or less perceptive officials who seem to have wished to make profits from the disaster.

The name of William Sharman Crawford has already occurred in this book as the landlord of the Brontë holdings both in Ballynaskeagh and Lackan. He had been MP for Dundalk from 1835-1837 and maintained his interest in his widespread Irish estates when he became MP for Rochdale from 1841-52. He became a Unitarian, and was praised by William Wright for his Christian attitude to his tenants; we have seen that Catherine Brontë was sufficiently confident in his interest to entrust any dissent among her children to his mediation. A trenchant opponent of absentee landlordism, he finally succeeded in his attempt to have legalised the Ulster system of tenant right. (In an unsuccessful attempt to introduce a similar measure in 1849, occasioned in part by his experience of the potato famine, he had failed.) The final provision prevented landlords from evicting tenants; it ensured a right for tenants to maintain their existing holdings even when the rent term expired.

It was probably the potato famine that caused James Brontë to travel to Haworth to seek help from his brother Patrick. Meanwhile Hugh is recorded by Wright as thinking that 'the devil' was causing the blight. This may seem a metaphor, but the notion of a devil causing late blackberries to become inedible was still common in folklore, and forms a parallel to this Brontë attitude – except that the devil was presented by Wright as a live belief for Hugh Brontë. There is no reason to doubt Wright's story of Hugh anathematising the devil as he carried rotten potatoes to the edge of the Brontë farm and hurled them down as a feast for the fiend. Hugh's energy is clear, and though Wright's description, based on the memory of a local man whom he had met, may seem weird and overdramatic, it is in line with other memories of the County Down Brontës at the time. Wright wrote:

> With bare, outstretched arms, the veins in his neck and forehead standing out like hempen cords, and his voice choking with concentrated passion, he would apostrophise Beelzebub as the bloated fly, and call on him to partake of the filthy repast he had provided. The address ended with wild, scornful laughter as Brontë hurled the rotten potatoes down the bank.

The words of 'Shebna' concerning this kind of behaviour, contained in the 1918 article from the *Banbridge Chronicle* are 'She [his recent informant] told in a horror-stricken voice how if they were working in a field, saving hay, when rain fell they would lift their hands to heaven and denounce the Almighty. She said they tried to leave some potatoes in a field and say, "Now, Devil, you needn't be hungry"'.[5]

It is little wonder that from an opposing point of view Wright was told to have nothing to do with a family so apparently wedded to the idea of a personal devil; not 'in league with', certainly, but in close contact. Later Brontë family members, giving material to Ramsden and Horsfall Turner, tended to play down the wildness and superstition of the brothers, especially Hugh. Wright did say that he had earlier been strong in religious disputation, but later became 'superstitious'; Rose Heslip and Maggie Shannon defended him from this aspersion.

There are other anecdotes about the Irish Brontës which Wright recorded. There was some scepticism about them in the mid-1890s, but Wright gave some details of his informants, and I have no doubt that these accounts are in general factual. Some date from after the last known direct contact between the three Brontë sisters and their Irish relatives, but they are not irrelevant, since they show the character of the family members, especially Hugh, James and Welsh.

They show Welsh as both gentlemanly and pugnacious, Hugh as enormously vital but also a joker, and James as somewhat in the shadow of his elder brother.

The first set of alleged events concerns ghosts. It will be recalled that Charlotte Brontë featured a pseudo-ghost in *Villette*, and that Emily introduced the ghost of Catherine in a dream-like sequence in *Wuthering Heights*. Ghosts are prominent in Wright's account of the Irish Brontës and deserve consideration here. We have seen Hugh Brontë confronting 'the devil' during the potato famine and noted local comments about the devil, whom they took to be a reality. It is not certain that Hugh Brontë thought the same about ghosts; in fact it seems quite likely that at times he manufactured his own ghosts to scare the locals. The 'glen' opposite the Better House (which was later itself called 'The Glen') was clearly an eerie place by night, since a number of ghost stories centred on it. In reality, it seems to have attracted depressives; there was an disused quarry at one side, and the stream itself could produce gurgling noises and seem 'haunted'. Wright told us that both a murder and a suicide had taken place in these fields in an earlier age and that the local people were afraid of the associated ghosts.

The murder involved a young woman called Kitty, who had been assaulted and murdered by a lover, who had taken her to a fair at Rathfriland and there tried to strangle her. She had escaped, but was caught by the murderer in the glen and killed. The event became the subject of a typical ballad, allegedly made up by Patrick (but here I think Wright exceeded the evidence), and was the subject of one of Hugh Prunty's stories in the kiln cottage. This eerie and frightening subject matter sounds very like the kind of material Patrick is said by Ellen Nussey to have regaled his daughters with at breakfast time. Orally transmitted ballads of this kind were, and until recently still have been, common in many parts of Ireland.

From Hugh Norton, who lived near David McKee, comes a story relating to Sarah Prunty, later Collins (Charlotte had heard of her as 'Aunt Collins'). Sarah allegedly married a Simon Collins in a registry office. It is doubtful whether this could be the case. Sarah was born about 1793, a twin with Rose. Civil registration for non-Catholics began in 1845, and for Catholics in 1864. Either Sarah Collins or, barely possibly, Rose, had a daughter, who would have to have been born in the 1810s or at the latest the 1820s. Wright's actual phrase was 'one of the Brontë sisters and her daughter lived in a house …' He then went on to write about the ghost of an old man who had died in the house. No husband of this sister is mentioned. Nothing whatever has come down to us about the life of Rose, though Sarah named one of her children after her. No facilities such as registry offices seem to have existed at that time, and we may suppose that Sarah Prunty/Brontë will either have been married unofficially or not at all. Simon Collins, her alleged husband, was not mentioned by Wright. When J. Horsfall Turner went to Ballynaskeagh in 1897/8, he talked to Maggie Shannon, who had already met and given details to Ramsden. The phrase 'runaway wedding' has several times been used of the Brontë-Collins union, and Turner gave a list of the Collins children: Stewart who died and was replaced by another Stewart, and then eight others who all bore names of the Prunty brothers and sisters except for 'Paggie'. Rose Heslip, born Rose Ann Collins, was the seventh child, and married David Heslip, later relocating to Yorkshire. Nothing is said about Sarah's previous daughter, if indeed she was the sister referred to by Wright, and not Rose. Maggie Shannon herself was of course a granddaughter of Welsh or Walsh Brontë. Another contact of Horsfall Turner's, who may perhaps have given him minor information was Dr Joseph May. Turner had already had contact with Dr May, who was also a J.P. and who attended late nineteenth-century members of the Brontë family. His practice was in Rathfriland.

Norton's story began in a house where Sarah lived, previously inhabited by the man called Frazer who had hanged himself. His ghost was supposed to haunt the house. Hugh once again exhibited his rhetoric by taunting the ghost and ordering it to face him; this the ghost refused to do. Next Hugh took his fiddle and tried to coax the ghost out. According to Wright, from Hugh Norton, Hugh became very agitated and went to bed defeated, only to be attacked by the ghost during the night. This was supposed to have caused his death, but a more prosaic reason for the death was provided by others, who said it was due to internal injury following lifting a very weighty sack of corn.

Both these stories suggest some kind of belief in ghosts by Hugh Brontë. However, a tale of a headless horseman has a character much more light-hearted. Wright gave a supposedly verbatim account, in the voice of Caleb ('Kaly') Nesbit, whom we have met as a neighbour of the Pruntys, living on a farm opposite the kiln cottage. It was Nesbit's daughter who had been Wright's nurse in his childhood, and it is possible this story comes via her recitation. The horseman of the story had only a stump instead of a head and rode through the Brontë glen at dead of night. Wright gave us the story with tongue in cheek, suggesting that Kaly, though a 'good' man, was too fond of whiskey to be always believed. Though he himself was of a romantic turn of mind, he felt that the generation of late Victorians for whom he was writing would have been much more sceptical.

Yorkshire commentators such as Horsfall Turner were not persuaded by Wright's account.[6] He summarised the Norton evidence by saying that 'Old Norton's tales were not trustworthy', but despite a partial retraction in the next sentence, he did not believe what Norton said. I have tried to make a distinction between the common 'headless horseman' tale and the others. It is also very important to note that the English writers of the 1890s did not live in the same world as the earlier nineteenth-century sources. Horsfall Turner did not like the remote 'Hugh Prunty origins' story. He talked to both Maggie Shannon and Rose Heslip, who were almost the only Brontë descendants to produce any evidence, though there were many descendants living in County Down. By the time he went to Ireland it seems that local residents were becoming tired of visitors asking the same questions again and again; they therefore told nothing.

One well authenticated event occurred on 22 September 1833, at a time when Charlotte Brontë was at Roe Head School. This was the death by drowning of the younger Welsh/Walsh Prunty in the River Bann while collecting peat from the Lackan bog. Ramsden is our authority, though he did not give the names of his informants. Welsh was Patrick's nephew and Charlotte's cousin. Ramsden heard that he was not sober at the time, but this was denied. He was a good swimmer, but the 'water-spout' caught him suddenly, overturning the cart where he was to carry the peat. The horse escaped but Walsh's body was found 40 yards down from the ford. J.B. Lusk was told that on that evening the three brothers, Hugh, James and Welsh 'went along the road to meet the corpse tearing their hair and wailing with long-drawn cries'.

Walsh was engaged to a girl called Ann McClory. Horsfall Turner mentioned a ballad dealing with this event in which the drowned man is called 'Walch Brunty'; we shall follow up this ballad in the next paragraph. J. Ramsden, in *The Brontë Homeland*, gave a composite text of the ballad. It is a typical locally made ballad, of which there were many. Specimen stanzas are as follows; it is worth stressing that Ramsden's is a composite, and no firmly accurate version can be found; this ballad may never have reached print.

> Ye nymphs and swains of tender fame,
> Come with me sympathise,
> You lovers all, on you I call
> To sing the obsequies.
>
> 'Tis of youth of candid truth
> Who did my heart trepan;
> But alas! Of late his cruel fate
> Was in the river Bann.
>
> 'Twas little he thought 'twould be his lot
> When he from home did steer;
> The Bann to cross, for Lacken Moss,
> Thinking no danger near …
>
> But here's to those who only knows
> The woes of weeping Ann;
> For, from the grave there's no retrieve;
> O cruel river Bann! …
>
> The Christian name I will explain
> With letters just and true;
> The first you take, make no mistake,
> It is a W.

With A and L the next you spell
With C and H you'll scan.
The Christian name it is the fame
Of the deep river Bann.

B R and U next comes in view,
And N T Y also,
It mentions he who heareth me
Great sorrow, grief and woe.

But here's to those who only knows
The woes of weeping Ann,
And from the grave there's no retrieve
O cruel river Bann! [7]

Ramsden printed sixteen stanzas, commenting that the writer was given a half-sovereign by Walsh Brontë and each of the brothers and sisters paid half a crown. It would be interesting to know whether a half crown was sought from Patrick in Yorkshire, or whether he was even informed of the death of his nephew. Recalling that this was in 1833, one wonders whether the Brontë sisters too were told of it.

James Brontë's comment on the existence of fairies has been mentioned. There is abundant evidence of a belief in fairies in Ireland during the lives of the Brontë brothers, but much of this comes from far distant counties. Lady Wilde collected some of these in a publication, the revised edition of which was issued in 1919.[8] It has been followed by methodical research in Ireland. There can be no doubt that the belief in fairies would have been common in Ulster as well as other parts of the land, and indeed James' refutation of the notion indicates both his rationalism and the prevalence of the belief in general. As the younger brother, James seems to have followed Hugh in his exploits, but this comment shows that he was not quite prepared to exploit the supernatural views of his neighbours as much as was Hugh. 'Shebna' heard from his informant that the Brontës had left out bread and butter at nights for supernatural guests.

Modern commentators have wondered whether some of the stories connected with the Irish Brontës are due to leg-pulling by Hugh, who had a reputation for practical joking. He played tricks on the locals by scooping out a turnip, putting a candle in it and roaming the fields trying to convince them that the furze was on fire.[9] Ghosts such as the headless horseman may well have been created by Hugh. Nevertheless, I hope I have shown that for many of the details given by Wright throughout his book there is supporting evidence.

On one occasion, much later, Charlotte Brontë asked her uncle a question about 'the Knock Hill' (see chapter 26). This is Knockiveagh in the townland of Lisnacreevy. It reaches 780 feet at its highest point, and Charlotte's interest in it shows that the Prunty family knew it. Patrick had the reputation of walking many miles with or without accompanying pupils. Charlotte also asked about Lough Neagh which has no Brontë associations, and is of course a major feature of the Ulster landscape, about which the young Brontës could have read or they might have seen it on maps. However, it can be seen on a clear day from the top of Knockiveagh. There is a circular cairn on the summit of the hill, just in the adjacent townland of Edenagarry, which has been excavated by archaeologists. Most of the cairn seems to be made of granite. Along with the many 'forts' in the district this ancient construction produced tales of fairies.

19

THE RELIGIOUS POSITION OF THE IRISH BRONTËS

In County Down during the nineteenth century, religious affiliation was important and generally static. Political attitudes had superimposed themselves on the religious, and it was very rare for people to be unattached or neutral. Hugh Prunty seems to have had no religious loyalty at all after arriving in the Boyne Valley, and then, as a non-Catholic, he had married a Catholic in a Church of Ireland church. All this is established. We also have to remember that different reporters and commentators at the end of the nineteenth century had their own partisan views, and there was a tendency to pull the Irish Brontës into their own camp.

We know that the all the early Prunty children, from 1779 on, were baptized at Drumballyroney church. Wright stated that the brothers followed Patrick into Glascar Presbyterian Meeting. William went to fight at Ballynahinch, an action which suggests a Presbyterian or Catholic background, but some Church of Ireland clergy were not against this movement. Patrick next worked as a teacher for Thomas Tighe, and tradition says that family members were finally interred at Drumballyroney church (though as has been said, they are not registered). But then 'Shebna', quoting an informant of Revd J.B. Lusk, said that in a riot that took place on 12 July (no year known) 'Ayles' (old Alice) took the Catholic (Thresher) side. A ballad was written about this particular fray.

Lusk's manuscript goes on:

> James Brontë applied to join a local 'Ribbon' or 'Thresher' lodge. For some reason the application was not successful. He next offered himself for initiation in the neighbouring Ballynafern Orange Lodge. The Orangemen heard of his previous overtures to their hereditary opponents, and it was considered surprising that they did not accompany their refusal to him with a physical chastisement for his easy laxity of convictions.[1]

The manuscript also suggests that the conformity of Ayles to Hugh's religion 'was only nominal'.

As we have seen, Hugh may well have had no clear religious allegiance anyway, except his undoubted interest in the Presbyterianism of the Harshaws.

The pugnacity involved in the 12 July riots is matched by a story relating to Welsh/Walsh Brunty, told as almost a legend around Ballynaskeagh and the surrounding district – perhaps even at Rathfriland. This is recorded in Wright's Chapter 21 as 'The Great Brontë Battle'. The Great Brontë Battle is authenticated by Horsfall Turner, as is the confrontation between Hugh and another man at Rathfriland. Turner said, 'there is nothing more generally known about the Brontës than this duel' [between Welsh and Sam Clarke]. We shall therefore be justified in taking Wright's story as authentic, though Turner was cautious about some of the detail. Wright was told the details by John Todd, who lived in Croan, a townland between Wright's birthplace at Finnard and the church at Ryans. Todd is likely to have told Wright about this fight when Wright was growing up. According to Wright, the feud between Welsh/Walsh and Clarke began because a young boy from the Campbell family, somewhat disabled, was being bullied by Clarke. At the time, Welsh was courting one of the Campbells, given by Wright as Peggy, but in other sources as Elizabeth. The date is therefore in the late 1810s, perhaps about 1818. This family later had a holding at the Ballynaskeagh end of Lisnacreevy, and it seems probable that this was the home of Peggy at the time of the fight.

We are not given the name of the bullied boy. He was clearly not so disabled that he could not walk, since Wright said he went to school in Ballynafern and used to walk back from there after school 'on crutches'. Welsh therefore hid himself in the bushes near the glen when the boy was coming home from school. The scholar was ambushed by Clarke's friends and pushed into a local pond where he stood up to his neck in water. The others then taunted him. Welsh is said to have waded into the pond and rescued the little boy, then forced the Clarkes to carry him home. Exaggerated rumours about the affair were then spread round the district. This story of rural bullying illustrates the kind of petty strife which prevailed, and perhaps it adds to the impression that the Pruntys were regarded with suspicion. Welsh's action in stopping the bullying so forcefully and compelling the Clarkes to take the little boy home shows the authority the family had.

This was not the end of the affair. As Turner agreed, a fight took place. This was set up with rules and a professional referee. The word 'mongrel' was used of Welsh, allegedly in a short speech of encouragement by Sam Clarke's mother. We need not follow Wright in his detailed account of the fight, which may well be one of the episodes in his book which caused critics to disapprove of him; however, we should note that Wright knew his informant well, and was intrigued by stories of the Pruntys. The word 'mongrel' was again pronounced, but in the end Welsh beat the older and heavier Clarke. Wright's account closed with a comment by William McCracken, who met Welsh later, and recorded his comment that this was '[All] folly; but folk won't see their folly in time'.[2] Though Wright did not say so, the use of the 'mongrel' insult does suggest there might have been an element of sectarianism in this episode.

A second pugilistic encounter concerns Hugh and a man he met at Rathfriland fair. A number of fairs were held in Rathfriland, mainly for the sale of cattle. These cattle fairs took place seven times a year.

A market was held every Wednesday, but this episode is more likely to have happened at a cattle fair, when Hugh might have been in the town to sell a cow. An offensive remark having been offered, Hugh knocked down the man who made it. When his son came to avenge the attack, he took one look at Hugh and decided it wasn't politic. Horsfall Turner was told of the event, and called it a 'skirmish'. We are not sure whether this was a 'religious' difference, but it does underline the large stature of Hugh, the very sight of whose body deters an avenger (his nickname was 'the giant').

In the 1890s, the spotlight was on the remaining Brontë relatives, especially Alice, Patrick's only remaining sibling. She died on 15 January 1891, the then incumbent at Drumballyroney church writing to *Notes and Queries* to say that she had been buried on 17 January. Alice appears to have been living in Dromorebrague (Glaskermore) with an Eliza Brontë and her son Welsh, not to be confused with any previously mentioned Welsh. I have not been able to trace Eliza, but in the 1901 census she gave her age as 60 and, like her son, was a member of the Church of Ireland. Her husband was evidently dead by 1901, the earliest census we have. Griffith's 'Valuation' revision books show that this branch of the Brontë family moved into Dromorebrague about 1889, and that a Welsh Brontë was the holder of the tenancy. Whether this was the very young Welsh shown on the 1901 census is unclear. Alice's coffin was taken on a ceremonial journey to Drumballyroney, though Dromorebrague is in Aghaderg. The tradition that all the Brontë brothers and sisters attended Drumballyroney church is thus strengthened. Revd J.B. Lusk commented, in the article already quoted, that people had told him that the Pruntys 'only became Protestants when Patrick was ordained in the English Church'. This does not seem likely in view of the reminiscences of Ayles taking part in 12 July activities 'on the Thresher side'. Possibly 'mongrel' was not such a misleading term after all.

20

PATRICK BRONTË'S CULTURAL INHERITANCE

As a very small child Patrick lay in the kiln room of the small Imdel cottage and watched the fire.

As Wright said, 'From the earliest moment of intelligence the child had the opportunity of becoming acquainted with his father's tales, and even before he could take in the meaning of the narrative he used to listen with the rest'. Hugh's first language had been Irish, though he must have learned English in the Boyne Valley, if not at least a smattering before. In Imdel, Hugh would have needed to use English to be understood by the County Down farmers and millers. This would be a version of English from County Louth or Meath, influenced later by the local idioms of Aghaderg. The little boy, Patrick, would hear the rise and fall of the narratives, the rhetorical flourishes Hugh is said to have used, the tense action portrayed in Hugh's delivery. The very lowest layer of Patrick's cultural experience was oral, the sounds of Irish English, with native Gaelic interspersions.

Hugh had struggled to read. On the other hand Eilís is said to have written letters to him and deposited them in the hollow tree near the lake side at Loughorne. If she was literate this was unusual for the time and place, but we cannot rule it out, since, as has been said, the McClorys were rather above average in status.[1] Neither she nor Hugh insisted on the correct Christian name being put in Drumballyroney register when the children were christened. However, the record we have may not have been made up in the presence of the parties recorded. The question arises, how did Patrick first learn to read? Authorities generally cite three books from the house at Lisnacreevy: the *Poems* of Burns, *The Pilgrim's Progress*, and a copy of the New Testament with 'Allie Brontë' written in it. There is no telling when Eilís acquired this, but Hugh's Presbyterian allegiance suggests that he would also have had a Bible somewhere around the house. It is not unlikely that Patrick learned to read as many a poor pupil did, by working through the Bible. The Scottish Burns is an important piece of evidence, since the Brontë children loved his work. This may be the seed of their enthusiasm for Scottish culture, though of course Sir Walter Scott was also a major factor.

Traditional songs and ballad making (still oral rather than written) were an important influence. We have the example of the ballad on the death of the younger Welsh; though this dates from 1833, the eighteenth-century style is notable, with its invocation of nymphs and swains. The internal rhyme scheme pervades the song, and, monotonous as it is, stays in the mind. Wright credited Patrick with ballad making. We have to regard this as an unsubstantiated possibility; he certainly did write poetry in his youth. Most interesting perhaps is the possibility that he wrote 'The Vision of Hell' and, as previously stated, its similarity to Brian Merriman's 'Midnight Court', which suggests the possibility that Hugh had memorised some eighteenth-century Irish poetry.

When the Prunty family danced in the glen opposite the 'Better House', they accompanied their dancing with the fiddle. The brothers could all play and Wright asserted that Patrick could also do so.[2] This must be a certainty. This would have been orally transmitted music; there was no question of Patrick being sent to a music teacher to learn to read music. Wright glancingly mentioned 'Sir Roger de Coverley' as the *kind* of dance which would be performed. He was thinking here of a ballroom, and of conventional country dances. A little later he mentioned 'a long bout of Scotch jigs', and perhaps Scottish tunes may have been played on the Prunty fiddles, but is likely that they would have been interspersed with native Irish tunes. The dancers were 'whirling and spinning airily over the grass'.[3] The great Irish music collector, Edward Bunting, was born in the city of Armagh in 1773, and was an official at the Belfast Festival of Harpers in 1792. His local collector was the Irish scholar Patrick Lynch, who came from Loughinisland in County Down and kept a diary of his travels in 1802. Loughinisland is the next parish north of Drumgooland. Lynch collected words of songs from County Mayo, but was also active in County Down. This whole revival movement of Irish music seems to have been unknown to Wright, but we can surely presume that the dances and music performed by the Pruntys in the Imdel glen were from this background.

The versions of traditional Irish dancing seen in twenty-first-century-Ireland reached their final development in the early nineteenth century; the description of the Prunty dances as we have them from Wright's informant may predate these polished forms, though Wright does stress the 'exquisite grace and courtesy' of the dances, in which 'there was nothing of the rough peasant or the country clown'.

Emphasis was placed by William McCracken, Wright's informant whose mother had attended Glascar school, on *Paradise Lost*. This was the poem Patrick was reading one summer day during his weaving period when Revd Andrew Harshaw found him stretched out on Imdel 'fort'. Harshaw approached the reader, who was lost in his book, reading pieces out and saying to himself some of the lines he was reading.[4] The pair are said to have walked 'arm in arm' round the fort discussing the poem. Harshaw fired Patrick's enthusiasm for education, and this is claimed to have been the start of his ambition, soon to be fulfilled in the Glascar teacher's post. Milton retained a strong influence on Patrick.

Both Glascar Meeting and Drumballyroney church would have encouraged communal hymn singing. This would have been very Scottish, in the case of Glascar certainly using metrical versions of the psalms. These might go back in structure and tone to the metrical version of the psalms first made by Thomas Sternhold in 1549 and continued up to 1553 by John Hopkins. Unfortunately we do not have any evidence about the actual psalm or hymn books used at Glascar. Drumballyroney church under Thomas Tighe is more problematic. Having regard to his friendship with Wesley, it is possible that he would have introduced Methodist hymnology to his congregation. Certainly Anne Brontë was very attracted to Wesleyan hymns and the family as a whole knew them. It would be most interesting to know whether this was part of Patrick's tradition. Wright said that in the night school which Patrick ran in conjunction with his school at Glascar, 'a number of Church tunes were sung, each pupil repeating the words he wished to be sung, and raising his own tune.'[5] Wright also said that Patrick 'assisted in conducting the music' at the regular services. All this, as well as the fiddle playing, argues a sharp ear; we can guess this already from the way in which Hugh told his stories.

It may seem strange to include alcohol as a cultural influence. It did, however, play an important part in the lives of the Haworth Brontës, and is worth examining here. Both Welsh/Walsh Prunty and William are credited with opening 'shebeens'. The Irish word '*síbín*' originally referred to a small quantity of ale, then came to imply that the ale was inferior. This was home-brewed beer, not necessarily inferior, but beyond the reach of the law. The word began to be used for these illicit establishments in the 1780s. References in Wright to spirit or beer consumption are frequent. Preparations for the wedding between Joe Burns and Eilís McClory, a wedding which never happened, involved importing whiskey from Banbridge. There was 'whiskey and strong language without measure'. The Brontës' whiskey was 'as good in quality as their roads' (p. 122). Wright went on to say that he feared that 'they were among the heartiest consumers for their own commodities'. This was especially after Walsh opened his public house, possibly a shebeen, in the lane next to the Better House at Ballynaskeagh. This was in the space between it and the house now shown as the house where Alice (Ayles, Eilís) grew up. Wright said the foundations of this public house were still visible in his time, while Horsfall Turner described this as 'the lower house'. A suspicion hangs over the character of Cornelius, Walsh's son, whom we have mentioned as the father of an illegitimate child, Margaret Barr. Wright's harsh view is that he was a 'drunkard', but this was denied by descendants who spoke to Turner.

William also ran a house which has been called a shebeen. He did not occupy a house opposite the glen, but lived in Lisnacreevy. There does seem to be some evidence that he drank too freely. To quote Horsfall Turner:

> Late in life [William] kept a public house on the Knock Hill ... and it is very probable that he patronized his own traffic to his own injury in body and pocket, and on the advice of Rev. Mr McKee, he is said to have retired from the public-house and lived with a son in Ballyroney ... Miss Shannon tells me he died at the age of 83.[6]

Ramsden investigated this story and printed the following version. William's residence was an 'off-licence'. One day a customer failed to take the drink off the premises and, because of the rain, drank his drink in the shop. The police discovered this and presented him with a summons. After this, local people 'would afterwards refer maliciously to the shop as a shebeen. William does not appear on the Sharman Crawford rent roll (though another William does). It is possible that he took over the previous Prunty lease and this may have been a subletting from the Ratcliffe family; Ramsden's phrase 'in trust' suggests that William was a sub-tenant.[7] One may or may not accept the exact truth of Ramsden's account, which may have been supplied to him by Maggie Shannon or another Brontë descendant. It appears that the Irish Brontës were, like much of the rest of the population, drinkers of whiskey almost unlimited.

The Pruntys' obsession with light, causing them to play the tricks mentioned with candles and turnips, may have descended from Hugh's corn-roasting. This activity provided intense light for much of the night, certainly in the time when Patrick was a young child, but lasting to a lesser extent into the childhood of William, who is almost certain to have been taken along the road to the old kiln, where the blacksmith opposite was constantly heating up his forge for his horseshoeing. Sparks were inevitable, but also dangerous, and the Prunty children must have learned that although one could play with candlelight, fire was destructive, as when the Welsh Horse allegedly came to set fire to the Prunty thatch, as they may well have done to other properties in the neighbourhood. Wright said that cottage fires were raked out at night with half-burnt turf preserved. Fire and light were to play their parts in Brontë writing.

There are several references to woollen clothing in Wright and elsewhere. Hugh's woollen clothes were exchanged for corduroy on the road to Drogheda. The Prunty sisters dressed in wool; Wright said, 'Their home-made dresses though of plain woollen material and simply made, fitted them well, and were in perfect harmony with their rustic surroundings.'[8] Animals of all kinds were a constant presence in the Prunty home, as in other cottages: pigs and cows were almost everywhere. They were, of course, to be eaten, and there is no evidence of any sentimental attachment between the family and its livestock. We have no information about dogs in the house at Ballynaskeagh, but Hugh is alleged to have mentioned a dog which formed an attachment to him in the Boyne Valley, and a favourite dog appears in Patrick's *The Maid of Killarney*. 'Fish' usually means herring in the Irish diet; other fish were available in Newry market but there is no mention of them in any Prunty reminiscences.

An activity which would not have pleased Charlotte, Emily and Anne, if they had known about it, was cock-fighting. This is an authenticated pastime of the later Brontës (perhaps the earlier ones too, though we have no evidence). Wright knew of the Brontë 'cockpit' in the northern part of the glen opposite, and thus on the land of Hugh and James. Not for the only time he suggested that the Brontës in Ireland suffered a 'decadence', in which they took to such rough pursuits.[9] Sunday afternoons were the most likely time for these contests. As he said, no one noticed any difficulty with the contests, and bets were laid on them just as on the long bullets game. Cock-fighting had a long history, allegedly having been practised as far back as ancient Greece. It had even been a royal sport, King Charles II having built a cockpit at Whitehall. It became illegal in the nineteenth century, but the law was not always observed anywhere in the British Isles.

THE BRONTËS
AND DAVID MCKEE

We may agree that one problem with Wright's book is his determination to show that the Irish Brontës were closely involved with the writing of the Brontë novels. In Part II of this book, I hope to show how the novels, poems and juvenilia were indeed influenced by the Irish Brontës. However, Wright exaggerated this, perhaps unwittingly; he made claims which cannot be substantiated. Whereas *Wuthering Heights* does have a strong relationship in parts to Hugh's narrative, Wright spoiled his argument by seeming to claim direct links between events in County Down and *Jane Eyre*. He suggested that an early copy of Charlotte's novel found its way to Ballynaskeagh, a view which cannot be accepted. That a later copy did reach Ireland is certainly true; before examining this event we need to consider the authenticity of Wright's view of David McKee, a local Presbyterian minister. Wright had every opportunity to know McKee: he was his son-in-law.

David McKee is one of the most interesting of all the Prunty contacts in Ballynaskeagh. During his youth he had been present at the Battle of Ballynahinch, despite the dangers involved for a spectator. He arrived in Ballynaskeagh in April 1804, but was not ordained at Glascar but in the Presbyterian church at Annaclone. His manse, later, was near the sluice and mill opposite Glascar, but illustrations of the manse are probably incorrect, since for much of the time he lived in a single-storey thatched house. With it went a 44-acre farm. He was well read in Latin and Greek, and took a strong interest in contemporary English literature. A typical saying of his was 'In every plant destined for the food of animals, there is not only a grosser substance for the support and increase of their frame, but also a spirit or essence giving excitement to the powers of life, activity and enjoyment'.[1] He is reported to have carried a packet of sweets in his pocket to give to any children he met on his walks. If he encountered a beggar with not much clothing, he would go behind a hedge and take off one of his own underclothes to hand it over to the destitute man.

McKee was unconventional in dress. He would work manually on his farm wearing the clothes of a farm labourer. He was well known in the district, chatting happily to Catholics or Protestants without distinction. He was quite a horseman, and as he sped along the local roads he propounded a theory that men would learn to fly, and he would say 'If I had £10,000, I would have no scruple in laying it out upon the trial'. His own horses were his pride and joy, to the point where he was pleased to have a race along the country roads. He went on riding until he was at least eight-seven.

At an earlier point in his ministry he had a manse on the banks of the River Bann near Katesbridge. Here he formed a readers' circle to buy and discuss the works of Sir Walter Scott as they came out. When he had finished reading a book he would hurl it across the Bann to another of the circle. He also tried walking on the frozen river one winter, but it gave way and he nearly drowned, breaking his leg in the process. From the point of view of our understanding of the Irish Brontës, the important matter is his relation with William Wright. He was in close contact with Wright during his undergraduate days, when McKee taught his student to help with his college work.

An anonymous informant said of McKee, 'I have rarely heard anything in the way of translation more enjoyable than the rush and vigour of his translations from the Iliad'. Wright married his daughter Annie on 9 March 1865.[2]

When Wright was compiling *The Brontës in Ireland*, he contacted McKee's widow (his own mother-in-law), who had been present at a crucial interview between Hugh and James Brontë, and David McKee. She wrote, '[David McKee] recognised many of the characters as founded largely on old Hugh's yarns, polished into literature'. The occasion for this interview was the arrival at Ballynaskeagh of a copy of *Jane Eyre*, sent from Haworth with a covering note (on the book itself) from Patrick. This was a copy of the first cheap edition. The note explained why it was not possible to send him copies of all Charlotte's novels (their cost). Wright maintained stoutly that Charlotte had already sent copies, admitting that he could not trace the *Jane Eyre* copy, though he claimed to have seen copies of the later novels. He said she sent it without her father's knowledge. This is most unlikely and appears to be contradicted by the action of Hugh and James who took the 1853 book to Mr McKee to see what his opinion was. He was immediately absorbed in the story, took all afternoon to read it (or part of it?) and announced, according to an eye-witness – surely either Mrs McKee or Annie, Wright's future wife – 'the child Jane Eyre is your father in petticoats, and Mrs Reed is the wicked uncle by the Boyne'.[3]

It is impossible to check definitively the accuracy of Wright's report here. What we appear to have are two confirmations that Brontë work was influenced at least by Hugh Prunty's life story. They seem to agree that he gave these accounts, whether they were true or not. Mrs McKee supported the view that the novel's characters were based on *Hugh's yarns*. McKee's daughter, or wife, added *the wicked uncle by the Boyne*. Later members of the family, who had not heard Hugh tell his stories in person, omitted both 'the Boyne' and 'wicked uncle', substituting 'Drogheda' and 'an uncle'.[4] Wright expended pages trying to show that this gift from Patrick was not the first the Brontë brothers knew of the writings of their nieces, but it is doubtful whether his pleading argument is successful.

Wright credited McKee with being in the forefront of the Temperance Movement in Ireland. This may be so, but Ramsden heard a different story, which featured a chair 'in which the rev. gentleman used to imbibe the fiery liquid, which does not speak favourably of the inaugurator of the Great Temperance Reform'. This was in a house not far from Drumballyroney church. Ramsden continued with a gibe in which he alleged that this chair was pointed out to Wright, but he was too wrapped up in praising the Presbyterians. Ramsden's view is, as we have said, very hostile to Presbyterianism, and it is impossible to evaluate the story of the chair. It is interesting that the Brontë brothers chose McKee to provide an authoritative opinion despite not being Presbyterians. Worth noticing is the fact that Patrick kept up a correspondence with them but not with his second brother, William.

The thrust of this part of the book has been to trace the early life of Patrick Brontë as far as possible, and to present details of the family and regional influences on him. It is legitimate to ask why this has all been glossed over in the first 200 years since Charlotte died, and this matter will be explored, so far as she and her father are concerned, in the next chapters. Apart from their attitudes, two major factors seem to be in play. We have seen that MacKay, Ramsden and Horsfall Turner, were very concerned to stress the 'Yorkshire regional novel' aspect of the Brontë works. MacKay and Ramsden disliked Presbyterianism and wrote from a Conservative point of view. The second matter is the ease with which Wright's work could be impugned despite what I consider to be his generally honourable approach. It has to be admitted that he was partisan politically and that this appears in his work, and that he could at times romance an event, a technique he learned from William McAllister. In the late 1890s he became ill and doesn't seem to have had the energy to refute some of the scurrilous allegations made against him. Later Brontë commentators began to see Ireland as an alien place and adopted the attitudes of MacKay and the rest uncritically.

Yet Patrick Brontë had spent a third of his life in his home country. His origin counted both for and against him, providing him with the fluency and wide-ranging interests he showed throughout his life, but disabling him from reaching the social heights of his fellow students at Cambridge. In the next part we shall examine the ways in which an Irish background influenced Patrick and his family in England.

PATRICK BRONTË ABANDONS HIS IRISH HARP

According to Wright, Patrick Brontë had written verses in Ireland; a specimen was mentioned in Part I. Wright also claimed that poems later included in *Cottage Poems* were written before Patrick left for England. There is no way of telling whether this is so. *Cottage Poems* was published in 1811, and will be examined later; first we need to glance at Patrick's second published work, *The Rural Minstrel*, including a poem called 'The Harper of Erin'. Among elements of Irish tradition which were beginning to appear romantic rather than outlandish was the harp. The Belfast Festival of Harpers, held in July 1792, began this movement, which included gentlemen who hoped to 'preserve the music, poetry and oral traditions of Ireland'.[1] Moore's *Irish Melodies* had also helped to create the effect of civilising native music, an effect which crossed the Irish Sea. Beethoven and Haydn were amongst classical composers who added arrangements of Irish music to Scots and Welsh. Though we shall find Patrick evading and downplaying his Irish roots, these reputable versions of Irish song made their mark.

One poem in *The Rural Minstrel* requires special comment. 'The Harper of Erin' begins:

An ancient harper, skilled in rustic lore;
When summer hailed the mild departing spring;
High on a rock, on sweet Killarney's shore,
With flying fingers, touched the tuneful string.
A wildly sentimental grace,
Each feature marked, of his expressive face;
And whilst his fingers swept the mellow chords along,
In sweet accord, with his seraphic lyre,
His soul spoke through his eyes, its wild poetic fire;
And thus he raised his song.

I shall not sing of Erin, beauteous isle,
Nor of her courteous sons, for valour famed,
Nor of Killarney, queen of lakes, –
Adorned with nature's sweetest smile,
And every grace that can be named, –
To view whose charms,
Insensibility herself awakes …

The harper goes on to say that he will 'aspire' to higher notes: 'I'll sing the praises of my Redeeming God'. This he does ecstatically for nine stanzas. The final stanza of the poem ends with an evening scene and what appear to be reminiscences of Gray's 'Elegy', in which, after we read that 'Killarney, matchless lake, could scarce be seen,' and the harper 'homeward took his way,/Resolved to tune his harp, another day'.

Patrick appears to have settled on Killarney as the romantic and ethereal essence of the land he had left. He never saw Killarney, or, so far as we are aware or can guess, anywhere south of Newry. The lake, however, could echo the distant vision of Lough Neagh as seen from the Mourne Mountains. The harper's Irish songs are not disdained, but religious ecstasy is much more important. There is much in the poem about Nature; rocks and mountains, torrents, a 'sighing breeze'. These feature a good deal in later Brontë writing; however, they do not seem purely literary, but were included because they chimed with Patrick's experience in the hills

Traditional Irish Bard. (From *Poems of Thomas Moore*, Vol. 3, 1841)

of County Down. The harper of the poem is a self-identification, doing exactly what Patrick himself was doing, substituting religious poetry for Irish balladry.

In the antepenultimate verse we have a judgement scene where the 'hellish crew… gnash their teeth, in black despair'. This reminds us of Patrick's earlier poem in which he depicted a vision of hell seen through a rift in the ground. It distantly echoes Brian Merriman's poem. If they are judged unfit for heaven, 'See! opening hell, received the wicked throng'.

These poems were published in 1813, by P.K. Holden of Halifax, 'for the author' (then incumbent at Hartshead), which implies that Patrick paid for them.[2] As poetry, these rhymes have little to excite; they adopt eighteenth-century poetic conventions and language years after Wordsworth and Coleridge published 'Lyrical Ballads'. But they indicate clearly what Patrick's motive was: he would, like the harper, cease to write Irish poems and instead use his talent to evangelise. This process can already be seen in *Cottage Poems*, addressed to 'the lower classes of society', published two years previously. 'The Author's wish is, not to lead anyone, into an error, but to show to all, that he, who would be truly happy, must be truly religious'. Here we see, in addition to the stop-and-start punctuation, which is typical of Patrick's letters, the strong influence of the Harshaws and Thomas Tighe. Despite Wright's allegation that some of these poems were made up at Ballynaskeagh, Patrick claimed that he had composed them 'when released from his clerical avocations'.

'The Irish Cabin' is a prominent poem within this collection. In it, a traveller in December, 'when Nature seemed frozen in death' and snow covered the hills, sees a pale light emanating from a small cottage.

> Some called it the Cabin of Mourne:
> A neat Irish Cabin, snow-proof,
> Well thatched, had a good earthen floor,
> One chimney in midst of the roof,
> One window, and one latched door.

The traveller enters the cabin, and is kindly welcomed.

> The dame nimbly rose from her wheel,
> And brushed off the powdery snow;
> Her daughter, forsaking the reel,
> Ran briskly the cinders to blow:
> The children who sat on the hearth,
> Leapt up without murmur or frown,
> An oaken stool quickly brought forth
> And smilingly bade me sit down.

The family then resume their occupations: the reel 'clicked again by the door', and the woman 'turned her wheel in the nook'. The husband comes back from his work in 'the barn', puts down his flail and draws his stool up to the fire. This well pictured beginning leads to a religious homily. It is time for supper, and the family produces 'the mealy potato and herring' with spring water. A grace is said and the meal begins. When it is finished, there is another grace and the traveller departs.

COTTAGE POEMS,

BY THE

REV. PATRICK BRONTË, B. A.

MINISTER

OF

HARTSHEAD-CUM-CLIFTON,

NEAR LEEDS, YORKSHIRE.

All you who turn the sturdy soil,
Or ply the loom with daily toil,
And lowly on, through life turmoil
     For scanty fare:
Attend: and gather richest spoil,
     To sooth your care.

𝔥𝔞𝔩𝔦𝔣𝔞𝔵:

Printed and sold by P. K. Holden, for the Author.

Sold also by B. Crosby & Co. Stationers' Court, London;
F. Houlston and Son, Wellington;
and by the Booksellers of Halifax, Leeds, York, &c.

1811.

Cottage Poems, title page. (From Horsfall Turner's *Brontëana*, 1898)

The poet says he will make sure that 'Whoever reads verses of mine/ Shall hear of the Cabin of Mourne'. If he could sing, he would ensure that the cottage would 'smile whilst the world remains' ('world' needing two syllables to scan, as in Ulster pronunciation). The final two stanzas provide the clearest encomium of Ireland we have from Patrick Brontë's pen. They do perhaps give credence to Wright's assertion that the poem was written while he was still in Ireland, and then expanded to include the homiletic elements. Patrick continued:

> In friendship, fair Erin, you glow;
> Offended, you quickly forgive;
> Your courage is known to each foe,
> Yet foes on your bounty might live.
> Some faults, you, however, must own;
> Dissensions, impetuous zeal,
> And wild prodigality, grown
> Too big for your income and weal.
>
> Ah! Erin, if you [would] be great,
> And happy, and wealthy, and wise,
> And trample your sorrows, elate,
> Contend for our cottager's prize;
> So error and vice shall decay,
> And concord add bliss to renown,
> And you shall gleam brighter than day,
> The gem of the fair British crown.

We note here there is no echo of Hugh Prunty's strictures on the political and ecclesiastical powers. The tone of these last stanzas is in accord with the status of a Church of England clergyman.

There are serious criticisms of Irish culture as well as approval of the native character. Aspects approved by Patrick were the friendship and courage of the Irish, but he noted that the courage emerged through impetuosity. 'Concord' was what was lacking. In the final line he emphasised the tie with Britain, a position he would retain throughout his life, despite sometimes in Haworth trying to persuade government to act to right wrongs. He was on his way to adopting contemporary Tory principles (in saying which, we should be careful not to confuse twenty-first-century Conservatism uncritically with the views held by some Tories in the early nineteenth century).

With 'The Maid of Killarney' or 'Albion and Flora' we are once again in Killarney, far away from County Down. The beauties of its lake had become well known in England, partly due to publicity given in Arthur Young's *Tour of Ireland*.

It is most improbable that Patrick Brontë could have had any personal knowledge of Killarney, but he took it as a symbol of the beauty of his country. To Killarney, it appears, he transferred local knowledge of Ballynaskeagh and district. The first part of 'Albion and Flora' outlines national characteristics of the English, Scots and Irish, and the whole novella exhibits a satirical view of the Scots, personified by Mr Mac Farsin, who is represented as having a fierce eye on business potential.[3] Despite this, 'The Scotch … are plodding and sure', while 'The English [are] wary, phlegmatic, and profound', says Albion. '[T]he Irish are free, humourous [*sic*] and designing; their courage is sometimes rash, and their liberality often prodigal: many of them are interesting and original …' Here Patrick seemed to be credit-ing Albion with insight gained by experiencing the personality of such people as McKee, Harshaw, Hugh Prunty and himself.

The three men walk to an 'Irish cabin', described with its mud-hardened gables and turf-covered roof. Smoke emerges from a hole in the roof, and a few chickens and a goat are on it. (Mud cabins are said to be rare in County Down, where stone quarries are often found, including one in the glen oppo-site the Better House.) As in *Cottage Poems*, the three enter the cabin (it seems that members of higher social classes may enter the peasants' houses at will). The inside is less well furnished than the cabin of Mourne. It includes a table and chest, some stools and a bed on which an emaciated old lady lies. The old lady, a Catholic, is dying, but some of her attributes remind us of the situation of Eilís McClory. She has been anointed by the priest but has also been receiv-ing the attentions of Flora Loughlean, an evangelically minded and beautiful young woman who catches the interest of Albion before retiring from the cot-tage. (The name 'Loughlean' could come from Ossian's 'Loughlin'.) Flora has been talking to the old lady of salvation through the love of Christ, and though she wishes to die a Catholic she has taken on some beliefs that Mac Farsin and Albion recognise as Protestant. Mac Farsin 'could like you to be a member of the Kirk of Scotland', but is 'rejoiced to see what grace has done' for her. Albion is given no lines to speak. We recall the New Testament owned by Eilís McClory. On the following day, Albion goes back to the small cottage, only to find that the old lady has died.

Patrick used the next passage to explore the funeral customs of the native Irish community: his subtitle is 'Giving a description of an Irish wake'. Albion meets with a 'respectable looking gentleman' who turns out to be Flora Loughlean's father. He accompanies Albion into the cottage, where twelve elderly women are sitting round the corpse. Most of them are hired mourners, and Loughlean explains that the chant they begin is the 'Irish Cry'. '[I]t is used only at the funerals of Roman Catholics and is altogether a very unmeaning ceremony'. This remark, however, is one of only two critical comments made by Loughlean or the narrator.

The Real Killarney. (From *Handy Andy*, 1842)

The women are singing in Irish, and Loughlean tries to give a commentary, though he says it is difficult. The song is 'somewhat pathetic in the original, [but] it is but foolish and trifling'. The women address the corpse, asking why she died, and then suggesting that it was because 'they' did not give her enough 'butter, and milk, and potatoes'. They beseech her to open her lips and speak, but agree that she cannot. They wonder whether her husband has met her and welcomed her into another world. 'Speak, ah! Speak to your dear children, whose tears are falling on your clay-cold face'. The whole is a mixture of sadness and accusation, the old woman being apparently in part blamed for her own death. At least she should return thanks to Miss Loughlean, is their final point.

This description is a slightly distanced description of an Irish wake, included by Patrick surely not as a criticism but almost as an anthropological study. It seems likely that it is based on a real experience of Patrick's, perhaps dating from his childhood, witnessing a funeral of a McClory or one of their friends. At the end of this chapter there is a return to the Ascendancy focus when it turns out that Mr Loughlean served with the Duke of Wellington in the Napoleonic Wars. The Brontës were extremely interested in the Duke, and we shall follow up their interest in a later chapter. Albion is still thinking of Flora and is happy to be invited to dinner by Loughlean, who lives in Loughlean Hall.

Flora appears at the dinner party, after fulfilling her duties to the poor cottagers in visits to them. Also at the dinner table is 'Doctor Laurence O'Leary' 'uncle to Flora, by the mother's side'. It is interesting that he bears an Irish native name and is Flora's mother's sister; this may reflect Patrick's own circumstance, with native Irish uncles and aunts 'on the mother's side'. The discussion turns on Catholic Emancipation, however, where Dr O'Leary suggests that it would lead to more and more demands by the Catholics, eventually ending with a demand that a Catholic should sit on the British throne. Captain Loughlean softens his comments, maintaining that though the Pope 'will always be opposed to the British crown', he does not blame individual Catholics; 'the fault lies in their creed'.

He goes on, 'Many of them are good friends and neighbours, and none make better soldiers'. The talk then turns to the war and Wellington, of whom it is said, 'Ireland is certainly happy in giving birth to such a hero'. This is followed by 'Wellington, as a general, is wily, persevering, bold and rapid'.

After the dinner, Flora leaves the table and 'soon after was heard sweet music at a distance'. Flora is playing her harp. More of her music is promised after tea. This does eventually follow, Flora playing a composition of her own called 'The Tempest'. However, Captain Loughlean asks her to follow it with 'one of the songs of Zion', a psalm, which she 'obligingly' plays. Here we have an echo of the transition made by Patrick Brontë's Killarney harper, from secular to sacred songs. A musical discussion follows. O'Leary gives his opinion, 'Those performances have the most genuine music in them, which make us feel the most'. Albion agrees, adding that 'amorous ditties, and amorous novels' make mischief, to which O'Leary replies that novels are like Irish bogs; green, smooth and tempting on the surface, but concealing underneath, the miry slough, or deadly pool.

On another day Albion, Flora and her father take a walk round Killarney Lake, where 'romantic mountains raised their fantastic forms'. They take a voyage in a boat, rowed by Paddy O'Flanaghan, a description of whom is given. He appears to be rather like the ferryman Frank Prunty; tall, straight and muscular. He wears a loose greatcoat, and has large rusty waterproof boots on. He has black, strong hair with a broad-brimmed hat, and his face is 'vested with great good humour'. His speech, however, seems to be 'stage Irish'. As they approach the Eagle's Nest, Paddy takes out a 'large horn' provoking an echo; perhaps this was in imitation of the Brontë brothers' aurochs' horn in County Down. This Killarney episode is not a first-hand account, but uses material which Patrick had evidently seen in a tourist guide.

A further incident deals with a girl called Ellen Green who is solaced by her 'very large dog' wearing a red ribbon round his neck. This girl is wearing a dress 'simple and clean', but she has a 'pensive wildness in her dark eyes'. She sings a wild but tuneful song, with a line in which she introduces 'the Saviour'. In a little 'car' (a trolley or buggy) which the dog is pulling, are a Bible and a doll, to which Ellen can talk when she feels lonely. She had been helped by Captain Loughlean when 'rude boys and girls' had thrown pieces of turf and stones at her: something which had happened to Patrick in Ballynaskeagh. One day she 'strayed' into a church where the preacher was Mr Burnet, who 'speaks so plainly that people of the narrowest capacities may comprehend him'. The result was that Ellen 'abstains from every species of crime and reads her Bible frequently'. 'Burnet' is, interestingly, an anagram of 'Brunte'. It seems that Patrick put himself in the book. Later, Emily would use anagrams and word play in *Wuthering Heights*.

A stirring chapter follows, in which the hall is attacked by 'Whiteboys, or Robbers'. The meaning of the earlier word was always vague, and it is not surprising that Patrick follows it with the other. Though initially 'Whiteboys' was the name for a group of societies which had a political aim, later almost any violent group could be called by it, especially by the non-Catholic population. Taxation was always a sore point, and many 'Whiteboy' bands were protesting against landlords, whether or not they were honourable. Flora reacts firmly to the siege of her home. She picks up a large rattle and sets it going; it makes a tremendous noise and the attackers disappear. John O'Flacharty, the footman, has also played a valiant part, and he is invited by Loughlean to have his dinner with the master of the house and his guest. Then they all sing 'God save the King'.

There follows a discussion of the jury system of justice, with O'Leary making the point that 'If a jury be empanelled from a neighbourhood overrun by a banditti … who can expect that a robber will condemn a robber, or a rebel a rebel?' His conclusion is that juries should not be chosen from the area where the criminal lived. This clearly reflects Patrick's own thought about the issue, and shows his interest in political and social matters, which he continued to pursue throughout his Haworth days, and passed on to his children. In the next chapter, Albion goes home to settle the affairs of his father, thus allowing a 'cooling-off period' for his romantic interest in Flora. When he returns to 'the beautiful island' his feelings have not changed, and in his bed at night he dreams fitfully of Flora.

A bright morning ensues, in which Flora is going to visit the cottagers. Albion goes with her. They meet 'a poor old man, tottering under the weight of infirmity and age'. He begs them to enter his cottage. Here we are given another picture of Irish poverty. There are 'four or five' ragged children squabbling over a cold potato. Their father, an emaciated man leaning on a cupboard, says he cannot be angry with them, as they have eaten nothing for days. He turns out to be a schoolmaster, who is prevented from teaching at 'my little school' because of his illness. His wife has just given birth to twins. The cottage is like the Brontë kiln, having just two rooms. Beyond the partition is the wife, trying to feed her new children. 'My dear husband, who is a good scholar you know, for about a month past, has kept no school; and my poor father, who went out a bit ago, is able to do nothing'.

A good deal of the next passage is devoted to religious comment through the mouths of the characters. The teacher and his family are overjoyed to receive the charity of Albion. We learn that two of the children are called Mary and Pat. The wife is called Jenny. This scene leads on to another visit by Albion and Flora, to an old but 'very worldly-minded and discontented old woman'. She too is made an object lesson in how the poor should act. The chapter ends with a visit to the small cottage of Ellen Green.

There is little more in 'Albion and Flora' concerning the Irish or Ireland. Patrick Brontë's final paragraph summarised what he had shown us: 'lakes, cataracts, mountains … the intricate mazes of politics [and] the more sublime paths of religion'. The religious elements of the poem have been sincere and related to the Irish situation. Not surprisingly, Patrick used the romance of Albion and Flora to illustrate the values of Christianity, seen through the eyes of an Evangelical, influenced by Wesley and Tighe. Some of the Irish background is from first-hand experience, though the Killarney episode seems second-hand. Though he claimed a political aspect, the only issue treated is Catholic Emancipation, and even this does not give a genuinely two-sided account. Most Presbyterians were in favour of it in 1798, but Patrick was dubious.

PATRICK GIVES
AN EDITED ACCOUNT
TO MRS GASKELL

Patrick moved from Hartshead to Thornton and then to Haworth, where the rest of his days were to be spent. Gradually his Irish youth faded from his mind, and he became more and more an English clergyman. Yet he never achieved the kind of fulfilment his fellow Cambridge students found. Perpetual curate of a small Yorkshire village was not a high ecclesiastical post. He tended his flock assiduously, held meetings, lobbied authority and taught his children. What we now have to examine is how much and what he taught them of his origins. He did not forget Ireland, but he was uneasy about it, becoming as much a 'dissembler' as the character created by his daughter, 'Agnes Grey'.

Much later, Mrs Gaskell tried to get him to tell something about his beginnings. He stalled, writing:

> My father's name, was Hugh Brontë – He was a native of the South of Ireland, and was left an orphan at an early age – It was said that he was of an Ancient Family. Whether this was, or was not so, I never gave myself the trouble to inquire, since his lot in life, as well as mine, depended, under providence, not on Family descent, but our own exertions. He came to the North of Ireland, and made an early, but suitable marriage. His pecuniary means were small – but renting a few acres of land, He and my mother, by dint of application, and industry, managed to bring up a family of ten Children, in a respectable manner. I shew'd an early fondness for books, and continued at school for several years – At the age of sixteen, knowing that my Father could afford me no pecuniary aid I began to think of doing something for myself – I therefore opened a public school – and in this line I continued five or six years; I was then a Tutor in a gentleman's Family… [he then continues to describe his move to Cambridge][1]

It may be thought that this is rather a late stage to examine what Patrick himself said about his inheritance. But as we have seen, other witnesses revealed much more about it than he did. Does he actually add anything? Does his account tell us anything about his wary glance back at himself?

He started by giving us information which misled commentators for a many years: his father's name. It was 'Hugh Brontë' only after Patrick himself decided to call himself 'Brontë'. The rest of the family followed, hence Wright's understanding that the name had always been 'Brontë'. Of course, this is in some ways a quibble, since the sound of his father's name was quite close to 'Brontë'. Still, it is not strictly accurate.

Hugh was 'a native of the South of Ireland'. Did Patrick believe this? What did he mean by 'the South'? Hugh came to County Down via Dundalk from Drogheda, a fact known to his sister Alice.

Patrick, as we have seen, romanced about Killarney, though he did write a poem about the cottage 'of Mourne'. Beyond Drogheda, we think, lay Fermanagh. Had Patrick ever heard a whisper of this?

Drogheda is not 'the South', though it is south of County Down. Readers will make up their own minds whether Hugh knew where his father lived, or whether Patrick knew. Patrick was right in saying his father's pecuniary means 'were small', but he married Eilís McClory whose pecuniary means were better (if not much). It was indeed a 'suitable' marriage, though it is not clear that it was 'early', since Hugh was probably 26. It is not clear what Patrick meant by saying he 'continued at school for several years'; we have no record of systematic schooling, though this may be a lacuna in other evidence; possibly he went to some school run by the Harshaws (merely a guess). We have seen him as a blacksmith's assistant and a weaver. At 16 he said he opened a school; this was Glascar, and we have no reason to doubt him. Finally, we read that he was a 'tutor' in a gentleman's family: Thomas Tighe is meant. Tighe's sons denied that this was so, as we have seen.[2]

Was Patrick 'of Ancient Family'? This is a puzzling statement. There seem to be four possibilities, all dubious. (i) It is sometimes said that Ó Pronntaigh is a branch of the O'Neills. Even if this is not so, Pádraig was certainly a scholarly scribe, who may have perhaps had Maguire backing. (ii) Possibly the 'Welsh' story hides an illegitimate scion of Drogheda (Moore) descent. (iii) The Hilltown link may imply some connection with the Hills, later Marquesses of Downshire, or – perhaps much more likely – the O'Neills. (iv) The McClorys, as we saw, were old inhabitants of the three local parishes in County Down. They may possibly have had a claim to be an 'ancient family'. None of these seem at all certain, the first being the most possible. What rumour Patrick had heard can probably never be discovered. It is likely that he had heard *something*, and this may well have meant *something*, but we do not know what. Altogether, this is a concealing but varnished account of Patrick's ancestry.

A major question now arises, which we have been trying to solve throughout the factual quest in Part I. As we consider Patrick's first 25 years of life, lived in a country area of Ireland, a district where the inhabitants and culture were made up of native Irish elements, Scots-Irish elements, and an influential but locally not large English element, how did all this affect the attitudes and writing of his four children? This is a special problem in the light of the kind of account Patrick gave to Mrs Gaskell, presenting himself in a way he thought would be acceptable to her readers, mainly in the United Kingdom. We shall see that Charlotte, his oldest and most protective daughter, took on his mantle. Exploring the issue is particularly difficult, since the only authentic outside source close to the family for many years was Ellen Nussey, Charlotte's friend. We thus see the Brontës of Haworth through two prisms: Ellen Nussey giving us what Charlotte wished us to know, and indeed, what she wished her to know. The results included the alarmed and hostile responses we have seen from such critics as Angus MacKay, J.D. Ramsden and Horsfall Turner.

Despite all this, Ellen was the first to give us any hint of the transmission of the culture of County Down and beyond to the Brontë children. She did this with great caution, carefully tailoring the scope of the information. She did not discuss the influence of Thomas Tighe or the Harshaws on Patrick's religion, and I shall also omit much discussion of these matters. Ellen first visited Haworth in 1833, when Charlotte was in her mid teens and the other sisters in their early teens. By this time Charlotte had written a good deal, much of it in co-operation with Branwell. Emily and Anne had in all likelihood begun their Gondal stories, though it is impossible to pin down the precise date when this happened. It was much later that Ellen found herself the focus of biographical curiosity about the family, and had the task of constructing a coherent narrative about them. We need to look at her evidence, bearing in mind all the caveats I have just mentioned.

The first intimation we have of Patrick's narratives, which often occurred at the breakfast table, come from Ellen Nussey's reminiscences, beginning in 1833. It was nearly forty years later that she touched on these stories in her 'Reminiscences' for *Scribner's Monthly*, May 1871.[3] By 1833, Patrick had presumably been telling this kind of story to the children for at least thirteen years, and of course, we have no idea which of his own or Hugh's experiences he told.

> Mr Brontë at times would relate strange stories which had been told to him by some of the oldest inhabitants in the Parish, of the extraordinary lives and doings of people who lived in far off out of the way places but in contiguity with Haworth – stories which made one shiver and shrink from hearing, but they were full of grim humour and interest to Mr Brontë and his children; they revealed the characteristics of a class of human beings, and as such Emily has stereotyped them in her 'Wuthering Heights'.

No mention whatever of Ireland here, but the scene will gradually move in that direction.

Six years later, in 1877, Ellen's help was acknowledged by T. Wemyss Reid, as he gave an expanded version of her evidence:

> Though he habitually took his meals alone he would often appear at the table where his daughters, with possibly their one female friend, were breakfasting, and without joining in the repast, would entertain the little company of school-girls with wild legends not only relating to Yorkshire during the last century, but to that still wilder life which he had left behind him in Ireland. A cold smile would play round his mouth as he added horror to horror in the attempt to move his children; and his keen eyes sparkled with triumph when he found he had succeeded in filling them with alarm. Emily listened to these stories with bated breath, drinking them in eagerly. She could repeat them afterwards by the hour to her sisters; and no better proof of the deep root they took in her sensitive nature can be desired than the fact that they led her to write *Wuthering Heights*. Thus the paternal influence, strong as it was in the case of all the daughters, was particularly strong as regarded Emily; and we can gauge the nature of that influence in the weird and ghastly story which was brought forth under its shadow.[4]

Writing in 1883, A.M.F. Robinson thanked a series of Haworth residents, including William Wood and the Brontë servants. The passages in which she mentioned the breakfast-time stories are:

> Some months before his wife's death he had begun to take his dinner alone, on account of his delicate digestion; and he continued the habit, seeing the children seldom except at breakfast and tea, when he would amuse the elders by talking Tory politics with them, and entertain the baby Emily, with his Irish tales of violence and horror. (p. 18)

> Emily cared … for fairy tales, wild, unnatural, strange fancies, suggested no doubt in some degree by her father's weird Irish stories. (p. 27)

> At breakfast … Ellen used to listen with shrinking amazement to the stories of wild horror that Mr Brontë loved to relate, fearful stories of superstitious Ireland, or barbarous legends of the rough dwellers on the moors; Ellen would turn pale and cold to hear them. Sometimes she marvelled as she caught sight of Emily's face, relaxed from its company rigour, while she stooped down to hand her porridge-bowl to the dog: she wore a strange expression, gratified, pleased, as though she had gained something which seemed to complete a picture in her mind. (pp 50-1).

On p. 160 Miss Robinson discussed *Wuthering Heights*. She wrote:

... Emily, familiar with all the wild stories of Haworth for a century back, and nursed on grisly Irish horrors, tales of 1798, tales of oppression and misery, Emily, with all this eerie lore at her fingertips, would have the less difficulty in combining and working the separate motives into a consistent whole, that she did not know the real people whose histories she knew by heart.

For the first time we have here a hint of what some of Patrick's stories were about. Setting aside those relating to Haworth, we find at least two types of Irish story: tales of the 1798 rebellion, and another group, variously described as 'weird', 'violent', 'fearful', 'grisly' and tales of 'horror'. These were not, then, contemporary stories of what the brothers were doing laughingly on Caldwell's fields. They sound like the Ulster cycle, or traditional epics which Hugh perhaps told in the corn kiln.

There is one more small and intriguing point about Patrick's breakfast-time stories. In 1828, Aunt Branwell gave the children a New Year present consisting of Scott's *Tales of a Grandfather*.

This was a book suitable for children, giving narratives about Scottish history. What Patrick was telling his children was exactly that; tales told by their grandfather. It is just worth wondering whether Aunt Branwell felt that Scott's book might have contained more edifying stories than Hugh Prunty's. (There is absolutely no evidence for this, but it is an interesting speculation.) Alternatively, we might wonder whether Scott's title caused the children to enquire about their own grandfather. The effect of the book, enhanced by their early acquaintance with Burns' poems, may have turned the thoughts of the children towards the Scots-Irish elements in Ulster, and formed a counter-balance to their native Irish heritage.

CHARLOTTE, EMILY, ANNE AND THE IRISH LANGUAGE

We now revisit a matter which we touched on in an earlier chapter. Did Patrick know Irish, and did that percolate down to his children in Yorkshire? In *The Maid of Killarney* he alluded to the language, which the mourners were using. It seemed more than possible that this was based on an actual experience of Patrick's. This brings us to the question of Hugh Prunty's language and what he passed on to Patrick and the others, and also to the language profile in late eighteenth-century Drumballyroney and Aghaderg. In my earlier work I had felt that the Presbyterians and Church of Ireland adherents would have spoken mainly or entirely English. (There were Irish speaking Presbyterians in the Dundalk area, but no evidence from Glascar suggesting that they had an influence there.) Much of Patrick's time was spent with Presbyterians or Church of Ireland ministers. But the native Irish population of these parishes was probably in the majority, though we have no precise figures for that period.

There is no doubt that the Irish language and culture were prominent in Dundalk and the surrounding district at the time when Hugh lived there. Séamus Ó Casaide had much to say about the language in County Down. Inevitably, he concentrated on written Irish, and there seem to be no detailed comments on the spoken forms at that time in that place: hardly surprising when we only have written types of record. Before we look at the possibility that the Brontë children knew any Irish words, we need to examine the likelihood of Irish being spoken in the households round Imdel and Ballynaskeagh. We shall have to begin with John O'Donovan, the Irish scholar who helped to trace Irish names for townlands and parishes during the preparation of the Ordnance Survey maps and reports in the 1830s. He arrived in Rathfriland in April 1834, to a district he called 'the Irish district'. He had travelled from Newry, walking behind a coach in which there were three drunks; he dared not get on the coach because of the poor driving. Whiskey, he thought, was the ruin of the people in the whole district. His aim was to find details of the old townland names in Drumballyroney, Drumgath and Clonduff.[1] On 15 April he went to meet Thomas Tighe's successor at Drumballyroney, Revd John Dubourdieu, at Ballyroney Glebe. The following day he set out towards Annaclone.

O'Donovan was particularly interested in the written and standard versions of Irish, and sought out the oldest inhabitants everywhere. He almost always found such people, but did not veer from his major aim. He found suitable memories of local names in all the townlands round Imdel, but it is not clear that he found actual speakers of the language as a living entity. This does not necessarily say anything about the Pruntys and McClorys. Six years after Patrick left for England, Dr William Neilson, a classical scholar, published an Irish grammar book, the writer of his 'memoir' remarking that in 1804 he felt called to a language daily fading from the land, 'the venerable Gaelic of Erin'.

'The sweet mother tongue was rarely heard amid the green hills, and on the wide plains round Dundalgan [Dundalk]; and those who understood it, neither spoke it with precision, or read with due accent'.[2] This was Dundalk in 1804; it is not unlikely that the same was true further north near Rathfriland.

John Martin of Loughorne, neighbour and relative of the Harshaws, was interested in the preservation of the Irish language. In a letter to a Miss Thomson, staying in Biarritz, at the very late date of 1860, he wrote that he had given £200 towards the production of an Irish dictionary. He was obviously quite involved in this project, though despairing about the response from wealthy people. John O'Donovan was one of the two people he considered most likely to organise such a publication. He admitted, however, that 'I am as ignorant of Irish myself as is the Emperor of China'. This seems to imply that there was no Irish spoken around Loughorne when he was a child in the 1820s.[3]

We have seen in a previous chapter that Hugh Prunty was almost certainly an Irish speaker. The McClorys may have been so, though we have no evidence. Patrick was in a position to hear Irish from his father, as well as from such events as the funeral wake. Examining carefully some of the writings of the Brontë sisters, we may come to the conclusion that at least individual words of Irish were passed down to them. Such words may have formed part of Patrick's breakfast-time entertainments. In 1829 the Brontë children created an imaginary town called 'Glasstown'. The Irish word *glas* means 'green'. A year after this the name was changed to 'Verreopolis' or, even a little later to 'Verdopolis', i.e. still 'the green town' but this time with French taking the place of an Irish element. (The French for 'glass' cannot be ignored, but where does the letter 'd' come from?) Kathleen Constable went a little further than this, deriving 'Angria' from *an-ghracha* (*an gradha?*) which may represent the young Brontës' idea of the Irish for 'love'.[4]

In the Gondal saga, one of the islands is called 'Ula'. This may represent the Irish word, *Uladh*, the name for Ulster, the final letters being unpronounced in Irish. This word seems likely to have been one Patrick would have known if he had only a small knowledge of the language. The word Gaaldine is odd, the spelling perhaps indicating a lengthened or repetitious 'a'. The second element certainly seems to be the Irish for people or mankind (*daoine*). The first part could be '*geal*' which could mean 'fair' or 'good'. Gaaldine could then be the land of good or fair people. Gondal was Emily's island, so we suspect, and Gaaldine Anne's. (However, Juliet Barker's transcription spells the word 'Garldin': *The Brontës*, p. 454.)Of all these instances, the strongest is certainly Ula, which can hardly come from any other root; but several reach the point of likelihood. We may add to them one extraordinary coincidence (or proof that the young Brontës knew of Hugh's story, through their father): a personage called The Marquis of Ardrah'.

Ardrah was the son of Parry, Emily's arctic explorer hero. Ardrah became characterised as 'the rascally Scot', but we may consider his name carefully and think he is more likely to be Irish.

Constable thought his name may have come from *ard* + *righe* (high king), but we recall that Hugh Prunty probably lived for eight years at a place called Ardagh. I would cautiously advance the theory that Patrick knew this, and mentioned the name to the children. Emily would turn out to be the most Hibernophile of them, and she gave this name to her hero's son. We recall that when she listened to her father's stories, she sometimes 'wore a strange expression, gratified, pleased, as though she had gained something which seems to complete a picture in her mind'. Emily was building a jigsaw, while the others were merely being entertained.

We turn for a short while to look at the names in lists of Gondal people. Anne wrote out two lists at unknown dates. Among them are the surnames Hybernia, (six times), MacElgin, Campbell, MacRay and 'Fizher' (possibly FitzGeorge?) and the Christian names Isabella and Una. Some of these could be more Scottish than Irish, reflecting the Scots elements in County Down. We shall examine some of Emily's nomenclature when we look at the Gondal saga in more detail.

A related point concerns the rapidity with which the young Brontës took to any language experience. As we have seen when commenting on Verdopolis/ Verreopolis, they liked the sound of French when still very young. Charlotte was to be attracted by this alternative to English for the rest of her life, scattering French throughout her novels. This was despite her dislike of French matters in general, doubtless as a consequence of the Napoleonic Wars. It is too much to say that the young Brontës grew up bilingual, but they were very open to the idea that there was more than one tongue in which to express oneself. This surely echoes Patrick's own interest in language. There is one further point linked to this, namely the oral tone of much Brontë writing, especially *Wuthering Heights*. Words spoken and placed in inverted commas are often in lively clusters. We shall look later on at Patrick's perceived accent and manner of speech, but for now we note that the oral mode is prominent in Brontë writing, and follows from the orality learned by Patrick in Ireland.

CHARLOTTE'S JUVENILIA

We should dearly like to have some juvenilia from Emily and Anne, but there is nothing before the 1834 diary paper, written when Anne was 14. However, Charlotte and Branwell left a great deal of material written before the publication of Charlotte's work. There are plenty of traces of their Irish heritage in this collection. For the exploration of this mountain of writing we have to thank Christine Alexander, who has worked tirelessly at the very extensive archive, and previously Winifred Gerin, who was also interested in some of Charlotte's early work. Anyone dealing with the juvenilia owes a heavy debt to Ms Alexander, whose investigations I shall chiefly follow in this chapter.[1] The young Brontës' written output is amazing in its volume, vivacity and the way in which it draws on all sorts of material, from newspapers and periodicals, to old geography books and accounts of political and historical events, mediated by Patrick and Aunt Branwell. There are many literary traces, showing the family as avaricious readers as well as writers. From all this I shall try to extract Irish influence.

Overshadowing much of the narrative content is the adored figure of the Duke of Wellington. Born in Dublin, he acquired a typically Irish musical interest from his father, Garrett Wellesley. His military career was spectacular, culminating in the victory at Waterloo, a battlefield which Patrick later visited. Also prominent was Robert Stewart, Viscount Castlereagh, the latter both close to Ulster opinion and active in Irish politics. His surname was taken up by Emily and Anne in Gondal matters. Castlereagh was in favour of Catholic franchise in the late 1790s, but also involved in the passing of the bill for Union in 1800. He represented County Down from 1800-05. Charlotte's early teenage years were taken up with the controversy over Catholic emancipation, which had been a parallel issue to the Act of Union. Patrick and his Presbyterian friends had been in favour during his last years in Ireland, and he retained this view at the end of the 1820s. The Duke of Wellington became prime minister in 1828. He was faced with an impossible situation in Ireland, where emancipation had been long delayed and dissention was gathering round the figure of Daniel O'Connell. The Duke of Wellington, guided by Robert Peel, had no option but to pass the emancipation bill in 1829. This ferment kept Ireland in the minds of the young Brontës, and was no doubt in the forefront of their discussions with Patrick.

An Irish literary influence was James Macpherson's *Poems of Ossian*. These were represented as Scots Gaelic, and it is generally thought that the versions of the epic Fingal (Fionn Mac Cumhaill, however spelt) were adapted rather than translated by Macpherson. Some of the elements may well be smoothed-out versions of stories which Hugh Prunty knew and retold from oral tradition. Branwell was particularly interested in these episodic narratives; in 1829 he wrote what he called a 'commentary' on them. Unfortunately, their existence makes it hard to be sure whether some elements in Brontë work came from Macpherson's versions of the narratives or the 'weird' Irish stories Patrick told

The Duke of Wellington. (From Alexander's *Life of the Duke of Wellington*, Vol. 1, 1839)

at breakfast. In his footnotes, Macpherson did include Scots versions of Irish words, but I have not found examples of the words mentioned above. Nor can I see much similarity between the Gaelic-type names used by Macpherson and the names adopted by the Brontës for their imaginary countries.

Charlotte's juvenilia and other writings unpublished in her lifetime provide many examples of Irish interest. One of her earliest narratives, contributed to the *Young Men's Magazine* which she and Branwell wrote jointly, is called 'Liffey Castle'. In this article she takes the reader on a small tour of southern Ireland, but does not touch the north. In a narrative known as *Mina Laury*, written as late as 1838, and continuing the Angrian saga, Mina is the mistress of the Duke of Zamorna (based on the Duke of Wellington). One day an associate of the duke, Lord Hartford, oversteps the bounds of friendship and declares passionate love for Mina. He kisses her 'furiously rather than fondly' and proposes. She turns him down: '[S]he sobbed – not in tears – but in the overmastering impulse born of a warm & Western heart – again she looked up – her eyes had changed – their aspect burning with a wild bright inspiration – truly, divinely Irish …'

In the same narrative she included a character called Ryan O'Neill, an Irish accountant whose accounts are 'a specimen of mathematical correctness'.[2] There is a crucial encounter between them which explains a lot in the poetry of the Brontës, especially Emily:

> 'Ah!' said Miss Laury smiling – 'You and I are Westerns, Mr O'Neill – Irish, & we favour our Countrymen…'

Here we have a firm assertion that when talking of the west or 'westerns', the Brontës would probably have meant 'Irish'. A few pages later Mina Laury witnesses a coach accident, as a result of which Mrs Irving ('my husband is a minister in the Northern Kirk') swoons.[3] 'What is to be done?' is the question asked. Mina Laury answers 'with Irish frankness', 'Bring them all into the house – let the horses be taken into the stables & the servants – how many are there?' The footman does not know, but Mina goes on, 'Well, you have my orders, bring the lady in directly & make the others comfortable'. When Mrs Irving is revived, Mina Laury tells her that the Duke of Zamorna (though she doesn't mention his name), whose mistress she is, is a 'Gentleman of Western extraction', and a distant relative of the Pakenhams; this family were Earls of Longford. By this time Angria had grown difficult to manage geographically, as it clearly has strong African elements confused with the British Isles; Mrs Irving, for example, with her Scots surname, is clearly a Presbyterian minister's wife. In the search for surnames, Branwell and Charlotte were eclectic: one of the characters is General Mac Terroglen, and another FitzArthur. As we have already seen, the 'Fitz' prefix also fascinated Anne and Emily. Another minor character in the Angrian story is Maurice Flanagan, his first name apparently coming from James FitzMaurice, a prominent Irish noble who sought help from Spain in the sixteenth century. Maurice Flanagan is no noble, but a servant.

Mina Laury considers the proposal from Lord Hartford. She refuses and he asks, 'Do you despise me?' Her reply and demeanour are worth repeating:

> 'no, my lord' [she replies], and then, she paused and looked down – the colour rose rapidly into her pale face she sobbed – not in tears but in the over-mastering approach of an impulse born of a warm & Western heart – again she looked up – her eyes had changed – their aspect burning with a wild bright inspiration – truly, divinely Irish…[4]

Summing up Charlotte Brontë's attitude to her Irish heritage in 1838, we may say that it was part of a huge and complex nexus of influences, whirling round her head and issuing on paper, as it had done for ten years. She made no clear references to County Down and, like her father, selected romantic and patrician elements of Irish society in which to express her loyalty to her background. While he wrote of Killarney, she chose Wellington, Pakenham and Castlereagh. Like him, she wished to find generalised Irish qualities, which she named as frankness, warmth, wildness and brightness. She also blurred a little the Irish with the Scots, perhaps helped by her reading of Ossian. Though I have found no overt references to Sir Walter Scott in the juvenilia, he was a favourite of the young Brontës, and elements of their work may have been influenced by him. It is not at all sure whether they might have seen any difference between the Gaelic of Ossian and the borderland of Scott.

Ellen Nussey described Charlotte's dramatic performances at school. They partook greatly of her father's (and Hugh's) horrific intensity. When another girl was ill, Charlotte apparently tried to entertain the company as well as the ill girl with ghostly stories. 'A shivering terror shook the recovered invalid,' said Ellen.[5] Thereupon Charlotte was full of remorse. Like her father before her, she had not realised her own narrative and dramatic strength. It was another friend, Mary Taylor, who noted, 'She was very shy and nervous, and spoke with a strong Irish accent.' No doubt this was deployed to great effect in the rhetorical performances.

THE UNCLES
VISIT ENGLAND

Charlotte Brontë said almost nothing about her Irish relations. However, their influence can be detected in her work. Two of her uncles, Hugh and James, visited the family in England, though they did not visit together, but on separate occasions. Their visits influenced *Wuthering Heights*, Gondal and perhaps earlier material by Charlotte, and – perhaps in a negative way – *Jane Eyre*. One of the most difficult problems, however, is that of precise dating. There are three alleged visits. One was by Hugh, apparently in the 1830s. One was by James, in the mid-1840s. A further, most mysterious visit is alleged to have been made by Hugh in the later 1840s. This visit is much disputed, with reason. We shall examine each in turn, trying to assess the primary sources.

Before doing so, we need to look at the evidence provided by Maggie Shannon, Rose Heslip and Patrick's sister Alice, taking up our story from the references in Part I. First, we review material given by Maggie Shannon, the granddaughter of Welsh/Walsh Brontë, Patrick's youngest brother. She met J.D. Ramsden on his journey to Ireland before he wrote *The Brontë Homeland* in 1897. He noted similarities between Maggie and Charlotte:

> There lurked the fiery streaks in the deep-set, dark eyes; the voice was tune-fully modulated; the quiet movements, and shy, nervous manner – all these reminded me of the word-painting of Charlotte Brontë. Seen in the profile, the face impresses one with a sense of beauty and repose, and on that brow I felt that the hand of a Brontë had laid its hallowing seal; the somewhat hollow cheeks, and large, firm mouth, truthfully determined the peculiarities of her race. The slim figure, neatly robed, further indicated the refinement so notable in the three English sisters.[1]

Maggie Shannon wrote to Wright, giving some details about the visit of Hugh. Details of this visit were filled out subsequently by Rose Heslip. The main points made by Maggie Shannon were: Hugh had visited London and seen 'the Queen', and been taken to visit Sir John Armitage (Armytage), where he tried on Robin Hood's helmet. He was given a silver pencil case, and there was one for each brother, with a silver thimble for each sister. Rose Heslip used to work for her Uncle Hugh. She confirmed that he had come to England, and worked at corn-threshing and at a sugar factory. She supported the Robin Hood story, and said he was given ten guineas at Haworth. Neither of these cousins gave any clear date.

Stories of Robin Hood are confusing. Some authorities suggest there were two men of the same name, one in Sherwood, one in Yorkshire. There is no doubt, however, that his grave was often pointed out at Kirklees, part of Patrick's early parish at Hartshead, where Maria and Elizabeth, Charlotte's two older sisters, were born. Sir George Armytage was thus Patrick's parishioner; one of the family, James Armytage, was one of Patrick's churchwardens. (This area was well known to the Brontës; Roe Head, the school where Charlotte and Anne were educated is half a mile away at the top of the hill, and Mirfield, where Anne was a governess, not far away.) Patrick's lodging was with a family named Bedford, who had been lodge keepers at the hall.[2] Brontë biographies are generally silent about Patrick's relations with Sir George Armytage, but he surely knew him, so that he was able to take Hugh into the park, and possibly to meet the Baronet. Robin Hood's grave had been mutilated many years previously, but it was still there, and there is no doubt that Hugh saw it. Hood's helmet was presumably kept in the hall itself, so we can suppose that Hugh was given a tour round the big house. Such were the people and places where this successful elder brother shared acquaintance.

The year 1836 was a bad year for the Armytages, since both the father, Sir George Armytage, and his son John died this year. The new baronet was only 17. It is not sure that Patrick would have known him, but he could perhaps have obtained entry to the hall through the Bedfords. Hugh tried on the helmet once allegedly worn by Robin Hood. Hood, it was said, went to Kirklees to be cured of an illness by blood-letting. This was done by the prioress of the convent, his cousin, but she treacherously abused the cure, and he was killed.[5] It is not clear that this was why his helmet had dire properties, but it was said that if anyone tried on Hood's helmet they would lose their hair. Hugh tried it on, and did lose his hair. Ramsden, depending on Maggie Shannon, wrote:

> Hugh laughingly placed the helmet on his [head], and, a strange coincidence, when he got back to Ireland, all his hair began to fall until there was not one left. In fact, it was as bare as an infant's. However, after a while, the hair grew again.[6]

It is most unfortunate that we cannot date Hugh's visit more closely, since it may have influenced the writing of the sisters and Branwell.

Our big difficulty with this issue is to try to pin down the date of Hugh's visit. Rose Heslip appears to have been the most authoritative, as she was of the same generation as Charlotte. She said Hugh visited 'when a boy'.[3] She claimed to remember Hugh's visit, but it cannot have been when Hugh was 'a boy'; Rose Heslip was not born until 1821. Hugh was four years younger than Patrick, and would thus have ceased to be 'a boy' not later than about the late 1790s, by which time Patrick was still in Ireland. What could Rose have meant? Maggie Shannon supported the information that Hugh had been to England, and had been to London and seen 'the Queen'. She did not mention the corn-threshing or sugar factory. Like Rose, she had seen the silver pencil cases he had brought back, and indeed had kept one.

If Rose Heslip actually remembered Hugh's visit to England, she must have been at some age older than about five or six, which puts the visit later than about 1826; by this time Patrick was in Haworth, and had lost his wife and two children. Apart from this confusing clue, we have only the reference to 'the Queen' and the silver pencil cases and thimbles. To Rose Heslip and Maggie Shannon in the 1890s 'the Queen' would surely have meant Queen Victoria, although to Maggie Shannon this was reported, not first hand. Two probably unanswerable questions arise: (**A**) Did Hugh see Queen Victoria or the dowager Queen Adelaide? (**B**) What were these silver pencil cases and thimbles? Silver thimbles and pencil cases were common gifts in Victorian England. Ramsden actually saw one of the Brontë specimens in 1897, and wrote:

> Years before, when Charlotte was but a child, Hugh Brontë visited Yorkshire, and he also visited London with his brother Patrick, who took him to all the places of interest. When he returned to Ireland, he took mementos from Patrick in the shape of a silver thimble for each of his sisters, and to the brothers handsome silver pencil-holders, each set in the end with a stone of different colours. It has been my good fortune to see one of these pencil-cases, which, needless to say, is greatly cherished by its owners.[4]

The phrase 'when Charlotte was but a child' may be helpful. Charlotte could have been called a child until about the early 1830s. In which case, did Hugh see Queen Adelaide, not Queen Victoria? King William IV and Queen Adelaide were crowned at Westminster Abbey in September 1831, but it seems likely that if Hugh had seen or been present in London at this event he would have called it 'the coronation'. It may seem more likely that his visit took place at a time when Queen Victoria would have been 'the Queen', and this would put the visit in 1837. On the other hand, we shall discuss below whether Hugh transferred some of the detail of this visit to another (probably imaginary) visit which he claimed he undertook in 1848. A crucial point here, which will be discussed below, is the fire which destroyed parliament in 1834.

We are on slightly more certain ground with the later visit of James, though even here there are tantalising questions. The clearest evidence about this visit from an English source is the note received by Horsfall Turner and reproduced on p. 300 of *Brontëana*. Ellen Nussey told him:

> Charlotte described an uncle from Belfast, who visited them, as a staid and respectable yeoman, of good personal appearance, and she also spoke of an aunt Collins, of whom she knew little, to her regret.

This is amazingly all Charlotte reported. The respectable yeoman must have been James, then in his early sixties. Dating this visit is slightly easier than that of Hugh, since rather more details are known about the circumstances. The primary source is Alice Brontë, talking to Revd J.B. Lusk and given by Wright in *The Bookman*. She said, 'Jamie was over in England with Patrick' and he told them about Charlotte when he came back. 'She was terrible sharp and inquisitive. She was fit for nothing but ornamenting a parlour.' She had asked particularly about the Knock Hill and Lough Neagh. Alice mentioned that 'Ann' had wanted to come 'home' with Jamie (though this had earlier been reported of Hugh's visit).[7] Wright expanded this to '[S]he threw her long slender arms around his neck and called him her noble uncle'. Rose Heslip gave much the same evidence in an article for *The Sketch*.[8] She confirmed that Charlotte 'was very inquisitive and wanted a heap of news'. Rose added that Charlotte had 'a very wee foot and small arms and was "sighted" [dim of sight] but her eyes were as clear as diamonds'.

I have already mentioned Charlotte's questions about Lough Neagh (see p. 104). It may be worth noting the fact that this huge Ulster lough had strange stories clinging to it. One such was that Finn McCool (Fíonn Mac Cumhaill) picked up a large handful of soil one day and threw it into the sea, where it became the Isle of Man, and the hole left became Lough Neagh. Lady Wilde, writing in 1887, said that 'mysterious influences still haunt the locality all round Lough Neagh; for it is the most ancient dwelling-place of the fairies …[9] She went on, 'Deep down, under the water of Lough Neagh, can still be seen, by those who have the gift of fairy vision, the columns and walls of the beautiful palaces which were once inhabited by the fairy race …' It is easy to see how Charlotte and the others would have been intrigued by this mysterious lough.

Wright added to this account, perhaps making use of a further interview, details given to him via Lusk. He slightly modified the comment about Charlotte to 'had eyes that looked through you'. He added that Jamie was not impressed by Branwell: 'he was too small and fantastic, and a chatterer, and could not drink more than two glasses of whiskey without making a fool of himself'.

This is slightly less authoritative than Rose Heslip and Alice Brontë, but likely to be correct. Jamie had needed to bring Branwell back from the Black Bull 'on more than one occasion'. Dating this visit by James requires a little conjecture, but we may note the following facts:

(A) Patrick, Charlotte, Branwell and Anne were all at home. Emily may have been, but is not mentioned.
(B) Comments about Charlotte, and one comment about Anne are from primary sources.
(C) Comments about Branwell, especially Wright's expansion, may be slightly more suspect.

This visit may be tied in with the potato famine. If the 'Branwell' description is correct, he was at home, going to the Black Bull, and in a poor state. This places the incident after Branwell's return in 1845.

Later 1845 is a likely date for the visit, but 1846 might be better. If we argue from absence of other known activity by the Brontës, we find spaces in September 1845 (18th to 1 October) or in the early part of September 1846 (before 14th). If 1846 is the right year, it is strange that Patrick's eye operation was not mentioned (though just conceivably it might have been one of the reasons for the visit). If 1845 is correct, there had been great turmoil with Branwell, and the Black Bull episodes are explicable. There is really no way we can decide between these options.

A third visit was described by Wright. Unlike the other two, this has been vigorously disputed, and with reason. Wright claimed that Hugh made another visit to England, to chastise the reviewer of *Jane Eyre* who had written a damning critique. Intrinsically this meets several major stumbling-blocks. As we shall see, it is doubtful whether the Irish Brontës knew of the publication of *Jane Eyre* before 1853. Some of the details printed by Wright look very much as if they have been transferred from the earlier visit.

Briefly, the story goes that Hugh got hold of a copy of the negative review in *The Quarterly*, dated December 1848. He was determined to avenge the slight, prepared a shillelagh and travelled to London to exact a penalty. He sailed from Warrrenpoint on the *Sea-nymph* and reached Haworth on a Sunday. Wright then ascribed his reception to 'Martha, the old servant'. He was here confusing Tabitha Aykroyd with Martha Brown. Tabby was about 77 at this time, while Martha was 20. Hugh said (to Wright, direct?) that he had been refused entry at first, but then, as he began to walk down the lane towards the church, he was called back and asked to wait until the family returned. This sounds genuine. Afterwards, Hugh went to London and talked to the publishers. He gave some detail about this encounter.

Altogether, this has many improbable aspects. My own view is that Hugh transferred some of the details of his earlier visit to this alleged one. In the 1830s Tabitha Aykroyd would have been 'old'. If we accept this, we may also add a few points to the earlier visit. Hugh did try on Robin Hood's helmet, but nothing is said about his hair falling out. In London, Hugh had seen the Queen and such sights as the Tower and Houses of Parliament. It is a pity he didn't say more about the Houses of Parliament, since they were destroyed by fire in 1834, and rebuilding was not complete until 1847. Surely Hugh would have noted that these were new buildings if he had seen them in 1848. He had lodged there for a while with friends of Branwell. This in itself is odd, since Branwell would only have been 16 in 1833. His exploits were apparently told to David McKee, because Wright tried to confirm this through his wife, who was McKee's daughter. She said she had talked to Hugh about it, but 'He would talk freely about what he had seen in England, but grew silent and dangerous-looking when pressed as to the subject of his journey'. She admitted to Hugh that she had heard the story, and he replied, 'Then you don't need to hear it from me'. Wright tried again to get more detail, but 'the conversation came to an abrupt end'. We can, I think, be sure that there were two visits by Brontë uncles to England, but the third one is doubtful.

PATRICK:
HIS IRISHNESS
IN ENGLAND

It has been suggested that Patrick did not advance according to his talents because his Irishness, amongst other things, stood in his way. In this chapter I wish to discuss how this was shown, apart from in Patrick's writings, which we have already examined. The first evidence of this, of course, was the well-known registration as 'Patrick Branty'. We note two points here about the pronunciation: the initial plosive, P, is changed to B, and the vowel is nasalised to a dark A. This is consistent with Northern Irish pronunciation. In December 1805 Thomas Tighe was asked for a certificate of Patrick's age, which he provided by quoting the baptism of William, no register having been kept at Drumballyroney at the time of Patrick's baptism. This was accepted. The following year Hugh was asked to send an affidavit of Patrick's age and replied,

County of Down,
Ireland

I Hugh Brontë of Ballynaskeagh Parish of Aghaderg, In said County, do swear that my son Patrick Brontë late of St John's College Cambridge England is twenty eight years of age,

Hugh Brontë
Sworn before me,
This 25th of September 1806   John Fury[1]

Prior to this, Henry Martyn, the Evangelical fellow of St John's had written to Revd John Sargent in January 1804 and said, 'An Irishman, of the name of Brontë entered St John's a year & a half ago as a sizar. During this time he has received no assistance from his friends who are incapable of affording him any …'

Martyn asked for some form of financial help for Patrick, and the 'friends' referred to are presumably the Prunty family.[2]

At Hartshead, Patrick perhaps wrote work under the pseudonym of 'A Cottage Writer' for John Buckworth's *Cottage Magazine* in 1812. Lock and Dixon say this was 'believed to be' Patrick. Juliet Barker says she does not think this is Patrick's work, though it is by an Irish Evangelical from Yorkshire. She hesitates to accept its authenticity on grounds of style. There is no specifically Irish content in the articles.[3] This was the year of the Luddite riots, in which Patrick protected himself with pistols, but some also add a 'shillelagh'. Prominent figures in the area were threatened, and one, William Horsfall, was murdered by the Luddites. There are echoes of this in *The Maid of Killarney.*

Two incidents reported from Patrick's Thornton days recall events in Ireland, though they do not actually mention Ireland. One day Patrick was accused by a parishioner of shaving on a Sunday, anathema to some dissenters. His reply, spoken no doubt with a serious face, but recalling Hugh Brontë's tale of the pursuit of the reviewer, was, 'I should like you to keep what I say in your family, but I never shaved in all my life, or was ever shaved by anyone else. I have so little beard that a little clipping every three months is all that is necessary'. Photographs do not confirm this, showing him at 56 with fluffy patches on his cheeks. A second episode reminds us of the earlier incident on the Mourne Mountains when Patrick took his party of children to safety in very bad weather. On this occasion he was taking about sixty youngsters to Bradford to be confirmed. Snow began to pour down, but as the party passed the Talbot Hotel, Patrick went in and ordered hot dinners for the whole lot of children. The dinners were ready after the service, and while the storm raged, his charges 'spent three or four hours' in genuine enjoyment. The fondness and care for children shown in this episode echoes the care for his pupils shown at Glascar.[4]

The issue of Catholic emancipation, close to Patrick's heart, is a little beyond the scope of this book. In the mid-1830s an argument raged about whether the Church of England and Ireland should be disestablished. The Irish aspect of this was based on the Irish Temporalities Act of 1833, which reduced the number of Church of Ireland bishoprics. Meanwhile a long dispute developed over the payment of tithes, when in Ireland especially the vast majority of the population adhered to Catholic or Dissenting churches. This caused a war in Ireland, with Sharman Crawford even more radical than O'Connell, pressing for the abolition of all tithes. (The tithe issue was hotly debated in Yorkshire also, but cannot be dealt with here.) In fact the Church of Ireland was disestablished and divided from the Church of England only by Gladstone in 1869. In 1835 Patrick entered this controversy, calling his church by its legal name, 'The Church of England and Ireland'. He also referred to the 'superstition' of the Irish without naming them:

I have never been able to discover, that because an orthodox church was but ill attended by a superstitious people, averse to its doctrines, that it could be pulled down, especially where the inhabitants are numerous. The greater their mental darkness, the greater is their need of gospel light …[5]

He went on, 'Though charitably disposed towards all Christian churches, I believe the Church of England and Ireland to accord best with Scripture'. His pamphlet is worth reading because of its breadth of tolerance, surely learned from his experiences with Church of Ireland, Roman Catholic and Presbyterian groups in County Down.

The following year provided Patrick with an opportunity to argue against a Baptist about the right time for Baptism. Here he quoted Thomas Tighe's friend John Wesley, to assert that the New Testament accepts 'pouring or sprinkling' as just as appropriate as 'dipping'. He supported the Catholic doctrine on this issue, saying:

This church, notwithstanding its present errors, was once pure: and boasts of higher antiquity than any other church whatsoever. It traces its origin from the times of the apostles. And by tradition and other means, must have a shrewd guess in regard to the best time and mode of Baptism.[6]

It was necessary to clip the wings of 'Peter Pontifex', his Baptist adversary, on the matter of Irishness, which it seems Peter had impugned. Patrick wrote:

You break some of your jokes on Irishmen. Do you not know that an Irishman is your lord and master? Are you not under the king's ministry? And are they not under Mr O'Connell, an Irishman? And do not you or your friends pay to him a yearly tribute under the title of *rent*? And is not the Duke of Wellington, the most famous and the greatest of living heroes, an Irishman? And dare you, or your adherents, take one political step of importance without trembling, lest it should not meet the approbation of your allies in Ireland? Then as an Irishman might say to you, refrain from your balderdash at once, and candidly own your inferiority.

The humour here is similar to that of the 'no need for shaving' remark. Daniel O'Connell, nicknamed 'the Liberator', had gained enormous support in Ireland, using legal means to pressurise the British Government towards Catholic emancipation. Patrick suggests that he has them under his control. The tithe situation was dealt with. As for the Duke of Wellington, we have seen the whole Brontë family in England absorbed with the victories, heroism and political success of this Dublin-born soldier.

We owe Dudley Green thanks for printing a letter from Patrick to Hugh written on 16 November 1843. This does not seem to be in answer to a letter from the family in Ballynaskeagh (written 'Ballinasceaugh' on Patrick's envelope). He asked after the whole family at the Brontë and McClory farmland, and was clearly alarmed at the prospect of a civil war breaking out. At this period Anne and Branwell were in Thorp Green and Charlotte away in Belgium. This perhaps unexpected renewal of concern about a 'civil war' may possibly reflect a conversation with Emily, who was often writing about such wars in Gondal. Without preamble, Patrick began, 'I wish to know how You are all doing in these turbulent times', as though he had been urged on by some agency, perhaps his favourite daughter. He recommended 'all' Protestants in Ireland to arm themselves and make proper plans. Here he was much more antagonistic to the Catholics than in his 1836 pamphlet. 'Should the Romanists Gain their ends, they will destroy, and utterly exterminate, both churchmen and Dissenters'. However, the family was not urged to do anything rash. He specifically asked for William's address, since he did not know where he lived. We have noted that William did not live with the rest of the family in Ballynasakeagh.[7]

Juliet Barker takes up the issue of Patrick's financial aid to the Irish Brontës.[8] She disputes Wright's remark on pp. 264-5 of *The Brontës in Ireland* that Patrick sent home £20 each year to his mother. Certainly he could not have afforded to do so at Cambridge, and Barker says his stipend at Wethersfield was £60. She may be correct for the early days, but one problem is that we have no idea when Eilís died. Rose Heslip, born in 1821, had seen her as a very old lady, with fair hair. This cannot have been much before about 1824 when Rose would have been 3, and could have been later. We therefore have to doubt the 1822 date usually given for Eilís' death. (Incidentally, Hugh cannot have died in 1808, the traditional date for this: Patrick's earlier letter 12 November 1808 stated that the family in County Down were 'all well'.) Barker also notes the support Eilís would have had from her other relatives. Mrs Gaskell said that the Hartshead living provided £202 per annum. The main point is, perhaps, that Patrick did send money, which Wright may have incorrectly put at £20 per annum.

Letters from Patrick to his Irish family have been quoted many times. In addition to the one already quoted, Dudley Green prints letters to Hugh and Mary from the 1850s. The earlier one to Hugh will be discussed when we deal with *Jane Eyre*. In the letter of 2 (or 20) December 1858, Patrick acknowledged a letter from his sister Mary, which has not survived, and hoped that Hugh's health was better. Evidently Mary had expressed a view that Hugh was finding the farm work difficult, since Patrick suggested that James might help out. He then diverged into general comments on Irish 'quarrelling with each other': If the Irish would leave off this activity and 'attend to the improvement of their country', Ireland could have been, instead of a degraded country, 'one of the most respectable portions of the globe'. There is no further reference to the Brontë family at Ballynaskeagh.

In his letter to Mary of 1 February 1859, Patrick began by expressing his regret that Sarah was not well. We have no idea what illness Sarah was suffering; Patrick sent her £1 and hoped she would be comforted and supported by God. This letter was in answer to one from Mary, sending 'boyish papers' which reminded Patrick of 'old times'. A man called David Cruikshank was mentioned, but I have not yet traced him. In his will, dated 20 June 1855, Patrick said he had given considerable sums to his brothers and sisters in times past, and now left forty pounds to be divided equally among them.

He directed that the money should be sent to Hugh at 'Ballinasceaugh, near Loughbrickland'.

It is clear that Patrick kept in contact with the family through Hugh, and that William, though he was his eldest brother, was not close to him. In these letters and messages, we see Patrick mentioning every one of his brothers and sisters except Rose. She is the mystery child of the family, about whom nothing seems to be known except her name.[9]

Various attempts were made to describe the version of English spoken by members of the Irish Brontë family, including Patrick. Mrs Gaskell, writing to a correspondent probably John Forster, mentioned Patrick's 'old-fashioned compliments', and said he spoke with a 'strong Scotch accent (he comes from the North of Ireland)'.[10] However, in Chapter III of *The Life of Charlotte Brontë* she seems to have contradicted this by writing, 'Mr Brontë has now no trace of his Irish origin remaining in his speech; he never could have shown his Celtic descent in the straight Greek lines and strong oval of his face'. Mr William McCracken told Wright that old Hugh Prunty 'spoke with a distinctly Scotch accent'. Alice Brontë's obituary in the *Banbridge Chronicle* contained the remark that Alice's accent was 'different from the present vulgar tongue of the locality…It had that decidedly Scottish flavour for which the inhabitants were formerly remarkable'.[11] These comments do not help us with the problem of Hugh Prunty's origin, and we are in any case relying on the ears of the commentators. To untrained ears Ulster pronunciation does sound Scottish, and perhaps this is all the two previous extracts mean, but one supposes that the *Banbridge Chronicle* writer had a close acquaintance with County Down accents. All that can be said is that Patrick grew up in a very rural and conservative area, and that he and Alice may well have retained some of the sounds of the very local inhabitants. The *Banbridge Chronicle* writer may have made his judgement relying on the Banbridge local sounds, which could differ to some extent from those at Ballynaskeagh. As for Mrs Gaskell, she seems to have adopted Charlotte's stance by playing down anything Irish about Patrick. It is not clear what she meant by 'Celtic'. In these several comments we see part of the same aversion which caused Charlotte to claim Scottish affinity rather than Irish.

When Arthur Bell Nicholls became Patrick's curate in May 1845, Charlotte wrote that he 'appears respectable, reads well' and she hoped he would give satisfaction. We do not have Patrick's response at this time; there had been Irish curates before this. However, as time went by he grew to distrust Nicholls, and was deeply opposed to his proposal of marriage to Charlotte. Surely one reason for this was that Nicholls would have known much more about social structures in Ireland, and would have discovered that Patrick's background was far from being a traditional Ascendancy one. It would hardly be possible to conceal the Catholic origins, despite the family's current fitful adherence to the Church of Ireland. This must have constituted a considerable block between the two clergymen, but we have no hint of this aspect of Patrick's wariness in the records.

MOORE AS WELL AS WELLINGTON AS 'RESPECTABLE IRISH'

The Brontës were very interested in all the Romantic writers, and, as we have already mentioned, Scott and Burns could have represented 'Northern Irishness' for them. As Mrs Gaskell said, Patrick spoke with 'a strong Scotch accent'. Nevertheless, the family was still interested in Dublin-born Irishmen, as we have seen with the Duke of Wellington. Pursuing this connection we need to examine the influence of Thomas Moore, the minor, perhaps underestimated Romantic poet, and – perhaps importantly for the musical Brontës – writer of songs.

Thomas Moore was born in Dublin just over two years after Patrick Prunty was born in Imdel (1779). He was from a higher social stratum but did much the same as Patrick in covering up anything he knew about his ancestry. It is known that he came from a Kerry family, but little else. His biographer Ronan Kelly states that he remembered the toast, 'May the breezes of France fan our Irish Oak into verdure', but it is unlikely that the Brontës knew anything about that.[1] He entered Trinity College, his religion being given in the register as 'Prot[estant]', though he certainly was Catholic.

There is plenty of evidence about Moore's hold over the Brontës. In her well-known advice to Ellen Nussey about what she should read, Charlotte included Moore's 'Life of Sheridan', actually *Memoirs of the Life of the Right Honourable Richard Brinsley Sheridan*. She would hardly have been recommending it if she had not read it herself, and it is full of intrigues, wit, bad debts and treachery. This book was written in 1818. More important for Charlotte was the 'Life' of Byron, the full title of which was *Letters and Journals of Lord Byron, with Notices of His Life*. This was published between 1829 and 1831. Charlotte did not go on to recommend to Ellen, Moore's *Life and Death of Lord Edward Fitzgerald*, which dealt with the aristocratic and rebellious life of the peer. We do not know clearly that she read it, but it would certainly have proved interesting reading for Emily and Anne. Nor do we have direct references to Moore's *History of Ireland*, another book which would have been illuminating. *Lalla Rookh*, with a subject far from Ireland, was a favourite with Charlotte, who referred to this 1817 poem in all her major novels.[2] She seems to have been particularly interested in the *Life of Byron* for the information about Byron, not the author. She also copied plates from illustrated versions, Alexander and Sellars giving their view that the Brontës may not have owned such an edition, but had access to a *Byron Gallery*.[3] The Byronic influence on the Brontës has been many times mentioned; it is interesting that some of this came through Moore.

Whereas for Charlotte, Moore was only a channel for Byronic or Arabic romance, for Emily and particularly Anne, he was much more an author they valued in his

Thomas Moore. (From *The Poetical Works of Thomas Moore*, 1850)

The Vale of Avoca. (From *Irish Pictures*, 1888)

own right. Before 1833 they knew *Irish Melodies*. This was the series of poems which came out in stages, beginning in 1808 and ending in 1834, containing poems composed by Moore to traditional but modified tunes. Opinions of these poems have varied over the years, and they are not, at the time of writing, always high on the list of those performing Irish music. Their pervasive influence in the nineteenth century cannot be underestimated. Among their number are patriotic songs, romantic songs, songs of friendship and mourning and other topics. 'The Meeting of the Waters' was in the earliest published group. It celebrated the 'Sweet vale of Avoca', in County Wicklow, where the Avoca and Avon rivers meet. The poem, a small gem, links the landscape at the confluence with the peace of friendship,

> Sweet vale of Avoca! how calm could I rest
> In thy bosom of shade, with the friends I love best.
> Where the storms that we feel in this cold world should cease,
> And our hearts, like thy waters, be mingled in peace.

The words were set to a traditional air modified by Sir John Stevenson. As with many Moore songs, the music seems part of the words, the two fitting closely. The younger Brontës clearly loved this poem, as they used its name for a confluence of becks on Haworth moor.

Anne Brontë's choice of a Moore song from *Irish Melodies* is from a later numbered volume. It is 'Has sorrow thy young days shaded?', which she copied into her manuscript music book about 1843. We cannot be certain which songs of Moore were known at the parsonage; they could be from music copies rather than texts of poems alone. We cannot be sure, therefore, how many other poems from *Irish Melodies* they knew. It seems unlikely that these two were the only ones. The 'first and second numbers of the melodies' had a preface by Moore in which he quoted a letter he sent to Sir John Stevenson discussing Irish national music, in particular the tunes. Part of it reads:

> Even in their liveliest strains we find some melancholy note intrude, – some minor Third or flat Seventh, – which throws its shade as it passes, and makes even mirth interesting. If Burns had been an Irishman (and I would willingly give up all our claims upon Ossian for him), his heart would have been proud of such music, and his genius would have made it immortal.

The link with Burns, another great Brontë favourite, is worth noting. We recall that one of Wright's informants thought the Brontës in their glen were singing Burns songs; as I suggested, I am sure they were not exactly Burns songs, but the original folk songs from which he made his own. If Emily and Anne did see whole copies of the *Irish Melodies* booklets, especially numbers one and two, they will have read 'Remember the glories of Brien the brave', 'The harp that once through Tara's halls', and 'Rich and rare were the gems she wore' in Part I and 'Let Erin remember the days of old' in Part II.

Anne was interested in Moore's *Sacred Songs*, which began to be published in 1816. The full title is *A Series of Sacred Songs Composed and Selected by Sir John*

'The Little Genii'. (From *Poems of Thomas Moore*, Vol. 2, 1840)

Stevenson and Mr Moore. She copied four of these into her music manuscript book about 1844. Moore's biographer Ronan Kelly notes that some of these are very similar in vocabulary to *Irish Melodies*, listing 'certain keywords', '"fragrant", "sparkling", "bright", "glow", "beam" and "tear"'.[4] Some of these words are frequent in Anne's own work. While writing these songs, Moore was struggling with *Lallah Rooke* and the death of his own baby child Olivia. Moore's biography was not particularly well known in the lifetime of the younger Brontës; he was thought of in general as a less interesting poet than the major Romantics, perhaps more useful as a commentator and preserver of other poets' life histories than in his own right. Like Patrick, he settled in England, successively in Leicestershire, Derbyshire and Wiltshire.

The Brontës were fond of *Blackwood's Magazine*. Articles by John Gibson Lockhart began to be published there in 1817, were later reprinted in *Noctes Ambrosianae*, and included discussions on Moore. *The Life of Byron* was enthusiastically awaited by the 'company' whose fictitious conversations were recorded in these pieces in Blackwood's. Moore was here said to have 'feeling, fancy and genius'; enough to recommend him to the Brontës. From this series of articles the Brontës developed an interest in the poetry of James Hogg, 'the Ettrick shepherd' who is presented using dialect throughout the series. Charlotte and Branwell in particular, but the others to a lesser extent, saw this Scots milieu as their own, seeing Northern Ireland as almost an extension of Scotland. However, this did not obliterate, especially for Emily and Anne, the Irish flavour we find in their work.

29

CHARLOTTE, *JANE EYRE* AND DAVID MCKEE

It is well known that Charlotte gave a most dispiriting picture of Ireland in *Jane Eyre*. The key passage comes in Chapter 23, where Rochester agrees with Jane's suggestion that she must leave Thornfield when he marries Blanche Ingram. He says:

> I have already, through my future mother-in-law, heard of a place that I think will suit [you]: It is to undertake the education of the five daughters of Mrs Dionysius O'Gall of Bitternut Lodge, Connaught, Ireland. You'll like Ireland, I think: they're such warm-hearted people there, they say.

Jane objects on the grounds that this is a long way from 'England and from Thornfield: and …"From *you*, sir".' She bursts into tears as Mrs O'Gall strikes cold into her heart. Rochester goes on, in answer to Jane's 'It's a long way'.

> It is, to be sure; and when you get to Bitternut Lodge, Connaught, Ireland, I shall never see you again, Jane; that's morally certain. I never go over to Ireland, not having much of a fancy for the country…[1]

Here he is speaking for Charlotte, who had lost her enthusiasm for Irish things many years before.

In Chapter 28 of *The Brontës in Ireland* Wright described the interview Hugh Brontë had with David McKee at his manse in Ballynaskeagh on receipt of a book purporting to be, in Wright's view, a first edition of *Jane Eyre*. We can have no doubt of the accuracy of this report, since it was witnessed by McKee's daughter, who became Wright's wife. It has been usual to look at this reported interview as another folly of Wright's, but there may be more points to note before dismissing it.

Wright claimed that he had seen the 'three volumes of the first edition' of *Jane Eyre*, sent direct from Haworth by Charlotte to the farm at Ballynaskeagh. He claimed to have 'in my possession', first editions of *Shirley* and *Villette* also sent to the farm. Much of his chapter, however, deals with a single-volume edition which certainly was sent from Haworth. This volume still exists. Wright's claim is that of Charlotte's six complementary copies from the publisher, 'she would certainly send one to her friends in Ireland'. Unfortunately this weak, unsubstantiated statement is as far as he went. It seems to me that he is far from proving either that Charlotte did send a first edition, or that she was in any case concerned with these alleged Irish friends.[2] As we have seen, Anne's attitude was rather different.

The disappearance of these first edition novels is problematic for Wright. It is one of several assertions he made in the book which have caused the whole work to be dismissed.[3] A more likely explanation is that he saw with his own eyes the 1850 one-volume edition sent by Patrick and jumped to an unscholarly conclusion. Since Wright had another chapter in which he retold the story about a vengeful expedition by Hugh Brontë dated to 1848, he had to provide an explanation evading the clear implication that the 1853 gift from Patrick is the first time the Irish Brontës knew of their niece's writing.

We cannot dismiss all Wright said, however. David McKee was his father-in-law, and he had ample opportunity to talk over with him the attitudes of the Brontë brothers, especially Hugh and James, to their relatives in England. Annie McKee was his wife, present at the interview to be discussed.

Wright filled up gaps in the story with romantic detail, but the core of his account must be based on fact. Since he wished to assert the early arrival of *Jane Eyre* at Ballynaskeagh, he wrote of the three volumes being tied up in a red handkerchief and taken to Mr McKee's manse. The interview, he wrote, 'took place in a large parlour which contained a bed and a central table, on which Mr McKee's tea was spread out'. Hugh Brontë then explained 'in a low voice' the sad tale of his niece's 'indiscretion' in publishing this book, so different from *Pilgrim's Progress*. Hugh was invited to 'draw up to the table to partake of the abundant tea that had been prepared for Mr McKee, while the latter proceeded to examine the book'. The three books tied in a red handkerchief have now become one. For the rest of the afternoon McKee read the book. 'Brontë sat still at the table, watching the features of the reader as they changed from sombre to gay, and from flinty fierceness to melting pathos'. The reading continued until 'both men' were sitting silent in the gloaming.[4]

The verdict of Mr McKee is often overlooked. He broke the silence with the verdict, 'Hughey… the book bears the Brontë stamp on every sentence and idea, and it is the grandest novel that has been produced in my time'; and then he added, 'The child Jane Eyre is your father in petticoats, and Mrs Reed is the wicked uncle by the Boyne'. Remembering that Annie McKee was in the house, and that 'the servant' had just gone into the room to take away the empty tea-cups and light the candles, it seems likely that these words are more or less verbatim. The picture in general is likely to be accurate.

What are we to make of these words of McKee's? If we transfer them to 1853, and discard the 1848 mirage, we may make some sense of the report.

The first thing to note is that McKee confirmed the 'Boyne Valley' part of the Prunty story. He had heard of 'Welsh' and his behaviour towards Hugh. The next matter is to interpret what McKee says as 'the Brontë stamp on every sentence and idea'. He likened Jane to Hugh Prunty. As we saw, Mr McKee was a devotee of Scott. He was not necessarily a literary critic and could not back up his statement with quotations. Nevertheless, he sensed something about the book which reflected Hugh Prunty's attitude. We are not required to suppose that Charlotte was deliberately basing her character on that of Hugh Prunty (though she may have been unconsciously echoing his life story). Though she surely knew all about his travails, Jane's experiences are in part gathered from Charlotte's own life and those of her sisters, as well as some literary exemplars. McKee's 'every sentence' is incautious, but he surely recognised an attitude in the book which was similar to that of the Brontës in County Down whom he had known for years. We may go a little further and note similarities between Hugh's story and Jane's.

What McKee saw was independence of mind. Jane is fiery and will not suffer injustice. Hugh Prunty suffered as a child, just as Jane does. Hugh revenged himself by abetting Welsh's downfall and then made a life for himself after wandering about. He had been farmed out to an uncle as Jane is adopted by an aunt. Jane's aunt is bitter and unkind, as was Welsh. Jane makes her own way in the world by adopting a trade she has observed, as did Hugh. Jane's values are based upon honour, and she reacts violently against anything unjust, as Hugh apparently held radical views on monarchy, aristocracy and undue power.

We now return to Wright's penultimate chapter, claiming that Hugh Brontë made a deliberate attempt to castigate the reviewer who had damned *Jane Eyre* in the *Quarterly Review* of December 1848. As suggested, it is unlikely that the novel had reached Ballynaskeagh by this date, or indeed for some years. So where did Wright find this extraordinary story and is there any basis for it at all?

Naturally, the chapter was treated with scorn by Angus MacKay, using rhetorical questions and an exclamation mark.[5] He quoted Maggie Shannon: 'Until we saw the account of Hugh's visit to thrash the reviewer we never heard of it, nor do we believe it'. Rose Heslip also added that at the date Hugh was in England, the Brontë novels 'had not been written nor thought of'. Yet Wright, a Presbyterian minister, is not likely to have deliberately tried to mislead his public.

As suggested on pp. 143-4, some of the details given by Wright are clearly attributable to Hugh's uncontested first visit to England. This was a celebratory visit, during which he was feted by Patrick, taken to London and Kirklees; these episodes were transferred by Wright to this later narrative. We have a build-up to the story in an attempt to explain how Hugh Brontë would have got to know about a review in a London magazine.[6] This is not really very convincing. Hugh then went to Mr McKee and he showed him the review. Yet it is only three years later, in 1853, that he described the single book on the tea table. Wright had got the whole thing very muddled in his own mind, and should have checked out the details. We might learn from his narrative that, probably after 1853, there were copies of a review in circulation in County Down, to which Hugh and James took exception. Wright's story continued with details of Hugh's preparation for vengeance, involving a shillelagh tempered with magpie's blood. As a descendant remarked, 'Sure, it makes him look like a heathen'.

Christopher Heywood has suggested that this story emanates entirely from Hugh Brontë's wicked sense of humour, shared, as we saw, by Patrick himself. We are not sure when William Wright met Hugh, but he did so. Perhaps Hugh told Wright this story then. Otherwise, perhaps Hugh put the story out round the neighbourhood and Wright picked it up second-hand. In any case, we cannot grant any credence to this tale. We do have, on the other hand, the copy of the single-volume edition which McKee read while Hugh drank tea on that exciting day in 1853. Written on one of the front pages is Patrick's 'letter' to Hugh. This has often been quoted and a fully accurate text is given in Dudley Green's *The Letters of the Reverend Patrick Brontë*.[7] Patrick explained about Charlotte's initial pseudonym and mentioned without naming them, *Shirley* and *Villette*. He suggested that Hugh let the other brothers and sisters read his letter.

There is one further point. I have suggested elsewhere that Charlotte, Emily and Anne discussed possible subjects when beginning their first trio of novels,

Patrick Brontë's letter to his brother Hugh. (From Wright, *The Brontës in Ireland*)

which became *The Professor*, [an early version of] *Wuthering Heights* and *Agnes Grey*. After Emily's novel was rejected, they began again. Is it possible that at some point they had discussed books based on Patrick's retelling of Hugh Prunty's story? Of course, we have no evidence whatsoever for this: it is pure conjecture. But both Charlotte's and Emily's novels centre on an orphan overcoming degradation. Jane was thought by David McKee to have been like Hugh Prunty, and we shall see that Welsh had remarkable similarities with Heathcliff. These links between the major novels may be pure coincidence, or from an unconscious background, but they exist and are worth pondering.

GONDAL PRINCES AND REVOLUTIONARIES

In an earlier chapter we looked at a small number of words in Brontë writings which might have been based on Irish words. In this chapter we shall examine Gondal, its names, story-line and small fragments (almost all poetry) which we have left. Many efforts have been made to produce coherent narratives from the poems, though I think this may be impossible for other reasons than lack of material. In Anne Brontë's 1845 diary paper, we find the remark, 'We have not yet finished our Gondal chronicles which we began three and a half years ago when will they be done?' From this I draw the conclusion that the two sisters had begun in 1841 to systematise their saga. Prior to this it became muddled, with changes being made retrospectively. Such efforts as that of Fannie Ratchford in *Gondal's Queen* have their place, but seem to me unsustainable for reasons I have often publicised.[1] As she admitted, names are changed in such a way that we cannot be sure if the initials attached to the poem refer to the same person as these initials did on another occasion.[2]

Going back to Emily's 1841 paper, we find that Gondalian royalty are important, while in Anne's 1845 paper we read that the Royalists are 'not quite overcome', though the Republicans are 'uppermost'. By 1845, the saga is in part played out between Royalists and Republicans, but we cannot be sure that this would have been the case earlier. For the moment, however, we shall leave the story itself and examine some of the names of the characters and places.

We have already noted Gaaldine. Where does the word 'Gondal' itself come from? It was probably coined about 1831, though we do not see it written until the 1834 'diary paper'. It has been conjectured to have an eastern, perhaps Indian, origin. We may guess (there is no evidence) that it was produced out of the subconscious of one of the sisters, perhaps Emily. If so, it is interesting that it shares one of it syllables with the townland of Patrick's birth: Imdel. I would not press this very far, but the idea is worth considering. A minor character is called Ierne, 'the Irish one'. The name occurs in Ossian, but may have been direct from Patrick.

Much more interesting is the name 'Geraldine'. There is also the variant Gerald for a prominent male character. A likely direct origin for this is Coleridge's 'Christabel'. Here Geraldine enacts a strange, rather sinister part, and Emily's Geraldine follows. We might risk the slightly uncertain view that she is the A.G.A. of many poems, whom Ratchford called 'Gondal's Queen'. A question which arises is how Emily Brontë knew Coleridge's poem. We cannot answer this directly, but there is internal evidence suggesting that she knew 'The Ancient Mariner'. In '*Noctes Ambrosianae*', 'Shepherd' (James Hogg) made disparaging remarks as follows: 'The author o' "Christabel" and the "Auncient Mariner" had better just continue to see visions – and to dream dreams – for he's no fit for the waking world'. This remark, from April 1827, may have been enough to send Emily and Anne Brontë looking for Coleridge's work. Nine-year-old Emily was already a deep dreamer.

However, there is an additional good reason why the two younger Brontës would have been interested in the name 'Geraldine'. We have noted Anne's Gondal list and the occurrence there of names beginning with 'Fitz'. This particularly Irish prefix was prominently displayed in the Fitzgerald family. Irish patriots would long remember the part played by Lord Edward Fitzgerald in the events of 1798. His exploits were the subject of legend, and the room where he was arrested was being shown as a memorial many years afterwards.[3] On 26 January 1793 Fitzgerald almost caused a riot in the Irish Parliament with his fervent support of the Volunteers who were on the point of arming themselves for rebellion. We cannot prove that Patrick Prunty knew of this, but it seems likely. Emily's forceful queen was a combination of the intense disruptiveness of Coleridge's Geraldine and the heroism of Edward Fitzgerald, though this is not to say that other influences were not involved also.

The Irish word 'glen' (*gleann*) is constantly used by all the Brontës. This was presumably reinforced by readings of Scott, Burns and Ossian, but we remember that Patrick was brought up near to the Prunty glen opposite the Better House in Ballynaskeagh. 'Glen' is combined in Gondal with Eden to make the name Gleneden. A number of other Gaelic-derived words may be originally from Ulster, though added to by Scottish influence: Rodric Lesley is the name of a character who may also be a lord, his first name possibly more Scots than Irish, but the Leslies were a well-known family of southern Ulster. These are possibilities, but no more. 'Douglas' could be another example, but, like 'glen' part of a Gaelic influence which had passed into common use. A strange word is 'Gobelrin', in the poem beginning 'Well, narrower draw the circle round', in which Douglas rides furiously along a steep path to encounter his enemies. This could be from Ossian.[4]

There are a number of other minor occurrences of words in Gondal which could relate to Ireland. 'Desmond' may be a place or a person. 'Rosina' could be a part-reminiscence of one of the Brontë aunts, Rose. 'Elmor' may contain the word for 'large' in the second element. These are hazardous identifications, and we must remember that there are many influences on Gondal names, outweighing Irish ones. The same is probably true of the story-line, so far as that is clear. Characters were invented by the two sisters, but their life histories develop as the story continues. In the Angria stories of Charlotte and Branwell, adultery plays a large part. In Gondal, we read much about faithlessness in general, civil wars and betrayal by close relatives. We shall next examine the implication that Irish character and politics, with Patrick's family history, played a part in this. I regard 'Why ask to know the date …?' as a special case and will leave it out for a while.

Quite early in the saga, we find factions plotting against royalty. Later, we read that some plotters are Republicans. From the days of the American War, Republicanism was on the agenda for Irish people.

Hugh Prunty's 'propositions' were cautious about this. He wished to limit royal power, but not, apparently, to eliminate it.[5] He was very suspicious of the authority of the Church and landlordism, but did not advocate violent means to overcome them. Uncle William, we know, fought for the cause of the United Irishmen, and Patrick was not far away from their cause through Samuel Barber. In a letter to the *Leeds Intelligencer* dated 15 January 1829, Revd William Morgan called Patrick 'a witness of the last Irish rebellion'.

Secretive as the Brontës, and especially Emily, were, we may ask whether she felt sympathy with these revolutionaries. Republicans entered the Gondal scene overtly in 1844, though Gondal material is so fragmentary that we cannot be sure they were not there previously. In a poem of 2 October 1844, Emily wrote:

> For face to face will our kindred stand …
> One must fight for the people's power,
> And one for the rights of Royalty.

In the following November, she wrote:

> For who forgives the accursed crime
> Of dastard Treachery?
> Rebellion in its chosen time
> May Freedom's champion be –
>
> Revenge may stain a righteous sword
> It may be just to slay;
> But, Traitor – Traitor – from *that* word
> All true breasts shrink away!

In her 1845 'diary paper' Anne wrote, 'The Gondals are at present in a sad state the Republicans are uppermost but the Royalists are not quite overcome'.[6]

I need to emphasise that there is nothing to show clearly that Emily and Anne were not interested in rebellion before this. We can, of course, also note the implications of David McKee's comment to Hugh Brontë about *Jane Eyre*. Jane can be seen as rebellious; so was Hugh Prunty. Gondal was a hotbed of rebellion, it seems, and by 1844/5 this rebellion was focused on the idea of Republicanism.

Patrick himself was a convinced Tory Royalist, but not therefore against reform. Emily, we know, had ideas which perplexed Charlotte.[7] Some emerge without direct statement in *Wuthering Heights*.

I have suggested in various publications that 'Why ask to know the date ..?' is a post-Gondal poem. We do not have any positive evidence that Gondal was finally abandoned, but this poem was written in part soon after the rejection of what I think of as the Ur-*Wuthering Heights*. It stayed in Emily's mind, as her poems were apt to do. After line 149, her ideas were put on paper without revision, which took place on the manuscript itself. The visit of James to Haworth had taken place, it seems to me, not long before this. Civil war, frequently hanging over Ireland, was in the air. In this poem, there are no Gondal names of people or places; it could as well refer to Ireland as to Gondal.

The poem begins with a question, which has often been ignored by commentators: 'Why ask to know the date – the clime?' Here Emily Brontë was moving away from Gondal, applying the poem to any circumstance in the world where civil war was taking place. Instead of their crops becoming a fine harvest, the peasants find horses trampling them. The ears of wheat were kneaded on the threshing floor 'With mire of tears and human gore'. The autumn of the poem is seen by 'famished eyes', not a direct reference to the Irish famine, but alluding to it. The narrator draws his 'alien sword' to 'free/One race beneath two standards fighting, for loyalty and liberty'. This is surely a hint that the combatants on one side were Republicans, while the 'loyalists' supported the current arrangements.

'When kindred strive, God help the weak!/ A brother's ruth 'tis vain to seek'. This civil war is reminiscent of Irish conflicts, bitter as Dolly's Brae, and symbolic of conflicts on a greater scale.

Emily also wrote of 'hearts hiding life-long secrets', just as many Prunty secrets were partly hidden from the world. The narrator will not tell about these secrets, reserving them for another time. As we shall see, Emily Brontë would part-reveal one in *Wuthering Heights*.

A royalist is captured and, severely wounded, denied merciful death. 'Our priest' declared that he had had his share of good things in his mansion, where he was now lying with the full moon 'beaming on his face'. We might ask why a 'priest' is involved: not 'our clergyman'; this may be a further indication that a quasi-Irish context was envisaged. The west wind (which we shall later examine more thoroughly) shines on the captive, while the narrator curses him and begins to fear God's justice for his contribution to 'the deeds that turn [God's] earth to hell'. The rest of the poem deals with the nobleman's child, taken prisoner by the rebels, and raises issues beyond the scope of this book. Emily Brontë did not finish the poem and revise it, but she came back in 1848 to the same work, showing how important she felt it to be. There are no place names in it whatsoever: it is a generalised picture of civil war and its consequences, but taking some of its power, I think, from her interest in Ireland.

My next section is speculative, though I shall try to produce evidence to support it. On a number of occasions I have suggested Emily Brontë's (and to a lesser extent Anne's) interest in Percy Bysshe Shelley. (In passing, we may notice that a prominent Angrian character is called Percy.) Internal evidence to support their reading of 'Epipsychidion' is strong, and first hinted at by John Hewish.[8]

This poem includes a startling line, 'Emily, I love thee'. It sometimes seems to anticipate Heathcliff's love for Catherine in *Wuthering Heights* and Patsy Stoneman has written about another aspect of Shelley's work which seems to have soaked into the Brontë novel.

We do not know whether the young Brontës were aware of Shelley's 'An Address to the Irish People', which he delivered in Dublin and had printed in 1812. Unlike 'Queen Mab', which we shall soon examine, it did not become well known. '*Noctes Ambrosianae*' did not find either Shelley or Byron interesting. All we can say is that Emily and Anne must have known that Shelley, whom they admired on other grounds, also had an interest in Irish reform. It is likely that he was mentioned during discussion of the Catholic Emancipation question of 1829, though I have not found a reference. Among the phrases occurring in this speech are, 'an Irishman prizes liberty dearly':

> I look upon Catholic Emancipation and the restoration of the liberties and happiness of Ireland, so far as they are compatible with the English Constitution, as great and important events; I wish you, O Irishmen, to be as careful and thoughtful of your interests as are your real friends. Do not drink, do not play, do not spend any ideal time, do not take anything that other people say for granted – there are numbers who will tell you lies to make your own fortunes.

It is not clear that the Dubliners took much notice of the speech of this young aristocratic Englishman, but it does make up part of the impression and reputation of Shelley which would pass down to the Brontë children.

QUEEN MAB
AND THE
WESTERN WIND

We return briefly to Charlotte's 'Mina Laury'. Mina says to O'Neill, 'You and I are Westerns, Mr O'Neill – Irish, & we favour our Countrymen' (we note Charlotte's familiarity with the name O'Neill). In her juvenilia Charlotte identified 'the West' with Ireland, and this is a clue to Emily's use of 'the west' in personal as well as Gondal poems, though in Charlotte's case the use is combined with an Angrian geography. One more point needs reiterating here: Gondal and personal poems were thought of differently by Emily Brontë, and though occasionally there was a crossover from one to the other, in general, she differentiated between the two groups, as shown by her categorisation of the two manuscripts, 'A' and 'B'.[1]

In *Shelley: The Pursuit* Richard Holmes has traced for us the history of Shelley's poem, 'Queen Mab'.[2] This was first published privately in 1813, but an enterprising radical printer and bookseller, William Clark, pirated it, and after it was given reviews in a number of magazines, it was taken up by the radical publisher Richard Carlile, who produced editions in 1822, 1823, 1826 and 1832, after which a further edition was printed by Watson and Hetherington's 'Chartist' edition of 1839. Holmes comments that through this poem, Shelley's name was assured currency in the working movement for the next twenty years. Charlotte did not quote the poem, but she did quote 'Prometheus Unbound', 'Adonais' and 'The Question'.[3] The first of these is in the 1839 work 'Caroline Vernon'. It seems to me that Shelley was an early influence on the two younger Brontë sisters, but that after the first collected edition came out in 1839, this interest was reinvigorated.

In view of Mina Laury's clear equation of 'Western' with 'Irish', repeated in various places in the juvenilia, it must be worth looking carefully at Emily Brontë's work where the west wind is important, and in anything comparable in Shelley, though we shall not suppose that every time he used the word 'west' it would necessarily mean 'Ireland'. However, in the case of Emily, 'west' often may have meant Ireland or Irish. We may start with a famous part of a Gondal poem, noted for its alleged 'mysticism'. I refer to the central section of the poem which either began as two poems or was later split into two; 'Silent is the house'. Suddenly, at line 69, this poem takes off from its Gondal background:

> He comes with western winds, with evening's wandering airs,
> With that clear dusk of heaven that brings the thickest stars,
> Winds take a pensive tone and stars a tender fire
> And visions rise and change that kill me with desire –
>
> Desire for nothing known in my maturer years
> When joy grew mad with awe at counting future tears;
> When if my spirit's sky was full of flashes warm,
> I knew not whence they came from sun or thunder storm ...

These words are put into the mouth of a young female prisoner in a dungeon. The 'He' in the first line refers to 'A messenger of Hope' from the previous stanza. No further reference is made to this 'messenger'; all we know is that it is a male and perhaps equal to the 'vision' in a later line. The 'western' wind takes Emily's captive back to her childhood or youth, and she speaks to a degree for her creator, even though this is a Gondal poem. Emily Brontë, beyond measure sensitive, was writing about her childhood and youthful ecstasy when she heard and felt the 'western wind'. To some this will seem a far-fetched notion, but we shall find other examples of Emily writing of the west wind, the Irish wind, to add to what we shall also discover about *Wuthering Heights*. To Irish readers it may not seem natural to talk about the west wind as an Irish wind, but to a Yorkshire woman who was well aware of her Irish ancestry, this is not so strange. We recall her 'strange expression, as though she had gained something which seemed to complete a picture in her mind' recorded by Miss A.M.F. Robinson, when her father told certain Irish stories.

'Queen Mab' was written in 1812 and revised for an edition of poetry which included 'Alastor', in 1816. The title comes from the Celtic queen (Irish and Welsh) who appears in Shakespeare and is taken up by Sir Walter Scott in *The Antiquary*. She is 'the midwife of dreams'. In Anglicised Irish, the name is 'Maeve'. Shelley's version is linked to Emily Brontë via her drawing or painting (we are not sure which) of 'Ianthe', a beautiful maiden who has died.[4] Her soul is awakened by Mab, and they fly through the air after 'the chains of earth's immurement/Fell from Ianthe's spirit.' She is taken through the heavens to see Palmyra, Egypt and Rome. There is much in the poem which would please Emily; such lines as 'Throughout this varied and eternal world/Soul is the only element'. However, we need to ponder her drawing, mentioned above. It is discussed in detail in *The Art of the Brontës*.[5] Emily copied the picture from a plate in Moore's *Life of Byron*. Alexander and Sellars say this picture was 'traditionally' called 'The North Wind'.

No doubt this was so, but one might wonder whether originally it was 'The West Wind', as the wind occurs in Shelley's 'Ode to the West Wind'.

These links between Queen Mab, Ianthe, Shelley's concept of Soul, the 'North Wind' attribution, and Emily Brontë's enthusiasm for the west wind are hard to untangle, since we have so little primary evidence. We have to leave the enigma and turn to Shelley's ode.

Winds in general interested Emily Brontë, but it was some time before she specified the west wind. At least 55 poems out of about 190 mention winds, and more mention breezes. The north wind is indeed mentioned in two earlier poems, and the south wind in two poems, while summer and winter winds are also included. Many other winds are 'wild', 'dreary', 'sweetest' and the east wind, mentioned once only, is 'bleak'. After 1844 there are three specific mentions of the west wind, but we also have the unnamed wind of 'Aye, there it is, it wakes tonight …'[6] Shelley's 'Ode to the West Wind' was first published with *Prometheus Unbound* in 1820. He noted that it was written 'on a day when that tempestuous wind, whose temperature is at once mild and animating, was collecting the vapours which pour down the autumnal rains'. In the first line he called it '*wild* west wind', an adjective Emily used to qualify winds at least eight times in her poetry. Perhaps we may suggest that 'wild' winds are 'west' winds, and therefore Irish winds, but this may be to take matters too far. However, we remember Charlotte's equation of the 'wild bright inspiration' of Mina Laury with Irishness, and this provides an argument for my suggestion. The 1839 edition of Shelley's works also included the 'Ode to the West Wind'.

In *Shirley*, Charlotte had a chapter entitled 'The West Wind Blows'.[7] In it, Caroline wakes from illness under the influence of the wind. Before this, there had been a 'dry', 'arid wind, blowing from the east'. Irishness is not mentioned here, but 'A little cloud like a man's hand arose in the west … wet and tempest prevailed a while … the sun broke out genially'. Caroline's youth now helps her to recover, as 'the pure west wind blow[s] soft as fresh through the ever-open chamber lattice …'

The west wind, early in Charlotte's work associated with the Irish, is seen as a comforting, life-giving wind.

Some readers may be dubious about the equations I have made between 'Irish', 'Western' and Shelley. To sum up, therefore, I admit that this is not a totally watertight theory, but we have seen Charlotte explaining in her juvenilia that 'west' and 'western' meant Irish. We have seen that she quoted Shelley's 'Prometheus Unbound', showing that the Brontës knew Shelley after 1839 (but elsewhere I have suggested that the influence from 'Epipsychidion' implies an earlier date). Shelley wrote 'Ode to the West Wind' as well as 'Queen Mab', linked to Emily through the 'North Wind' picture from Moore's *Life of Byron*, the title of which is traditional, not authenticated, and it could be the 'west wind'.

SHIRLEY, CHARLOTTE AND IRISH CURATES

Charlotte Brontë had come a long way from Mina Laury, whose expression when she turned down the proposal of Lord Hartford was 'wild' and 'bright' and 'truly, divinely Irish'. Mina Laury's account of Irishness had changed in *Jane Eyre* to Mrs O'Gall of Bitternut Lodge. In the interval Charlotte had been to Belgium and encountered a culture far different both from Yorkshire and Ireland. It was, however, a Catholic culture, and it is possible that she had associated aspects of Irish tradition with that of the Catholic Belgians. She had also encountered Irish curates.

The first Irish curate was the Revd John Collins, an assistant at Keighley, whose wife was a friend of the Brontës.[1] We first hear of him at a Church-rate meeting in 1840, when his 'Irish blood' was 'set in a ferment' and he was with difficulty persuaded not to attack the 'Dissenters' physically.

Collins went from bad to worse. He became 'drunken, extravagant and profligate', getting into serious debt and treating his wife and child viciously. His vices were, wrote Charlotte, 'utterly hopeless'.[2]

In 1847 Mrs Collins appeared on the doorstep at Haworth with a distressing tale of her separation from her husband and current success in running a lodging house in Manchester. She had no idea where her husband had got to.[3] In this encounter, Irish character was seen as 'drunken' etc; this view was reinforced by the presence at the parsonage of Branwell, who showed some similar signs without the heartlessness.

The second curate was Revd James William Smith, who arrived in Haworth and took up his duties on 12 March 1843.[4] He courted Ellen Nussey, but when she failed to respond he wondered if she had any money, and then left for Keighley, proceeding to Canada, with many debts left behind him. He had also embezzled charity money.[5] Charlotte was very unimpressed by these two Irishmen, and this may have coloured initially her reaction to the arrival of another, Arthur Nicholls, whom she eventually married.

Early in 1848, Charlotte summoned up the courage to begin a new novel to follow *Jane Eyre*. This would not have been easy; her favourite sister had followed her brother to the grave, and she did not wish to revisit the Gothic-influenced scenarios of *Jane Eyre*. She remembered Hartshead and the Mirfield region, and also wished to discuss some political and almost philosophical issues. Her lost sister haunted her; she wanted to redraw her as she might have been. I wonder if she thought of 'Shirley' as a name because of her sister's enthusiasm for Shelley (but there is no evidence, and it may be stretching a theory too far). Certainly her mind returned to thoughts of Ireland. Irish curates had been disastrous at Haworth, lacking all the robust and stalwart qualities of her own Irish curate father.

We meet Mr Malone in the first chapter, at dinner with his fellow curates who are not Irish. His portrait is not appealing, but gives us an idea of how Charlotte thought by this time of the Irish.

'More bread!' cries Mr Malone, in a tone which, though prolonged but to utter two syllables, proclaims him at once a native of the land of shamrocks and potatoes. Mrs Gale [the landlady] hates Mr Malone more than either of the other two, but she fears him also, for he is a tall, strongly – built personage, with real Irish legs and arms, and a face as genuinely national; not the Milesian face – not Daniel O'Connell's style, but the high-featured, North-American Indian sort of visage, which belongs to a certain class of the Irish gentry, and has a petrified and proud look, better suited to the owner of an estate of slaves, than to the landlord of a free peasantry. Mr Malone's father termed himself a gentleman: he was poor and in debt, and besottedly arrogant; and his son was like him.[6]

Charlotte had originally added 'as most of his caste are in Ireland', after 'in debt', but this was not printed.

We need to consider carefully what these words show of Charlotte Brontë's understanding of the various strands of the Irish population and where she got these ideas.

Since Mina Laury had told Lord Hartford they were 'westerns', there had been many developments in Ireland, so widespread that they had impinged, in some cases severely, on the English national consciousness. Charlotte's own knowledge of particular Irish clergy had affected her view of the Church of Ireland strand of Irish culture. On the one hand, the idea of the 'stage Irish' character had been developed. An important element in the development of this was the publication in 1842 of Samuel Lover's *Handy Andy*. Here Andy is shown as 'a blundering servant'. He has 'some redeeming natural traits: he is not made either a brute or a villain'.[7] This book and others like it conveyed an idea of the Irishman as likeable but 'bungling'. It tended to debunk romantic views of the country, as our illustration of 'The Party at Killarney' shows. The Irish famine also had a impact;

it shocked much English opinion, though Charlotte said nothing about it in her surviving letters to her friends.

Malone in *Shirley* exhibits a 'high featured visage'. He is not a 'Milesian'. The use of this word indicates that Charlotte Brontë was aware of the legend, based on fact, of an invasion from Spain, which had provided a dark colouring noted in some Irish faces. She specified Daniel O'Connell as an example of this kind of appearance. Her next sentences are bitter. Malone and his kind have faces 'petrified and proud', such as a slave-owner might have. These words and the following clause could have come from the mouth of Hugh Prunty. Charlotte contrasted the slave estates with the circumstances of a 'free Irish peasantry'. It is surely to be supposed that during the famine at least, if not before, Patrick talked in the tones of his father about the dire results of absentee landlordism. Malone's father was 'besottedly arrogant', i.e. drunken as well as remote and utterly selfish. However she had thought about the Irish character as 'warm' in the juvenilia, Charlotte was now excepting the landlords from this view.

There is satirical fun at Mr Malone's expense in Volume II, Chapter IV when Malone arrives at Shirley's house. He is challenged by the dog Tartar, and immediately hits it with a 'cane or whip'. He then runs up the stairs. He refuses at first to come down, then claims that it is his friend Donne who is afraid of dogs. Finally coming down the stairs, Malone slips and almost falls down, but 'he is no coward' and passes Tartar in 'suppressed fury'. His good humour returns, and he sits on his chair with 'his athletic Irish legs crossed'. He also performs tricks with a silk handkerchief. Charlotte's dislike of Malone has evaporated, and she allows him to cause the assembled ladies to smile. Irish joking has taken the place of Irish hauteur. The humour in this chapter and elsewhere is not confined to satirical portrayal of the Irish; Southern English also come in for some leg-pulling in the shape of Mr Donne, one of the other curates, who is mocked for his South English accent. One might characterise Charlotte Brontë's attitude here as 'Yorkshire Patriotic', and this explains to some extent the protective feeling against foreign (including Irish) elements, which surfaced in the work of Ramsden and Horsfall Turner.

How far was this new attitude of Charlotte's influenced by her father? We have seen that Patrick had a somewhat ambivalent attitude to his Irish heritage and to Ireland. He told wild stories in the children's infancy, but outside the family circle he tended to conceal his Irishness. His attitude to the potato famine got no mention in Charlotte's letters (though we know Ellen Nussey destroyed some, and Mary Taylor's have not survived). Hugh Prunty's revolutionary stance had not affected Charlotte very much, though Emily and Anne had some sympathy for it. On the whole, it seems as though the mocking portrayal of Mr Malone (not a County Down surname) stems from literary influences rather than personal ones, with the exception of the experiences with the Haworth curates, both of whom were 'not Milesian', but both of whom were disloyal and self-centred.

BRANWELL
AND ANNE

Branwell had been named after his father. He was in full, 'Patrick Branwell Brontë'. We have seen that Uncle James was not impressed by him as he 'could not hold his drink'. In his juvenilia, he seemed to identify with Maurice Flanagan, as well as others. In the early work *The Secret*, for example, Flanagan is described as 'a broad, carrotty-locked young man of a most pugnacious aspect'. Superficially Branwell was a Yorkshire man, often writing short satirical passages on Yorkshire dialect. Nevertheless, he was seen by the neighbours as Irish, his (apparently rejected) name being a reminder.

In 2004 James Reaney contributed an interesting article to *Brontë Studies* in which he looked at Branwell's narratives from a different angle.[1] He raised two interesting issues. He noted the strange incidence among Angrian characters of the trade of driving cattle: cattle drovers. He noted a first appearance of this motif in *Letters from an Englishman* of 1831. In it, Branwell wrote that his hero was startled by 'the noise and bellowing of an immense drove of mountain cattle, which were going towards the city'. 'Charles Wellesley' adds that some cattle belonging to his father were sold back to him by a notorious person called Pigtail. As is usual in these narratives, 'Pigtail' soon disappears and the droving is taken over by 'Northangerland' ('Rogue') and a man called S'death.

Percy (another name for Northangerland) later spends vast sums on 'an immense concern in horses and horned cattle'. He becomes a leading player among 'drovers, cow-jobbers, cattle-dealers' in the legendary Africa where Charlotte and Branwell had set their imaginary world. Sir Edward Hartford also becomes involved in cattle-dealing, after Percy, representing 'the dregs of the Western aristocracy', has driven his cattle amid clouds of dust so dense that it was thought to be the smoke from hell. It is here worth noting our earlier point that for the young Brontës, 'western' could have meant Irish. By the time these elements of the rambling epic were written, the geography of Angria had become totally confused with that of the British Isles.

Reaney also discovers in Charlotte's 1840-1 'Ashworth' mention of Percy's role as cow-jobber. Three of Percy's helpers in the enterprise are Daniels, who could 'disguise a traitor's heart under the features of a jovial Irish gentleman', McShane, another Irishman, and the red-haired Robert King, also known as S'death. It is unclear which of the two, Branwell or Charlotte, contributed which elements to 'Ashworth', though Charlotte considered it hers enough to send early chapters to Hartley Coleridge for his opinion. Christine Alexander notes that later, 'Percy and Co' returned to cattle trading in North Yorkshire. McShane's earlier name was Arthur O'Connor.[2]

So far as I am aware, Reaney is the only commentator to notice this persistent element of droving or cattle trading in the work of Branwell and to a lesser extent, Charlotte. Of course, there were cattle drovers in Haworth, a main route from Lancashire to Bradford and Leeds going though the village. But there was no reason for Branwell to single out this kind of farming for his villains to espouse; in fact there was no reason why he should have allowed them to deal in farming at all. 'Welsh' and his family were cattle-breeders, however, and it seems certain that Patrick had re-told the 'Welsh' story to the children at one of his breakfast-time visits. A strong impression was clearly made on Branwell by the cattle-breeding aspect of his ancestral story, just as we shall see that a similar impression was made on Emily.

Other interesting possibilities are raised by the image of a copper cauldron, 'with a little old man in it', sailing across the sea in *Letters from an Englishman*. Irish hero legends are full of magic cauldrons. They are sometimes ornamented with precious stones, and are used as rejuvenation or even reincarnation vessels. Was Branwell influenced by these tales? Branwell's cauldron here is no ordinary cauldron, but a magic one in which a person may navigate. A final point to note about cauldrons is that a significant one was given by a hero (god of the underworld, but more common in Welsh mythology) named Bran, to the King of Ireland. Possibly it is a coincidence that Branwell's name is partly reminiscent of Bran, an underworld god, but it may not be; we have no way of knowing. There is more to be noted when we get to the 'Irish *Iliad*'.

During the 1835 election, the Brontës, as always, favoured the 'blue', Tory side. Patrick spoke in favour of their candidate but was heckled. Branwell was so riled, according to Winifred Gerin, that he shouted out a threat to anyone stopping his father speaking. 'If you won't let my father speak, you shan't speak'. After this, his effigy was burnt, holding a potato in one hand and a herring in the other.[3]

Other characteristics of Branwell may have had a genetic element; some of his behaviour was uncannily similar to that of some of his Irish relatives. This was not culturally transmitted, but some deeper part of his genetic heritage. One matter which does not seem to have any counterpart in the Irish Brontës was his stature, which was notoriously small. For this, he seems to have compensated with fierce attitudes. Branwell wanted to be a prize fighter. We recall how Walsh fought Sam Clarke in a famous battle. This is what Branwell aspired to. His talented cartoons showed him as a boxer, as well as in macabre drawings worthy of a ghost hunter in Ballynaskeagh.

Wright made a case for moderation in the drinking at Drumballyroney and the surrounding district.[4] However, he admitted that on St Patrick's Day and 12 July:

> [T]here was a large consumption of spirituous liquors, or rather of fiery water. It was made up of vitriol, and blue-stone, and copperas, and other corrosive ingredients, and was flavoured with *potheen*. The beverage was prepared in great quantities and sold cheap.

He added that Irishmen occasionally drink to excess, but 'when the drunken bout is over they become strict total abstainers till some circumstance calls them again to social hilarity'. However, William was allegedly a keeper of a shebeen (denied by others) and Walsh certainly did keep a small public house near the Better House at Ballynaskeagh. David McKee was a follower of Dr John Edgar, the temperance campaigner. There is no doubt that strong drink was seen as a problem in Ireland, as it was in England. Cornelius ('Neelus', Walsh's son) was, perhaps, an alcoholic. Branwell was notoriously sucked into this mode of behaviour.

'Neelus' had an illegitimate child. In a copy of *Brontë Studies* Sarah Elizabeth Griffiths explored the case for the possibility that Branwell also fathered a child.[5] This has nothing to do with Irishness in principle, but Ms Griffiths suggests that the mother of the child was Irish. She follows Juliet Barker in locating the event at Broughton, while Branwell was working for the Postlethwaites in 1840. She offers evidence that an Agnes Riley may have been the mother. 'Her surname is of Irish origin and may have instigated a shared sense of commonality for a relationship to develop between Agnes and the young tutor of Irish descent, three years her junior'. It has to be said that 'Riley' is not always an Irish-derived name, the second element being quite common in English surnames. The case is unproven but explored by Juliet Barker in *The Brontës*, pp. 334-5.

Anne also pursued the drink question when writing *The Tenant of Wildfell Hall*. It is not easy to see Irish elements in Anne beyond her adherence to Emily's Gondal world. As we have seen, she often used Irish-derived names in her Gondal output. Compounds of the element 'Fitz' have already been noted. Una Campbell is an Irish character, it seems, with a Scots heritage. Helen Douglas has a Celtic name which we have already seen used by Emily in Gondal.

From her Evangelical father, influenced by Thomas Tighe and John Wesley, Anne drew a mission in life, 'to do ... good in the world before I leave it', identifying good with adherence to Christianity, not a view adopted by Branwell or Emily. Hugh Prunty was a thinker and an enthusiast, with strong ideas about the health of the Irish nation as exemplified in his (perhaps orally transmitted) dialectic.[6] In *The Tenant of Wildfell Hall* Anne Brontë argued cases. She made Helen act rationally and support her actions by theory. In *Brontë Studies* for January 2013, Clare Flaherty examined a recently discovered manuscript by Anne, in which two characters discuss theology.[7] They are labelled 'S' and 'C', the first perhaps standing for 'Sceptic' and the second for 'Christian'. Here we see Anne debating, producing rational arguments for both sides of the discussion. Ms Flaherty points out the relevance to this discussion of Sir Humphrey Davy's *The Last Days of a Philosopher,* and suggests a solution to a puzzle in *Wildfell Hall* concerning an apparent anachronism which has been put down as an error by Anne. The reasoning displayed in this dialogue, with the logical questioning of Gilbert Markham in the novel, echoes Hugh Prunty's logic. There is no suggestion that Anne was deliberately following him; like Branwell's coincidental similarity to Walsh Brontë, Anne's similarity to Hugh was perhaps genetic rather than culturally transmitted.

Rather surprisingly, Anne did give an Irish flavour to a character in *Wildfell Hall* by naming Gilbert's brother 'Fergus'. Precisely where she found the name is not clear. Feargus O'Connor, the Chartist leader, was very different from the Fergus of Linden-Car. Perhaps Anne was taking on some aspects of Branwell's personality in this portrait, and felt an Irish name would suit him best. Fergus is light-hearted and irresponsible, but at this time Anne could not have supposed this was typically Irish; she had after all met James Brontë, the 'respectable yeoman' of Charlotte's report. The matter remains mysterious. Could the name 'Fergus' have been adopted from Irish mythology?

All the young Brontës died of consumption, Anne being the last. Meanwhile all the Ballynaskeagh Brontës lived to a ripe old age except for Patrick's sister Jane. They were all thought of as fine, tall, healthy men and women.[8] From the interviews given by Rose Ann Heslip to various papers after the Brontë heritage was investigated in the 1890s, and now unearthed by Imelda Marsden, it is clear that consumption was a scourge of the children of Sarah Collins (Patrick's sister). All but Rose Ann died of the disease, as did a younger generation. There will no doubt be further medical research into this strange fact.

THE MCALLISTERS, WILLIAM WRIGHT, EMILY BRONTË AND *WUTHERING HEIGHTS*

I begin this chapter with a lengthy quotation from Wright, explaining how it is that he felt competent to write his book on Brontë origins. We remember that he was born and lived in what is now known as 'The Brontë Homeland', an area between Rathfriland and Banbridge in County Down. He produced the following account:

> My first classical teacher was the Rev. William McAllister of Finard, near Newry… He used to take me for long walks through the fields, and tell me the story of Hugh Brontë's early life, or some of his other stories, which he assured me were just as striking and as worthy to be recounted as the wrath of Achilles or the wanderings of Pius Aeneas. These stories I would reproduce, sometimes in writing but oftener *viva voce*, with as much spirit as possible, dulness [*sic*] being the one quality my tutor would not tolerate.
>
> It thus happened that I wrote screeds of the Brontë novels before a line of them had been penned at Haworth; and I do not think Branwell Brontë meant to deceive when he spoke of writing *Wuthering Heights*, for the story in outline must have been common property at Haworth as it was largely the story of Grandfather Brontë … I read the Brontë novels with the feeling that I had already known what was coming, and I was chiefly interested in the wording and skilful manipulation of details, for I had become acquainted with the incidents of old Brontë's career, as well as most of his stories, real and imaginary.[1]

We have examined Wright's early life and his acquaintance with William McAllister, and noted that he was a member of the McAllister family of Aghaderg and Drumballyroney. We shall return shortly to follow up these points. Meanwhile, we need to analyse this extraordinary claim by Wright. Firstly, we think about McAllister's method of teaching and his materials. There is specific mention of two classical epics, the *Iliad* and the *Aeneid*. The first of these was standard literature in nineteenth-century Britain, and was particularly known for its stirring narratives of war, as well as the pathos in the lives of Hector and Achilles. The second, a much later work, was a complex narrative, with flashbacks, dealing with the Trojan War, the journey of Aeneas across the Mediterranean, and his struggle to establish Rome in Italy. By coincidence, Emily Brontë also read some of it in Latin.[2]

In this passage, Wright was comparing Hugh Prunty's stories with these two epics and said he himself was told to reproduce Hugh's stories both on paper and orally, as part of an exercise in rendering narratives in lively forms. Irish hero stories, such as those concerning Cúchulainn, were epics with some of the characteristics of the *Iliad*. There is actually an incident in what has been called 'the Irish *Iliad*' in which associates of Cúchulainn captured 'three cows of magic qualities and a marvellous cauldron in which was always found an inexhaustible supply of meat, with treasure of silver and gold …' These legends had been produced as oral narratives, though by this time some had been put on paper, notably by James Ferguson in the 'Ossian' version, as we have seen. But Wright's allegation is that McAllister retold Hugh's stories from oral tradition, and he himself told them again. When he read 'the Brontë novels',

Emily Brontë. (From
A Life of Emily Brontë,
Second edition, 2010)

he saw an amazing similarity. What did he mean by 'the Brontë novels'? He mentioned that he had copies of *Jane Eyre*, *Shirley* and *Villette* sent from Haworth to Ballynaskeagh. He did not say where and when he first read *Wuthering Heights*, but it is surely this book above all the rest which riveted his attention. We saw that David McKee recognised a similarity between *Jane Eyre* and Hugh's stories, but we shall find that *Wuthering Heights* has startling resemblances. My suggestion is that, as Wright maintained, Emily's novel has its roots in the family history.

Let us first note what Wright did not claim, and what I do not claim either. In April 2013, Christopher Heywood contributed an interesting article to *Brontë Studies* in which he makes a case for Emily Brontë mirroring in her poems facets of earlier Irish history. Wright did not, however, mention Emily's poems. Heywood also asserts that the 'Welsh' story and other aspects of Hugh Prunty's narratives were constructed by Hugh Brontë, Patrick's *brother*, not his father. There is a good deal of evidence against this, as we have already seen, but which I shall systematise below. Wright did seem to be confused by Hugh Brontë's narratives at times, in particular the garbled version of his trip to England, firmly rejected by Rose Heslip. This confusion should not be held to invalidate his account of William McAllister's walks in the fields, and reproduction of old Hugh Prunty's oral stories.

We can now move to *Wuthering Heights* and its complex genesis. This novel is enormously compressed and suggestive, having many elements gathered in Emily Brontë's mind over a lifetime, and constantly pondered. I have previously discussed some of these elements, e.g. in *The Birth of Wuthering Heights*. The fabric of the novel is oral. The story is *heard*, whether from the mouth of Lockwood, or those of Nelly, Joseph, or Catherine. Commentators have often noted the similarity of its spare, direct quality to ballads, for example in the way in which time is treated arbitrarily, and in the time-shifts which occur. If there is a 'hero', it is the 'anti-hero', Heathcliff. In his creation, it is alleged that Byron played a part, and that a Byronic figure can be seen throughout Gondal, emerging in the novel. There is no need to discard this element of the story, but I hope to show conclusively that this is not where Heathcliff originated.

Returning first to the Haworth breakfast table, we can consider small elements of which have been revealed to us by Ellen Nussey and Martha Brown, as reported by A.M.F. Robinson (Madame Duclaux). In Chapter 23 we laid out these passages, and now return to confront one or two of them more precisely. Emily was, said Madame Duclaux, 'nursed on grisly Irish horrors, tales of 1798, tales of oppression and misery'. At times she 'wore a strange expression, gratified, pleased, as though she had gained something which seemed to complete a picture in her mind'. Duclaux added, 'this was the same Emily who at five years of age used to startle the nursery with her fantastic fairy stories'. At these times Ellen Nussey would marvel, 'as she caught sight of Emily's face, relaxed from its company rigour'.[3] As for the content of the stories, we may remind ourselves of the murderous tales occurring in Branwell's juvenilia and later.

This account is largely that of Ellen, who disliked Mr Brontë and gave only a brief notice of these Irish stories. They were 'stories of wild horror', 'fearful stories of superstitious Ireland', which made Ellen turn pale and cold. Hugh Prunty's life story was not quite like this. His was characterised in the phrase, 'tales of oppression and misery'; perhaps one tale in particular, about which Ellen could have told much more; the treatment of Hugh by 'Welsh'. Anyone who considers that it may have been Hugh Brontë, the brother, who invented this tale, needs also to remember the comment by Mrs McKee, David's wife, who said that he had recognised that many of the characters were 'founded largely on old Hugh's yarns polished into literature'.[4] 'Old Hugh [Prunty]' was, in Mr McKee's opinion, a teller of 'yarns'. Luckily, the McAllister family were especially interested in some of these yarns. We now have two versions of their memories.

Though Wright used a number of primary sources for the parts of his book which deal with old Hugh Prunty's stories, such as the Todds and McKees, who all knew Hugh Prunty, the McAllisters are the closest to the original. We have just dealt with the tradition passed on by William, but in the Poyntzpass article we found evidence from other members of the family. William may never have heard Hugh personally, but Samuel, his father, did. It is quite certain that William was the son of Samuel of Derrydrummuck, a miller. There were other millers in the family, for instance at a mill in Imdel townland. We are not quite sure which Samuel was the one who contributed to the papers recorded in the Poyntzpass evidence. However, the evidence of these McAllisters together is safe and reliable. The Poyntzpass version is similar to, but significantly different from the Wright version, and this shows that they are related but independent. Before we examine their effect on *Wuthering Heights*, we shall once again revisit the Haworth breakfast table.

Ellen Nussey's recollections begin in 1833, when Emily Brontë was 15. She recalled the 'strange stories' Patrick told, but in her *Scribner* article, cagily, she did not associate them with Ireland.

Probing more deeply, after the deaths of all the family, Madame Duclaux unearthed the glimpse of Emily's concentrated expression as she put together the jigsaw of Hugh Prunty's life. She had told 'fairy stories' in her childhood; it is not totally clear what kind of stories they were, but in the light of what we saw about Branwell and his interest in cauldrons, it seems likely that Emily's 'fairy stories' were derived in part from Patrick's stories (we cannot discount *The Arabian Nights* or *Ossian*).

The same mixture will be found in *Wuthering Heights*. The novel makes use of motifs and characters previously used in Gondal, partly shaped by the Roman Horace, and derived from countless sources, though, as we saw, one element in Gondal is an Irish element.

Emily Brontë felt quite early an alienation from almost all the human race, though she had another side to her, which Charlotte later named 'ruth for others'.[5] She was, as Charlotte's comment implies, also very hard on herself. At Cowan Bridge, she was considered the 'pet nursling', but in her case the 'shades of the prison house', which Wordsworth noted, closed down early. If we combine this personality with the moving story of old Hugh Prunty's ordeal in the Boyne Valley, we can see how Emily might have been particularly interested in 'Welsh' and his treatment as an outcast, which turned him into a tyrant. The picture she was forming in her mind as her father spoke about Hugh, Welsh and the Boyne was beginning to haunt her. Each time he told more, she fitted his information into the jigsaw.

When she came to write *Wuthering Heights*, it appears that Emily Brontë began with many considerations in mind. The thread which runs through the three

Brontë novels begun in early 1845, which I believe to be the date when the three sisters agreed to write publishable tales, is 'our early experiences in teaching'. Anne wrote of her two teaching posts in *Agnes Grey*. Charlotte went back to Belgium, her most intense experience of education, though from the other side. Emily returned to the country round Halifax, where she had spent either three or possibly six months teaching children to whom she preferred 'the housedog'. But the orphan story of Hugh and Welsh could not be avoided. This lay at the bottom of her sub-conscious, and she wished above all to write about it. Her very sharp memory went over what she had heard her father relate, dwelling particularly on 'Welsh', whom (so it seems) she transferred to Yorkshire, just as her father, in the Haworth kitchen, had naturalised some Irish stories in England (this, at any rate, is the thrust of Ellen Nussey's earlier versions of what happened at the breakfast table).

We now take up the remark of Wright that, 'I wrote screeds of the Brontë novels before a line of them had been published at Haworth'. He was following out the instructions of his tutor, William McAllister. Unfortunately we have none of Wright's undergraduate compositions. What we do have are two discreet versions of Hugh's story, both from the McAllisters, but from different members of the family. Let us first look at the matter of Heathcliff's origin and compare it with that of Welsh.

Emily's account begins with old Mr Earnshaw telling Hindley and Catherine,

> 'Now, my bonny man, I'm going to Liverpool, today …'. [A few paragraphs later he returns] 'See here, wife; I was never so beaten with anything in my life; but you must e'en take it as a gift from God, though it's as dark almost as if it came from the devil.' [The narrator, Nelly, goes on] 'We crowded round, and, over Miss Cathy's head, I had a peep at a dirty, ragged, black-haired child, big enough to walk and talk – indeed, its face looked older than Catherine's – yet, when it was set on its feet, it only stared round, and repeated over and over again some gibberish that nobody could understand. I was frightened, and Mrs Earnshaw was ready to fling it out of doors: she did fly up, asking how he could fashion to bring that gipsy brat into the house, when they had their own bairns to feed …'

In the next paragraph, Nelly says that the child was 'starving and houseless, and as good as dumb, in the streets of Liverpool … Not a soul knew to whom it belonged … he thought it better to take it home with him at once … he was determined he would not leave it as he found it.' Thus Heathcliff comes to live at Wuthering Heights.

We now turn to the narratives of Wright and 'Poyntzpass', remembering that we have shown the latter could not have been influenced by *Wuthering Heights*, and Wright claimed not to have been. Wright said:

> On one of his [the alleged earliest Brontë (but it could not be a 'Brontë')] return journeys from Liverpool a strange child was found in a bundle in the hold of the vessel. It was very young, very black, very dirty, and almost without any clothing of any kind. No one on board knew whence it had come, and no one seemed to care what became of it. (p. 19)

Poyntzpass said:

> On one such occasion when they [the earliest 'Brontë' and his wife] were coming home from Liverpool, a child was discovered, abandoned on the ship. It was a swarthy looking little boy with prominent teeth and a squint and wasn't just everyone's idea of an attractive child. Some of the sailors actually thought it was bad luck and were going to throw him overboard but Mrs Prunty wouldn't hear tell of that. (p. 87)

The source uses the word 'gypsy' and asserts that 'Hugh' (presumably meaning the father of the family) called the boy a 'brat'.

Emily Brontë had enlivened the scene, but kept Liverpool as the origin of the child, discarded the sea voyage, and ascribed the rescue wholly to the man. She agreed with the sources in the child's description. Poyntzpass says that only a daughter, Mary, accepted this new addition. Wright's account does not make this point. In the novel Mary becomes Catherine, who does not welcome Heathcliff. In a short while, Heathcliff becomes 'the usurper of [Hindley's] parent's affections and privileges'. Wright said, 'He became a favourite with Mr Brontë', while Poyntzpass says '[T]he child, Welsh, and the father, Hugh, had almost a dog-master attachment'. Wright put the point as follows, 'He followed the master about while at home with dog-like fidelity'.

The next incident in Poyntzpass was wholly omitted by Wright, but is so interestingly close to *Wuthering Heights* that I feel both must be given verbatim. Here, first, is the Poyntzpass version, with the punctuation of the article:

> The incident of the two colts, has been told by different members of the family. It appears that Hugh, the father, having returned from a successful cattle sale, had given one of the boys and Welsh, enough money with which to buy horses for themselves. It was considered good training for them to purchase their own mounts even if it meant making mistakes. The son went to a local fair and Welsh to one further afield. On returning it was discovered that Welsh had made a mistake, his horse proved to be lame. As the two of them were dismounting at the stables, the surly Welsh, mad that some one had done better than him, and that he would look a fool, couldn't contain himself and went up behind young Prunty as he was about to hang up the saddle and knocked

him off his feet. However he had taken on more than he had bargained for, for in the fight, Welsh was badly bruised and knocked about. At last, he shouted, 'If you don't give me your horse, I'll tell Pa you beat me up.' Now young Prunty, knowing that his father would always favour Welsh, and that he would probably lose his horse anyhow, decided that discretion was the only way and he very grudgingly handed the horse over to Welsh. He said vindictively, 'I hope he breaks your neck!' And that nearly happened – a day or two later as he was forcing the animal to gallop up a hill, it threw him off and broke his collar bone. So Welsh got the best horse at least he paid for it!

This becomes in *Wuthering Heights*:

I remember [Nelly speaking] Mr Earnshaw once bought a couple of colts at the parish fair, and gave the lads each one. Heathcliff took the handsomest, but it soon fell lame, and when he discovered it, he said to Hindley, 'You must exchange horses with me; I don't like mine, and if you don't I shall tell your father of the three thrashings you've given me this week, and show him my arm, which is black to the shoulder'. Hindley put out his tongue, and cuffed him over the ears.

'You'd better do it at once,' he persisted, escaping to the porch (they were in the stable): you will have to, and if I speak of these blows, you'll get them again with interest'.

'Off, dog!' cried Hindley, threatening him with an iron weight, used for weighting potatoes and hay.

'Throw it', he replied, standing still, 'and then I'll tell how you boasted you would turn me out of doors as soon as he died, and see whether he will not turn you out directly'.

He threw it, hitting him on the breast, and down he fell, but staggered up immediately, breathless and white, and had not I prevented it he would have gone just so to the master, and got full revenge by letting his condition plead for him, intimating who had caused it.

'Take my colt, gipsy, then,' said young Earnshaw, 'And I pray that he may break your neck; take him, and be damned, you beggarly interloper! And wheedle my father out of all he has – only, afterwards, show him what you are, imp of Satan – And take that, I hope he'll kick out your brains!'

Heathcliff had gone to loose the beast, and shift it to his own stall. He was passing behind it, when Hindley finished his speech by knocking him under its feet, and without stopping to examine whether his hopes were fulfilled, ran away as fast as he could.

I was surprised to see how coolly the child gathered himself up, and went on with his intention, exchanging saddles and all, and then sitting down on a

EMILY BRONTE uses HUGH'S story

The incident of the two colts, has been told by different members of the family. It appears that Hugh, the father, having returned from a successful cattle sale had given one of the boys and Welsh, enough money with which to buy horses for themselves. It was considered good training for them to purchase their own mounts even if it meant making mistakes. The son went to a local fair and Welsh to one further afield. On returning it was discovered that Welsh had made a mistake, his horse proved to be lame. As the two of them were dismounting at the stables, the surly Welsh, mad that some one had done better then him, and that he would look a fool, couldn't contain himself and went up behind young Prunty as he was about to hang up the saddle and knocked him off his feet. However he had taken on more than he had bargained for, for in the fight, Welsh was badly bruised and knocked about. At last, he shouted 'If you don't give me your horse, I'll tell Pa you beat me up.' Now young Prunty, knowing that his father would always favour Welsh, and that he would probably lose his horse anyhow, decided that discretion was the only way and he very grudingly handed the horse over to Welsh. He said vindictively, 'I hope he breaks your neck!' And that nearly happened — a day or two later as he was forcing the animal to gallop up a hill, it threw him off and broke his collar bone. So while Welsh got the best horse at least he paid for it!

1 2 3 7 4 5 6

- Poyntzpass version (Hugh's own).

'The Two Colts'. (From Poyntzpass and *Wuthering Heights*)

1 As an instance, I remember Mr. Earnshaw once bought a couple of colts at the parish fair, and gave the lads each one. Heathcliff took the handsomest, but it soon fell lame and when he discovered it, he said to Hindley, **2**

"You must exchange horses with me; I don't like mine, and if you won't I shall tell your father of the three thrashings you've given me this week, and show him my arm, which is black to the shoulder." **4**

Hindley put out his tongue, and cuffed him over the ears.

"You'd better do it at once," he persisted, escaping to the **3** porch (they were in the stable) "you will have to, and if I speak of these blows, you'll get them again with interest."

"Off, dog!" cried Hindley, threatening him with an iron weight, used for weighing potatoes and hay.

"Throw it," he replied, standing still, "and then I'll tell how you boasted that you would turn me out of doors as soon as he died, and see whether he will not turn you out directly."

Hindley threw it, hitting him on the breast, and down he fell, but staggered up immediately, breathless and white, and had not I prevented it he would have gone just so to the master, and got full revenge by letting his condition plead for him, intimating who had caused it.

5 "Take my colt, gipsy, then!" said young Earnshaw, "And I **6** pray that he may break your neck: take him, and be damned, you beggarly interloper! and wheedle my father out of all he has-- only, afterwards, show him what you are, imp of Satan—And take that, I hope he'll kick out your brains!"

Heathcliff had gone to loose the beast, and shift it to his own stall He was passing behind it, when Hindley finished his **7** speech by knocking him under its feet, and without stopping to examine whether his hopes were fulfilled, ran away as fast as he could. *Wuthering Heights, Ch IV.*

WUTHERING HEIGHTS

bundle of hay to overcome the qualm which the blow had occasioned, before
he entered the house. (Chapter IV).

Emily Brontë retained the theme of hatred between the family members,
together with the imperturbability of the former waif.

Later, both Welsh and Heathcliff leave the scene and become changed per-
sonalities. Both Wright (p. 22) and Poyntzpass set this on a boat returning from
Liverpool, where the usual cattle transactions had taken place. In Wright's version
old 'Hugh' died on board, while in Poyntzpass 'he was found dead in his bunk'.
Emily Brontë set the disappearance of Heathcliff in a much more telling and dramatic context. Heathcliff has heard the declaration of Catherine that she cannot
think of marrying him. In the Wright and Poyntzpass originals, 'there was no sign
of Welsh or the money [from the cattle sale]'. There is a little more detail in this
version than in Wright's, but it is agreed that the money has gone.

But Welsh re-entered as a rich person: 'next day' Welsh arrived at the door
in a horse-drawn chaise, 'dressed like a gentleman' (Poyntzpass). He 'appeared
dressed up as he had never been seen before. He was arrayed in broadcloth,
black and shiny as his well-greased hair, and in fine linen, white and glisten-
ing as his prominent teeth' (Wright, p. 23). (Incidentally his teeth had not been
mentioned by Wright on his arrival, though they had been a feature of the waif
in Poyntzpass.) In *Wuthering Heights* Heathcliff stays away for a considerable time,
returning one night to surprise Nelly by his appearance:

> I was amazed to behold the transformation in Heathcliff ... He had grown a
> tall, athletic, well-formed man, beside whom my master seemed quite slender
> and youth-like. His upright carriage suggested the idea of his having been in
> the army ... His countenance ... looked intelligent, and retained no marks of
> former degradation.

The 'gentlemanly' appearance of Welsh is thus stressed in the originals,
and Emily Brontë takes this over in her novelistic development.

We now turn to the matter of ghosts, prominent in *Wuthering Heights* and
appearing also in the milieu of the Ballynaskeagh Brontës. Madame Duclaux
(p. 160) described the result of Patrick's stories as leaving Emily with a fund
of 'eerie lore'. We have seen that the main proponents of ghostly doings in the
glens and in Caldwell's Fields at Ballynaskeagh were Hugh and James, though
they betrayed a healthy scepticism when their practical jokes were challenged.
But Emily told 'fairy stories' as a child. Her feeling about ghosts was not precisely that of her uncles. We shall briefly look at the most telling ghost episodes
in the novel; the appearance of Catherine to Lockwood, and the rustic notion
that Heathcliff might haunt the moor at the end of the book. Catherine is not

'Mary', Welsh's wife and quasi-sibling to Hugh Prunty. She partakes a little more of Emily's eldest sister Maria, though some will dispute this. Her haunting is taken very seriously in the book, in a mode very different from Hugh's arranged hauntings. Yet the very notion of hauntings may come from Patrick's stories, augmented by tales told by the old Haworth servant Tabby.

Heathcliff haunts Wuthering Heights, 'There are those who speak of having met him near the church and on the moor and even within this house…' Nelly explains. This comment is left unevaluated.

There is one more important facet of *Wuthering Heights* which relates to Patrick's breakfast-time interruptions. Emily Brontë knew that what her father was telling was in part family history. She recognised, we may deduce, that the story told by Hugh had a personal implication for her. The Irish legends that he told were also part of her, and she could not rid herself of them any more than Heathcliff could leave Wuthering Heights after his death. The time setting of *Wuthering Heights* is different from those of Charlotte's and Anne's novels, though all go back to the past. From C.P. Sanger's *The Structure of Wuthering Heights* to Conal Boyce's 'Nested Narratives of *Wuthering Heights*' of 2013, many attempts have been made to clarify the chronology of the novel.[6] However the variants differ, the main action takes place between about 1778 and 1802. Patrick Brontë was born in 1777, a fact most certainly known by his children. He left Ireland in 1802. The similarity of dates can hardly be a coincidence. Emily Brontë probed further back, to imply dates for the birth of the old Earnshaws, and even cited the tablet over the gateway to Wuthering Heights recording the name of a Hareton Earnshaw from 1500. There is here a trace of Patrick's disavowal, or feigned lack of interest, in the proposition that he could be 'of ancient family'. Whatever he told Mrs Gaskell, he kept his children aware of their heritage through the 'tales of a grandfather' he relayed.

Another correspondence claimed by Wright may be mentioned, though I am much more dubious about it. He claimed that Joseph is partly based on the wily Gallagher of Hugh's Boyne Valley period. I am not convinced that Emily would not rather have depicted local Yorkshire models for this character. His dialect is amazingly rich and accurate, and I find it difficult to believe that Emily would have been able to marry the Gallagher character to the Haworth expressions. The two do not play the same part in their respective stories. Wright here was surely going well beyond the evidence.

The final link between Hugh Prunty's life and the plot of *Wuthering Heights* which I should like to note (there may well be many more) is the name, and elopement, of Isabella Linton. Isabella is the sister of Edgar (whose name may come from *King Lear*, but may also incorporate the name of a famous Ulster temperance reformer, Dr John Edgar). An Isabella Linton married James Stewart at Glascar about 1797 and had ten children. Simon and Sarah Collins made two attempts to have a first child named Stewart, using the surname as a Christian name. I have not been able to trace direct family links between Isabella and the Collinses, but the possibility is there. Emily Brontë's strange list of Gondal characters includes two members of a family written as Stwart, but presumably abbreviated.[7]

Emily's Isabella develops an odd infatuation with Heathcliff, and in Chapter 12 elopes with him. Some aspects of this mirror the runaway marriage of Hugh Prunty and Eilís McClory. The couple are not seen disappearing: news is brought by a third party. In Ballyanskeagh, on the morning of her proposed wedding to Mr Burns, Eilís and Hugh were seen along the Banbridge road as follows; 'a messenger on foot arrived, and reported that he had met Miss McClory and a tall gentleman galloping furiously towards the river Bann near Banbridge'. Poyntzpass says, 'A messenger came back to McCloreys [*sic*] with a letter and with the horse'. Emily Brontë wrote:

> One of the maids, a thoughtless girl, who had been on an early errand to Gimmerton, came panting upstairs, open-mouthed, and dashed into the chamber …
>
> [She went on] 'I met on the road a lad that fetches milk here' … 'and he asked whether we weren't in trouble at the Grange … Then he says, "they's somebody gone after them, I guess?" … [H]e told how a gentleman and lady had stopped to have a horse's shoe fastened at a blacksmith's shop, two miles out of Gimmerton, not very long after midnight! … the blacksmith's lass … knew them both directly – And she noticed the man – Heathcliff, she felt certain, and nob'dy could mistake him …' (Chapter 12).

Emily Brontë had embroidered the original, but there is enough left to see that she had clearly registered her father's narrative.

OBJECTIONS
AND QUESTIONS

The thesis of this book has been that the Brontë sisters and Branwell could not have written as they did without their Irish heritage. This has not, in my view, been given due weight (among many other influences), partly because of the speedy and firm response greeting the work of Dr William Wright in the 1890s (Wright unfortunately having left himself open to valid criticism in some of his assertions), and partly because of the attitude of Charlotte Brontë and Patrick himself, aware in the mid-nineteenth century of obstacles in the way of treating this Irish influence positively.

I hope I have shown that the Irish dimension was vital to the Brontës. However, it is likely that some degree of scepticism remains in readers' minds, and in this final chapter I should like to summarise what we now know for certain, what we may reasonably deduce, and what must remain conjecture.

There will be those who wish to see the Brontës' provincialism as bred by their Yorkshire birth and upbringing, and of course they are right. The Brontës were Yorkshire provincials. But a careful reading of their biographies will suggest that they were not always quite part of Yorkshire society either, and a residue of something anomalous remained. The three sisters had a reputation for shyness, as though they were not quite at home; we can compare this with the rooted family connections of Ellen Nussey, Mary Taylor, and their other friends. Patrick had made his own way in England; his daughters found it more difficult to do so.

First I wish to summarise what is definitely known about the family's Irish origins, which cannot rationally be challenged. Evidence for all this cannot be repeated here and will be found in the earlier chapters of this book.

1. Patrick Brontë was born 'Prunty' (written 'Brunty' at times) in a small cabin at Imdel, parish of Dumballyroney, County Down. This was at first challenged, but there is now no doubt; the cabin was later called 'the Brontë kiln'. His father was Hugh, his mother Alice (Eilís in an Irish form they

probably didn't know) McClory. There is no warrant for the 'Eleanor' written by the clerk at the Church of Ireland church where Patrick's siblings were christened (though it is interesting that Walsh/Welsh Brontë called his sister Eleanor in his will of 1865). Alice's name was pronounced 'Ayles' by the neighbours. The McClorys were Catholics, but had adapted to the point where they could rent substantial amounts of land.

2. Patrick was followed by nine other children, of whom William fought at Ballynahinch in 1798, Hugh and James remained all their lives to look after the farm, and Walsh or Welsh added keeping of public houses to his agricultural interests. Hugh and James became road menders. One sister, Jane, died early. Another, Sarah, married a Simon Collins, and had a number of children, the only survivor being Rose Ann, who married a Heslip and migrated to Yorkshire. Mary kept the farm with Hugh and James. There was also a 'Rose', apparently called 'Rose Anne'.

3. Patrick grew up as an unusual child, fond of reading. He became a blacksmith's assistant and a linen weaver, but at sixteen was taken on as a teacher at Glascar Presbyterian Church school. He was an imaginative teacher, fostering the education of both boys and girls. He was friends with other Presbyterians such as Samuel Barber, the reforming minister of a Rathfriland church. He left Glascar school and was noticed by Thomas Tighe of Drumballyroney, and then taught in his church school. All the while he was reading and had ambitions to leave the area, perhaps the country.

4. Hugh made his living by roasting corn, but before that he had worked at lime kilns near Dundalk (Mount Pleasant). He had come from 'Drogheda' an area which is not confined to the city. He had come north and at some point visited a relation at Hilltown. Hugh had been adopted by an uncle.

I should be surprised if any rational objection to any of these points could be made.

Strong objections have been raised to the version of the earlier part of Hugh's life given by members of the McAllister family of Glascar, Imdel and Derrydrummuck. This information was passed down though William McAllister, Wright's tutor, and other members of the family. These objections do not seem reasonable when we study the authorities. In the older generation, Samuel McAllister was a miller whose work took him to Hugh Prunty's corn kiln where he heard Hugh tell this story, and others comparable to the *Iliad* but located in Ireland. This is supported by a comment made by David McKee, a Presbyterian minister and Wright's mother-in-law, who recognised some Brontë work as 'old Hugh's yarns polished into literature'. We now have two versions of Hugh's story, descending through different members of the McAllister family. One incident, that of 'the two colts', recorded in the Poyntzpass version, is clearly the origin of an episode in *Wuthering Heights*. We may, therefore, take the story about his origin told by Hugh as certainly told by him, and can try to check its veracity.

Other family members had heard that Hugh came from 'Drogheda'. The Earl of Drogheda's estates included the area where Hugh claimed to have been brought up. There is no difficulty about accepting that he was brought up on land belonging to the Earl, not far from the River Boyne. Now, however, we move to the field of deduction and less certainty. Wright thought the farm which Hugh talked about was on the Boyne. In *The Brontës' Irish Background* I looked for a holding actually on the Boyne, but I now think Ardagh on the tributary, the Mattock, is more likely. Here a Welsh or Walsh family were primary tenants of Drogheda land. Branwell Brontë remembered the name 'Ardagh'. My deduction here is still open to question; proof may yet surface.

Hugh told, in his corn-kiln, a detailed story of his life before Drogheda. We have only Wright's version, as the 'Poyntzpass' version merely states that the journey from his early home took four days.

The task is to try to reconstruct a narrative which I am sure Hugh did tell, but of which the details are less firm. Poyntzpass says that the early home was 'mid-Ulster', perhaps near Enniskillen. I have not located it precisely there, but certainly in that part of County Fermanagh. This Poyntzpass information is tantalising. If we could be sure this was in the information originally occurring in the McAllister manuscripts, the matter would be settled. Unfortunately, we cannot rule out the possibility that 'Enniskillen' has crept in from a later theory, possibly even *The Brontës' Irish Background*, by some route or another. Poyntzpass also says 'there was a lake near'. A location in County Fermanagh seems almost certain, because the journey taken by Hugh will not fit logistically with any other distance or route. However, we have to keep a very small possibility of doubt here, since members of the Ó Pronntaigh family were also found in Armagh, near Loughgall, Monaghan, and Cavan. The surname is a rare one, found nowhere in the south of Ireland.

Ó Pronntaigh, variously spelt, is the original Irish version of 'Prunty'. An Irish poet and scribe, Pádraig Ó Pronntaigh, gave his origin in a colophon to one or more of his writings as 'the Erne'. He was later found writing about a farmer called 'Uí' [genitive of O] Labhraidh' (but see appendix for a caveat). This is the Irish for McClory, a name almost entirely confined to a few parishes in County Down. He seems to have reached Down via Ballymascanlan near Dundalk, where later Hugh was to work at the lime kilns. He was in Ballymascanlan in 1738. It would make sense if he was actually Hugh's father, but we cannot finally prove this. I personally think the evidence, though circumstantial, strongly suggests it. Irish Christian names were given on a traditional basis. This held in the Prunty family. Patrick was therefore named after his grandfather, who must also have been called Patrick (Pádraig). According to Wright, Hugh wished to become 'a great scholar' (p. 17). It is not easy to see how this ambition could be formed by a farmer's son, but Pádraig *was* a scholar. All these points are circumstantial, but it is very difficult to find any other explanation for them. Wright, for example, knew nothing about Pádraig Ó Pronntaigh, and was certainly not making up the 'great scholar' ambition to fit a theory.

One really interesting consideration, which I hardly dealt with in the earlier parts of the book, but which is raised by the recent discoveries, is the question of whether or not Hugh really had no idea where his family had come from, either in Fermanagh, Ballymascanlan, or County Down. This is highly speculative, and I raise it merely as a possibility, since additional facts have emerged which make the idea worth exploring. Wright was adamant that this was not the case. In Chapter 5 he said that when Hugh's parents agreed to the adoption, 'a solemn oath' was given 'by which the father agreed never to visit or communicate with his son in any way'. The same promise was given by Welsh and Mary. I am not sure that I believe Wright, who may well have heard this but failed to challenge his informant. The following are points which tell against Wright's confidence. When Hugh ran away from the 'Boyne farm', he turned north. Perhaps he remembered coming to Drogheda eight or so years previously and wished to retrace his steps. Perhaps, however, he knew where he was running to. He eventually arrived at Hilltown, after service as a lime-roaster in Ballymascanlan. This was 'to a relative of his mother'. If he knew nothing about his ancestry, how did he know to go to Hilltown? For that matter, how had he known that Ballymascanlan was a likely place to find clues to his paternity? If Mary had not told him, perhaps a neighbour in Ardagh or the surrounding district had leaked this information?

If Pádraig Ó Pronntaigh was Hugh's father, or very near relative, and wrote about a McClory, implying a knowledge of Aghaderg and Drumballyroney, perhaps it was not chance that Hugh cultivated the acquaintance of 'Red' Paddy McClory when he met him at the Mount Pleasant lime kilns. An alternative view might be that even as a small child he had heard his parents talk about Ballymascanlan, or his mother's relatives in South Down, though at that time there was no Hilltown. At this point we add speculation to speculation, and wonder who were his mother's relatives near Hilltown in the 1790s? Perhaps, but there is no clear evidence for this, the fact that while Patrick was teaching at Glascar, he took on as a pupil one David Lindsay from Bangrove, near Rathfriland, may indicate that David was a relation. Before Hilltown was built only the Lindsays and Morgans, it seems, lived in that area, then designated 'Eight-Mile Bridge'.[1] Since Pádraig Ó Pronntaigh was in the district at some point, did he possibly marry a Lindsay? This is a weak deduction, but worth consideration. The Lindsays were tenants of a good deal of land stretching from south of Hilltown to 'Bangrove', a name which disappears from documentation after the 1820s. John Morgan was born in the area about 1750 and lived near Hilltown all his life. The Lindsays have a slightly better claim to a link with the Ó Pronntaighs, because of David Lindsay's education by Patrick Prunty. However, I am becoming more and more interested in the possible O'Neill link, following the discovery that the O'Neills lived at Bannvale near Hilltown, but there is much more research to be done.

The issue of the origin of Welsh or Walsh is problematic. Wright and Poyntzpass agree that he was discovered on a boat returning from Liverpool. Since Hugh could not know this personally the story must have been mediated through Mary or a neighbour in the Boyne Valley. I shall deal with the 'Liverpool' aspect in Appendix 2. As in *Wuthering Heights* with Heathcliff, so here there is a suspicion that Welsh was an illegitimate child of his adoptive father. Heathcliff is favoured by Mr Earnshaw, while Welsh was favoured (extremely) by the landowner at the 'Boyne' farm. In both cases we may feel there is a cover-up. There is little chance of penetrating this authoritatively, in the absence or destruction of any records which might have existed.

Ellen Nussey followed Charlotte and her father in being extremely secretive about Patrick's breakfast time horror stories. At first she tried to give the impression that they all came from the Yorkshire neighbourhood, but gradually relaxed and admitted an Irish provenance. The internal evidence we have examined, including such matters as the 'two colts', shows that Patrick told the story of Hugh's upbringing. Little clue is given about the other Irish horror stories, other than their violence and frightening tone. Branwell and his sisters produced narratives that sound similar to Irish hero tales of magic and war. This is not conclusive evidence, but with William Wright's comparison between Hugh's tales and the *Iliad*, a likely thread does emerge. We shall examine these legends in more detail in Appendix 1.

The precise attitude of the Prunty family, and Patrick in particular, to the 1798 rebellion is unclear. William fought at Ballynahinch. Patrick was a friend of Samuel Barber. Later he was employed by Thomas Tighe, a clergyman with strong sympathies towards constitutional reform in Ireland. He perhaps taught Patrick to fire pistols. On one side of the argument, William differentiated himself from his brothers, setting up his home away from Ballynaskeagh, in Lisnacreevy. On the other hand, no secret was made of his participation in the 1798 rising. In my view, Patrick probably shared the understanding of both Presbyterians and Catholics at the time of the rising, but then drifted away from this, perhaps in accordance with the 'ambition' which is reported of him. This view is to some extent speculative.

APPENDIX 1

HUGH PRUNTY AND IRISH STORYTELLING

W e looked briefly on p. 44 at Hugh's repertoire and (A) the types of story he may have told, and (B) his method of delivery. In this appendix I should like to expand what has been said about these matters, and give more details about the possible repertoire available to him.

Before looking at this repertoire, it may be worth reminding ourselves of Wright's comments on Hugh's range and technique, linking it with the storytelling of a *seanchaí* such as Peig Sayers.

'Tyranny and cruelty of every kind he denounced fiercely' (p. 132); 'where girls had been betrayed, either the ghost of the injured woman or the devil himself in some awful form wreaked unutterable vengeance on the betrayer' (p. 132). The stories 'though sometimes rough in texture, and interspersed with emphatic expletives, after the manner of the time, had always a healthy, moral bearing' (pp. 131-2). While he was being tutored by William McAllister, Wright was told, 'some of [Hugh's] other stories, which he assured me were just as striking and worthy to be recounted as the wrath of Achilles or the wanderings of Pius Aeneas. These stories I would reproduce, sometimes in writing, but oftener *viva voce*, with as much spirit as possible …' (pp.7-8). Wright thus clearly associated Hugh's stories with Classical Greek and Latin epics, and regarded them as comparable.

The German visitor, J.C. Kohl, who visited Drogheda in the 1840s, listened to a storyteller reciting a story in Irish. The content of such stories will concern us later, but for now we may note the status of this man, and his manner of telling his story.[1]

> The reciter was … a simple and ignorant man, with a good deal of the clown about him. [His recitation was unadorned.] Sometimes, however, when carried away by the interest of his story manner and voice were animated and moving. At such times he fixed his eyes on his hearers as if demanding sympathy for himself and his poem.

These Irish stories were originally and normally in Irish. The native language of most of the Todds, McAllisters, and other Scots-heritage inhabitants of Imdel and Ballynaskeagh was surely 'Scots-Irish'. It therefore follows that Hugh would have translated in his own way stories which he may originally have heard in Irish Gaelic. Twentieth-century folk-tale collectors sometimes found Irish tales in English. In Hugh's case, it may be that some Irish words remained in the original. The evidence that Patrick knew some Irish words has been given above, but it is more than likely that the McClory family included Irish speakers, though this cannot be proved. One small point about Irish in Clonduff parish is that a John O'Neill who was buried in Clonduff graveyard in 1809 aged 80, was regarded as a splendid native Irishman. His home is given as Banville or Banvale.[2]

Where exactly did Hugh learn his apparently considerable repertoire of Irish stories? The Ordnance Survey 'Statistical Reporters' of the 1830s were asked to comment for each parish on 'the habits of the people'. They rarely did so in detail, but Lieutenant P. Taylor, surveying Devenish parish, not far from Enniskillen (County Fermanagh), wrote in 1834, 'Many long legendary tales are preserved among the tenantry in this as in every other county, more extravagant than the celebrated *Arabian Nights*.'

Unfortunately he gave no details, but this is one of the few indications of popular oral traditions in the area, so we must regard it as better than nothing. No corresponding comments were made in the case of Galloon or Drummully.

Hugh was either 6 or, more probably, 8, when he was taken by Welsh and Mary from his home in Fermanagh. Much later, he was to tell Irish hero legends comparable to the *Iliad*. One possibility is that he might have got some of these direct from his father, who may have been the scholar, scribe and poet, Pádraig Ó Pronntaigh. It is worth examining what Ó Pronntaigh wrote and anything we know about his life and productions. I shall first try to state what is actually known and what might credibly be deduced from the small remnants of his work which we have, then look at these productions in more detail.

The colophon asserting that Pádraig was from 'the Erne' has already been mentioned. He seems to have produced work in two phases, from 1732 to 1738, and from 1759 to 1772. Though he is regarded as a poet, much of his material seems to be stories in prose of a traditional nature. A celebratory poem is that for the new archbishop Brian Mac Mathghamhna (MacMahon) on his arrival at Ballymascanlan, from a previous post at Clogher. At this point, in 1738, Pádraig was indisputably a Catholic, writing for a Catholic audience. I have speculated that he may have been in some way patronised by the Maguires, but this is, of course, speculation. Then we have the foray into County Down suggested by the dialogue between the farmer Ó Labhrai (McClory) and a harper. This could have followed his sojourn in Ballymascanlan. In the 1760s Pádraig wrote what are described as 'tales', the last of which is dated 1772. My next sentence is bold guesswork, and would need a great deal of (probably impossible) research to find evidence. Is it possible that after the Ballymascanlan period he returned to Fermanagh and so provided the original home for Hugh, from which the little boy was taken to the Boyne Valley? There also seems some possibility that he taught at a school at or near Forkhill, perhaps before returning to the Erne.[3] There was a school in this parish run by the poet Peadar Ó Doirnín, who lived there until his death in 1768. During this period, penal laws were very slowly starting to loosen, but there was little secure employment for an Irish poet, and some scholars took to a wandering life.

Hugh then went to the Drogheda area along the River Boyne. As we have seen, even in the 1840s a German visitor would hear 'Ossianic poetry' in the neighbourhood. J.C. Kohl wrote that Drogheda was the last genuinely Irish town, 'the suburbs of Drogheda are genuine Irish suburbs … and a great many people are to be found in the neighbourhood who speak the old Irish tongue more fluently and more frequently than the English'. Visiting a priest's house, Kohl found some Irish harps and a young harper who could play 'Brian Boru's march'. We can only guess that Hugh, perhaps already interested in Irish traditional composition, would have visited this place in pursuit of his ambition of scholarship. It seems likely, but there is absolutely no proof. Surely he would also have been interested in the whole landscape of the area, knowing that the legendary hill of Tara was across the river, and that the strange mounds of Dowth, Knowth and Newgrange were at hand. Almost in the backyard of the farm was Mellifont Abbey.

Hugh's flight took him to Ballymascanlan, just north of Dundalk, the Dundealgan of the legends, home of Cúchulainn himself, the hero of the *Táin Bó Chúailnge*.

Not far away, near Forkhill, where Pádraig had taught, was Slieve Gullion, the site of many magic stories. A famous meeting of bards was held here in 1744. We cannot rule out the possibility that Pádraig Ó Pronntaigh attended, though that clashes in date with the chronology suggested above. These local parishes were culturally Irish, so that the Ordnance Survey accounts of them in the 1830s are very sparse. Forkhill and the other parishes are in County Armagh, the very centre of Ulster legend, where Conchobar ruled at Emain Macha, now Navan Fort, just outside Armagh city. Cúchulainn was the greatest hero, called by Alfred Nutt 'the Irish Achilles'. Back on the edge of County Louth, Samuel Coulter, the Presbyterian farmer, collected Irish manuscripts in his library. When Hugh entertained the farmers waiting for lime at Mount Pleasant with strange stories, it is hard to believe that Cúchulainn's exploits were not among them.

Having outlined the geography of Hugh's life (strangely similar to that of Pádraig) we can now examine in more detail some of the manuscripts Pádraig wrote.

A manuscript in the British Library, copied for Samuel Coulter, is a good example of Pádraig's versatile concerns.[4] It was copied by Patrick Lynch in 1800 from one of Pádraig's, written in 1732. It includes the wide-spread story of the death of the sons of Usna. Deirdre ('the Irish Helen') had dreamed that these young men had their heads sliced off. She doubted whether it would be safe to accept an invitation from Conchobar to Armagh. Nevertheless, she accepted it, and was lodged in the Red Branch House. In the night, Conchobar ordered it to be set on fire; after various interventions the three sons of Usna decided to escape from the house, but were captured. Conchobar condemned them to death, and their heads were speedily severed with a sword called 'The Retaliator'. Deirdre made a famous elegy for them, but she too soon met her death.

The tale of Ailinn, a fire-breathing goblin, took place near Tara and is from a different cycle. This was translated by Douglas Hyde from a 1763 manuscript written by Pádraig. Ailinn used to come from his fort near Tara every year in summer, and burn Tara. The king promised a vast reward to anyone who could kill the goblin. Part of Ailinn's success was due to a fairy harp which he played, producing magic music which lulled his opponents into trances. The hero Fionn stood up and promised to rid Tara of the goblin with fiery breath. Sure enough, next summer, Ailinn came out of his rath and made for Tara, playing sweet music on his magic harp. Fionn was almost overcome by sleep, but roused himself and threw an enchanted spear at Ailinn, which felled the goblin. Fionn beheaded him and fixed his head on the point of his spear, placing it on the ramparts for all to see. The king was as good as his word and made Fionn chief of the Fianna. The same manuscript carries other tales of legendary Ireland, dealing with fairies, heroes and kings. In the year 1759 Pádraig apparently wrote the Connspoid between the harper and the farmer, though this also appears in other manuscripts. The impression is given in secondary sources that this is Pádraig's own work, but we need to have a little caution in this respect.

A further example of an Ó Pronntaigh manuscript is one in the collection of the Royal Irish Academy. This is part of a group from the Ballymascanlan area, including pages from various dates. About 180 pages are in Ó Pronntaigh's hand, and dated 1761. Much of the content deals with armed conflict, 'black rages' and 'utter routs'. Sixty pages are given over to 'late, romantic, adventure tales of the Red Branch cycle'. It is from this manuscript that the colophon giving Pádraig's home as Lough Erne comes. A further manuscript, dated 1772, focuses on quarrels among Irish heroes and godlike men.[5] Very different is the poem Pádraig Ó Pronntaigh wrote in honour of the new Catholic primate of all Ireland, Brian, or Bernard, MacMahon, in 1738. MacMahon was 58 when elevated to this position, and we may consider the possibility that Pádraig had already known him, or known of him, in his earlier role, since the Clogher diocese covered the Fermanagh area where he lived. The manuscript heading, in translation, reads 'composed on the occasion of the Primate Brian MacMahon, and his brother, Ross MacMahon, Bishop of Clogher, coming to live at Ballymascanlan, near Dundalk.' Here are the first three stanzas in English translation:

Of welcomes ninety millions I give to thee,
Who comest with Christ's symbol in thy hand,
Gifted with wisdom and with power supreme,
To rule and guide the myriads of our land.

A glorious tree thou art, dispensing shade,
Sprung from the noble root of Heremon,
True essence of the blood of the Gaels
Whose sceptre ruled our isles in days long gone.

Rich jewel of the church of Innisfail
Successor of St Patrick, psalmist sweet,
Whose voice is loudest in the sacred choir
Praising the lord in strains most exquisite.[6]

Having in mind the comparison with the *Iliad*, we can see that it is quite likely that some of this material was told by Hugh to the farmers in the kiln cottage, though 'quite likely' is as near as we can get. We also need to remember that the Brontës had access to a copy of 'Ossian', which dealt with some of the same legends; we cannot rule out the possibility that some of Branwell's gory tales stem from that source rather than from oral tradition emanating from Hugh.

At this point it might be worth listing the types of Irish legend, placing the examples in their due location. They are (A) Remote times, including 'The Children of Lir'; (B) Cúchulainn, including the *Táin Bó*; our first example above was from this group; (C) Fionn and the Fianna, including Oisín (Ossian); our second example was from this group. We can gather that Pádraig Ó Pronntaigh knew all these. William McAllister saw Hugh's recitation of some of them as comparable to the *Iliad*, an observation (as we have seen) often made. They also measure up to Ellen Nussey's view of Irish stories as 'wild' and frightening.

In addition to these venerable legends, there are two other categories of oral composition or transmission which we have evidence for. Hugh's stories, we read in Wright's book, 'denounced tyranny and cruelty'. 'Falseness and deceit always met condign punishment in his romances; and in cases where girls had been betrayed, either the ghost of the injured woman or the devil himself in some awful form wreaked unutterable vengeance on the betrayer'.[7] In addition, Wright credited Patrick Prunty himself with poems and ballad-type compositions in English, drawn from the folk poem styles current in England and Scotland as well as Ireland. Emily Brontë used references to at least two ballads in *Wuthering Heights*.

There were Irish language scholars in the neighbourhood of Imdel well into the nineteenth-century. Seamus Ó Casaide records interviews by John O'Donovan, the Ordnance Survey worker deputed to discover Irish names for the local townlands, with influential Irish speakers. In Loughbrickland he met Dean McArdle, parish priest of Aghaderg, who considered there were now no Irish speakers left in his parish, but this was in 1834. The Donaghmore townland names were recalled by an old man, aged 100. John O'Donovan also met Mrs Con Magennis, aged 70, McArdle's sister, a repository of Irish legend, who gave him the townland names of Drumballyroney and Annaclone. A farmer called Hennan of Lissnacroppan, nearly 90, said that his native tongue was Irish. The parish priest of Drumballyroney Father McKay, was too old to help O'Donovan.[8]

Despite this evidence of Irish speaking at the beginning of the nineteenth century, and therefore at the end of the eighteenth, I still do not consider it likely that Hugh Prunty would have used Irish to communicate with his neighbours, and to tell his stories in the logie hole at the corn kiln. All the Irish tradition he passed down to Patrick and his other sons and daughters more probably came from earlier encounters in his life.

APPENDIX 2

THE WALSHES, CATTLE EXPORTS, LIVERPOOL AND SLAVERY

In this appendix I propose to tackle the remote story told by Hugh of events he could not possibly have witnessed, and consider the role of Liverpool in the Brontë story. Much of this ground is very speculative, and it will be necessary to differentiate between fact, supported deduction, and speculation.

According to our calculations, based on the evidence of the 1821 census copy, Hugh Prunty arrived at the Boyne Valley in or about 1758. By this time his 'uncle' Welsh was presumably about 40-45. I assume that one of the reasons why Welsh and his wife Mary had adopted Hugh was, at least in Mary's eyes, 'to make him [their] heir'. This implies that they had no natural heir, and they would not be concerned about this until they were beyond youth. In fact, Mary did apparently have another child, a girl, later. She brought this girl with her to Rathfriland, where a local shopkeeper fell in love with her. This suggests that she was not beyond the age of childbearing even when Hugh was adopted, but the question of whether she or Welsh was the elder is not clear. Poyntzpass says that Welsh was favoured by Mary, implying that this was as soon as he arrived, but this is not said precisely, and it may be that she simply grew fond of him as they grew up (this is the case with Catherine in *Wuthering Heights*). Welsh's exact age cannot therefore be calculated. All we can say is that he may have been found on the 'Liverpool boat' about 1715-1725. Even this is not sure, but we have to work with it as a hypothesis. Hugh was therefore relying on Mary, Welsh or local legend, for the story he told of his origins. That he did tell the story is certain.

There is little doubt that Hugh's uncle 'Welsh' was part of the family of Walshes who were major tenants at Ardagh on the banks of the Mattock, a tributary of the Boyne, their land stretching perhaps to the Boyne itself, rented from the Earl of Drogheda, and next door to land belonging to the Nettervilles. Wright was not an expert in Irish social history; both he and Poyntzpass give us a picture of the Walsh family as well-to-do, at least before their money was stolen (at any rate this is hinted) by Welsh. They made their money from cattle trading. Poyntzpass begins the article with an early 'Hugh Prunty' 'at about the beginning of the eighteenth century'. The date is probable, the name, as I hope to have shown, almost impossible. Several times the sources suggest that the name Hugh was traditional in the family, but in discussing Patrick's name we saw that native Irish families had a system for naming which makes this unlikely. That the Christian name was inherited is not so unlikely, as we recall the possible O'Neill link, but also Hugh is a name in both the Maguires and Magennises. But (I have to underline) we can surely rule out Prunty as a name for the family in the Boyne. So the head of the Boyne Valley family was very unlikely to have been called either Hugh or Prunty. Young Hugh probably saw the Boyne tenants as part of his family, which he *assumed* was called Prunty; however, this assumption might come from the McAllisters or other attendees at the Brontë kiln, who did not understand Hugh's references. In the corn kiln, Hugh would say, 'Welsh', 'the father', 'Mary' etc. When Mary came to Rathfriland and her daughter was found attractive to a Rathfriland tradesman, she would, of course, have been surnamed Welsh or Walsh. As we have no idea when this was, possibly her visit affected the naming of Welsh Brunty, Patrick's brother.

These wealthy residents on the Boyne were surely Anglo-Irish, non-Catholics, and of a social class to provide the 'ponies and carriages, and dogs, and guns, and fishing rods' promised to Hugh when Welsh and Mary were coaxing him to come with them.[1] I have no doubt that these adopting land-agents were called Welsh or Walsh. We have to remember that Hugh could not know personally how 'Welsh' arrived on the scene, nor how the family a generation before had prospered. Poyntzpass says '[Hugh] was not an ordinary farmer. He specialised in fattening cattle and exporting them from Drogheda to Liverpool'. There would be no problem in fattening cattle in this lush countryside, but they could not then be embarked on a boat for Liverpool.

In Chapter 7, I gave some details of the Walsh family. There is a good deal more which can make sense of Hugh's garbled story, transmitted through several narrators though it has been. The corn census of 1740 shows that a widow of the family produced 800 barrels of oats that year as well as wheat, meslin, rye and barley. She was no ordinary small farmer. The assertion that these Walshes were also cattle farmers is likely in view of the kind of land situated in this part of Ireland. Actual farming would have been in the hands of a sub-agent, since the main family members would have been out of the country, though not 'absentee landlords', since they were not *primary* landholders. Wright and Poyntzpass both try to explain what they had heard from the Hugh Prunty narratives of the family fortunes. We must be very careful about firm conclusions here, since the transmission is so shaky. But both these sources stress the high social status of the family. 'Education of the Prunty children was pretty good by the standards of those days. The Pruntys were well off financially, and in those days, if you had money you could buy your education, so Hugh Prunty educated the sons in particular' (Poyntzpass). Wright said of the 'Brontë' family, 'Their wants had always been supplied from their father's purse … They were well educated, and had been a good deal in England'.[2] These were not native Irish, but Anglo-Irish; they were not practical farmers.

The Walsh family distinguished itself in British history. Most celebrated was Lieutenant General George Walsh, who has a tomb in Westminster Abbey. He was the son of Richard Walsh of Ardagh and had a brother Anthony to whom he left part of the property on his death in 1761. We have already mentioned Anthony, the steward for the Earl of Drogheda; this seems likely to be either his son or a nephew. George left bequests to a nephew, also Anthony, and another nephew, Ralph. George Walsh had a spectacular career in the army, joining as an ensign in 1709 and working his way up to be colonel of the 49th Regiment of foot. However, some of his nephews were in the Royal Navy rather than the army. In 1740 Thomas, one of the Ardagh family, was in the Bahamas. He had three brothers also in the navy; Joseph, Bob (Robert) and Robin. Of these, Joseph had been in the navy for seven years and in 1740 was serving in the West Indies, while Thomas had just joined. Thomas' correspondent was Elizabeth, the oldest of his sisters, but he was to die in the West Indies in June 1744. General Walsh wrote to Elizabeth saying that money has been embezzled from Tom, and that 'that vile fellow Robin Walsh' had commenced a law suit costing above £50 to the family. Trench commented 'It was not a harmonious family'.[3] It is notable that in the traditional accounts money disappeared from the family through treachery: not exactly 'embezzlement' but fraud of some kind.

Because of the frequency of the surname, we need to be careful about identifying other Walshes with this family, but it we may think it likely that those named Anthony would have a connection. There was an Anthony involved in a land transaction in 1742 at Sheepgrange (very near to Ardagh), and several others in other parts of Louth or Meath. One leased land at Mellifont in 1752.[4] At various times Walshes appear on the lists of officials in Drogheda town. In assessing the relation between these rather grand, but not noble, Walshes and Hugh Prunty, we need to remember that he had been promised ponies and orchards, and that the family he was coaxed to live with *must* have been an Anglo-Irish family living at or near Ardagh. Wright's emphasis that the family 'were well educated, and had been a good deal in England' may imply a memory of such members as George. After their bankruptcy, the girls 'went into service' (Poyntzpass); but perhaps it was the men who went into, not 'service', but '*the* service' (the navy)?

The insoluble difficulty in accepting the story Hugh told, which he had surely been told in his turn by Mary or the neighbours at Ardagh, is that fat cattle could not be exported from Drogheda to Liverpool during the period when 'Welsh' had come into the family. Liverpool port books do not mention cattle being imported from Ireland, and it had been illegal to do so since 1680. Drogheda has no record of live cattle exports. What is possible is that the cattle could have been driven to Drogheda and slaughtered there, with the products (e.g. tallow) being taken by boat to Liverpool. Both Poyntzpass and Wright insist on Liverpool as a place visited by the 'Brontë/Prunty' family, where both say that the 'farmer's' wife went to Liverpool with him, and in the case of Poyntzpass, that this was thought of as a kind of holiday, in which they would buy 'trinkets' to bring back to Drogheda. Liverpool is also where Heathcliff was found, and the only city mentioned in *Wuthering Heights*. It enters the Brontë story on a number of occasions, while Leeds, Sheffield and Bradford are not mentioned by name. The impression is that Liverpool was particularly important to the Brontës in England, as it had been to Hugh's early family in Drogheda. Yet such members of the Walsh family as George Walsh do not seem likely to have been selling cattle in Liverpool, though they had been 'much in England'.

To try to make sense of this ancient story, we need to look carefully at English history, and the history of Liverpool, just before and after the death of Queen Anne in 1714, remembering that the date we have for Welsh's arrival is speculative and cannot be fixed exactly. Liverpool merchants entered the slave trade about 1700, when it was reported that the *Liverpool Merchant* carried 220 slaves from Africa to Barbados. Bristol and London were also prominent in this trade, but by 1740 Liverpool had outstripped both. Liverpool men also owned estates in the Caribbean, like Jane's uncle in *Jane Eyre*. (It is possible that this reference is also part of the Irish background.) We may wonder whether when Tom Walsh wrote back from Barbados he or the family owned property there; again, I have found no evidence for this, but it is a matter for serious consideration. Relationships developed between slaves and their owners and there were exploitative unions resulting in children. One possibility that has to be considered, therefore, is whether Welsh could have been the child of a slave, fathered by a member of the Walsh family. It may be worth noting, though it is not conclusive, that a Patrick Welsh, whose will was proved in 1739, gave his occupation at St Thomas, Jamaica, as 'Planter'.

Both Wright and Poyntzpass stress the 'master-dog' relationship between the Ardagh farmer and Welsh. Welsh was favoured by the castle farmer over the other children. This cannot have been for his beauty. Poyntzpass described the foundling as 'a swarthy looking little boy with prominent teeth and a squint … Some thought it was a gypsy because it was so dark and foreign looking'. Commenting on the perception Hugh first had of Welsh, visiting the family in Fermanagh, Wright said, 'they did not like the uncle's swarthy complexion and dark glancing eyes'. When first found, said Wright, the child was 'very young, very black, very dirty, and almost without clothing of any kind' (p. 19). Welsh, then, when small, was of a type not then thought attractive, and with facial characteristics which did not endear him to anyone. His first appearance is on the boat from Liverpool to Drogheda. There is a feeling in both Wright and Poyntzpass that though it was Mrs Walsh who took pity on the dark and untidy child, her husband had a special link with him. What on earth would persuade the Walshes to adopt this unattractive child, even if Mrs Walsh felt sorry for him, unless there was an overriding motive from the husband? These were the days of patriarchy, after all.

One possibility is that the 'Liverpool' boat could actually have been a naval vessel on which the Walsh brothers served in the West Indies. In some ways this is attractive. Possibly the dark boy at Ardagh was explained as a Liverpool foundling as a cover-up. We have no evidence for this at all; it is speculation. The problem is that this does not explain the Liverpool conundrum. Liverpool in the eighteenth century was certainly a place where cattle products such as tallow could find a ready market. The earliest Liverpool directory is Gore's in 1766. A random inspection of this book shows tallow chandlers (also boiling soap) in High Street and Key Street; there are many more. Liverpool was also the place to buy small gifts; there were trinkets and ladies' clothes to be had. One could buy tobacco at Davies and Holland, watches at Rowland Johnson's and Thompson's in Pool Lane, while Samuel Warren in Castle Street was a silversmith.[5] The emphasis on the family enjoying a kind of holiday each autumn is possible.

Huge changes were taking place in Liverpool in the early part of the nineteenth century. The Bluecoat School was founded in 1709, and a new dry dock was started in 1717. Three years later an Act of Parliament paved the way for the Weaver canal, opening up the Cheshire markets. By this time 130 ships belonged to the port of Liverpool. A butchers' shambles was established not far from the port, which suggests that though Irish cattle could not be brought in, there was a strong trade in all kinds of cattle, and we can always suppose that some might have been brought in illegally. By the end of the century William Moss reported that Liverpool markets were supplied from a very wide area; Ireland, for example, provided 'a great quantity of cattle and pigs'.[6] Here we recall Branwell's interest in cattle droving.

In *Wuthering Heights* old Earnshaw travels to Liverpool, where he finds Heathcliff. He is 'as dark almost as if [he] came from the devil'. As she peeps at him through an opening in his blanket, Catherine sees 'a dirty, ragged, black-haired child'. He is next described as a 'gipsy brat'. This passage is only a few pages away from the 'two colts' passage, and seems likely to be associated with it. In other words, this is a picture clear in Emily's mind: the dark, unprepossessing Welsh becoming the dark unprepossessing Heathcliff. She did not assert that this waif was a slave child, but the identification lurks behind the surface.

In 1840 Charlotte Brontë proposed to go to Liverpool to see the sea, and hoped Ellen Nussey would join her (it did not happen). In 1845, Branwell was sent to Liverpool to cure him of his fanciful wish to marry Mrs Robinson. Anne referred to this in her diary paper of 31 July. His companion was John Brown, who presumably also went with him to North Wales; Branwell mentioned in a letter of 4 August that he had by this time returned from Liverpool and North Wales. Later, Anne Brontë wrote to a Liverpool clergyman, Revd David Thom. We can do no more than suggest the possibility that there was a remote feeling in Haworth that Liverpool had been important in the history of the family; this is of course pure speculation and Manchester also occurs in the Brontë story; but Liverpool seems to have a strong hold.

APPENDIX 3

SMALL ADDITIONAL DETAILS?

In 1980 John Cannon published his *The Road to Haworth*, since reissued in a second edition. He based his work on Wright, but talked to a number of residents of County Down, including Brontë descendants. The book is written from a Northern Ireland perspective, and ignores Alice Brontë's evidence that Hugh came from Drogheda. Almost all events therefore take place in County Down. For example, the putative journeys to Liverpool start at Warrenpoint rather than Drogheda. The 'Brontë' farm is moved from the Boyne to near Newry.

However, we cannot totally sideline a few points which are made that might add detail to Hugh's narrative, which could conceivably have been transmitted by a different route from the McAllisters.

Like Poyntzpass, the account omits details of the journey from North-west Ulster. In fact, a vague 'south' is reinstated (p. 36) instead of the north later favoured by Wright. William McAllister is credited with knowing Patrick, though he was only one when Patrick went to England. On p.37 the suggestion is made that the Pruntys arrived in plantation times. The Mount Pleasant lime-kilns are said to be near Carlingford.

Nevertheless, we might note the following points which could have come down to descendants. On p. 34 it is suggested that there was a witness to the last minutes of the old [Boyne] farmer who had adopted Welsh, during which he spoke to his favourite. Mary's attitude to Welsh's courtship is more like that suggested in Poyntzpass than Wright. Her brothers are 'transported' for their actions against Welsh (p. 40). Red Paddy's parents are said to be dead by 1776, and he works the farm with his sister. Hugh's father is also dead when Hugh leaves his original home. Mary is said to be 'a weak person and hopelessly alcoholic' (p. 46). A strange detail which can hardly have been invented is that when Hugh arrives at the McClory house in Ballynaskeagh he 'clumsily banged his head on the door frame'. This sounds like a true memory. The vicar of Magherally is said to be a friend of the Harshaws. Of these, I feel that the description of Mary seems probable, and the 'door frame' also seems likely. The reader will make his/her mind up about all these details.

NOTES AND REFERENCES

Where full titles are not given here they will be found in the bibliography.

Chapter 1: South Down in the Late Eighteenth Century

1. In his testimonial of 30 December 1805, Thomas Tighe stated 'no Register was kept of Baptisms in this Parish for time immemorial until after Sept 1778'.
2. Pender's 'census', pp. 73-5.
3. Stevenson, p. 277.

Chapter 2: William Wright, Presbyterian

1. Harrison, *The Clue to the Brontës*, pp. 2-3.
2. Shorter, pp. 157-8.
3. S.D. Wright ('Uel') [1986].
4. Chitham, pp. 7-8.
5. It is unfortunate that Wright did not give precise details about what his nurse told him, since she may perhaps have repeated some of the Irish hero legends.
6. Henry McMaster to author, 14 July 1992.
7. Revd W. Dobbin in the sermon given in Second Annaghlone after McKee's death in January 1867.

Chapter 3: Publication and Controversy

1. S.D. Wright, p. 17.
2. *Banbridge Chronicle*, 7 September 1918.
3. Phone conversation Christopher Heywood and author, 2013, discussing his evidence for giving this date for Hugh's age in 'A Brontë Narrative: Hugh Brontë's Tale of Welsh' in *Durham University Journal*, July 1995, pp. 279ff. The reference is given at the foot of p. 286; the Lusk notes are unfortunately lost, and the Johnston Robb article referred to untraced so far. It does not appear to be in the Johnston Robb collection at PRONI. The Lusk notes were taken down by Heywood before the loss of the notebook.
4. Ramsden, p. 53.

5. Mackay, pp. 121-2.
6. *The Bookman*, Vol. 11, December 1896, p. 65.
7. 'Rose Ann Heslip (1821-1915): Charlotte Brontë's Cousin and her Descendants' in *Brontë Studies*, Vol. 35, No. 3, November 2010, pp.232 ff.

Chapter 4: The Family History According to Wright

1. McLysaght, p. 174.
2. Tithe Applotment microfilm available in The National Archives of Ireland, and there are microfilms in various places. I have not yet discovered a comprehensive microfilm of County Down. There is an Index in PRONI. Griffith is available through the website www.askaboutireland.ie.

Chapter 5: Searching the Erne District of Fermanagh

1. The 1,579 examples were chosen at random, having regard to what data was available. However, I do consider them to be representative.
2. Mr Barcroft's letter is printed in the 3rd edition of Wright.
3. Griffith's 'revision' books are available from PRONI on line and are numbered VAL/123/B and adjacent numbers.
4. British Library Edgerton 172, 1759.

Chapter 6: The Boyne Valley

1. Wright, p. 59.
2. Wright, pp. 21ff.
3. C.E.F. Trench, 'Brontë and the Boyne', in *Riocht na Midhe*, Vol. VIII, No. 4, 1992-3, p. 141.
4. Now Trinity College, Dublin, MS 10563.
5. OS first edition 6" map.
6. Under Cattle Acts of 1666 and 1680.

Chapter 7: A Fight Leading to a Flight

1. C.E.F. Trench, *Riocht na Midhe*, loc cit.
2. 'Aunt Mary' brought this daughter to County Down at an unknown date after Welsh died. See Chapter 3.
3. Hyde, p. 258.
4. Constable, p. 26.
5. Facsimile of a Macaronic piece in Constable, op. cit, p.32.
6. E. Charles Nelson, 'A Dundalk Farmer's Library', in *Irish Booklore*, pp. 14-16.
7. Edward Carolan seems to have been active around 1800.
8. Ó Casaide, p. 11.

Chapter 8: Astonishing Support for the Boyne Valley Narrative

1. This detail is not alluded to by Wright.

Chapter 9: Hugh Prunty Meets the McClorys

1. Ó Casaide, p. 11.
2. Ros Davies, quoting Davidson Cowan.
3. Patrick Brontë to Mrs E.C. Gaskell, 20 June 1855.
4. Wright, p. 94.
5. McKay, *The Brontës: Fact and Fiction*, pp. 121-2.
6. R. Quinn Duffy, 'Redmond O'Hanlon and the Outlaws of Ulster' in *History Today*, Vol. 32, 1982.
7. Taylor and Skinner, pp. 7 and 285.
8. Details of these O'Neills in Ó Casaide, pp. 12-13.

Chapter 10: Hired out to Presbyterians

1. For this section of his life, see Wright, pp. 95ff.
2. Wright, p. 96.
3. Davidson Cowan, p. 261.
4. Information from Wikipedia.
5. Wright, p. 96.

Chapter 11: Return to Imdel

1. Wright, p. 37.
2. Wright, *passim*, also in Poyntzpass.
3. Leo McNeill, 'The Parish of Annaclone' in *The Diocese of Dromore Past and Present*, Dromore Diocesan Historical Society, 2004.
4. *ibid.*
5. Wright gave this first name, but he is not always reliable about first names.
6. 'A Wedding Race' in *Tocher, Tales, Songs and Tradition*, Edinburgh, ND, pp. 372ff.
7. Diocese of Dromore.

Chapter 12: Patrick Prunty and his Early Upbringing

1. Crowe (Dundalk, 1978), chapter 10ff.
2. Wright (third edition), p. vi.
3. ibid., p. 228.
4. ibid., p. 230.
5. O'Sullivan, p. xxvii.
6. Robinson, p. 160.

Chapter 13: Glascar and Presbyterianism

1. *History of Congregations*, p. 496.
2. Wright, p. 256
3. Lock and Dixon, pp. 4, 6; Wright, pp. 230-1.
4. Griffith 'Valuation'; Wright, p. 256 (hinted only).
5. Ramsden, pp. 38-9.
6. Ordnance Survey Memoirs, Vol. 12, p. 5.
7. Wright, p. 242.
8. Lock & Dixon, p. 224; Wright, pp. 248-9.
9. ibid., pp. 184, 228.
10. ibid., p. 248.
11. ibid., p. 253.
12. ibid., Chapter XVI.
13. Ordnance Survey Memoirs, Vol. 3, p. 4
14. Wright, p. 85.
15. ibid., pp. 254-6.

Chapter 14: The Prunty Family in 1798

1. Wright, Chapter XVI. Andrew Mackay was the lead critic, but almost all subsequent commentators have failed to understand this element of the Prunty/Brontë heritage. Brian Wilks redresses the balance somewhat in an article for *Brontë Studies*, Vol. 39, No. 2, April 2014, pp. 93-105.
2. See article in Wikipedia. Tacitus was a pro-senatorial writer born in 55 BC. He was bitterly opposed to the imperatorial system. His writing was sharp and punchy: Barber followed him in these characteristics.
3. See Wikipedia.

Chapter 15: Thomas Tighe Employs Patrick

1. Harrison, p. 11. The Brontës at Haworth also absorbed much Wesleyan influence from Maria Brontë (née Branwell), whose sister, Elizabeth, has wrongly been associated with Calvinism.
2. *Notes and Queries*, 5th series, Vol. 12, 26 July 1879, p. 65. This produced a very short reply, dated 20 September 1879 (p. 234), in which the correspondent briefly discussed Patrick's degree. Tighe papers, including comments on the 1798 rebellion, are in PRONI.
3. *ibid.*
4. Griffith's 'Valuation', Parish of Drumballyroney, townland of Aughnavallog, pp. 86-7.
5. *Notes and Queries*, as note 2.
6. Clarke, *Round about Rathfriland*, Chapter IV, p. 25. 'At that same library' is a little ambiguous, and possibly the books in Tighe's library had been sold.
7. Clarke, *City set on a Hill*, Chapter XI.
8. Patrick Brontë to William Campbell, 12 November 1808; Green, p. 24.

Chapter 16: The Brontës in Ireland

1. Wright, pp. 173-4.
2. Paterson, p. 90.
3. Stevenson, p. 277.

Chapter 17: After Patrick went to England

1. Sharman Crawford's rent Roll 1851-1864, PRONI D 1759/3B/4. A copy of a letter written by J.B. Lusk is attached to the front of the roll, with other letters relating to Brontë descendants in Ireland.
2. Wright, p. 267. The matter of whether Patrick visited more than once is debated; there seems little evidence. Would he have come back for the funerals of his parents? It seems possible. Meanwhile the only authenticated visit is that described in Chapter 16.
3. Green, *Letters*, p. 278.
4. Wright, p. 174.
5. Aghaderg Parish Register, 11 May 1851.

Chapter 18: Unconventional Features of the Irish Brontës

1. Ros Davies, freepages.rootsweb.ancestry.com/~rosdavies.
2. The bill received Royal Assent on 26 June 1846.
3. Information on famine in County Down from Ros Davies, County Down website.
4. *ibid*.
5. *Banbridge Chronicle*, 7 September 1918
6. *Brontëana*, p. 289.
7. Ramsden, pp. 81-2.
8. Lady Wilde, 1919, reissued 2006.
9. Wright, p. 29.

Chapter 19: The Religious Position of the Irish Brontës

1. 'Shebna the Scribe', reporting verbatim a communication of J.B. Lusk, loc. cit.
2. Wright, p. 104.

Chapter 20: Patrick Brontë's Cultural Inheritance

1. Wright, p. 101; Poyntzpass also tells this story.
2. ibid., pp. 162, 172.
3. ibid., pp. 168ff.
4. ibid., p. 231.
5. ibid., p. 242.
6. *Brontëana*, p. 286.
7. Ramsden, p. 85.
8. Wright, p. 168
9. ibid., p. 189.

Chapter 21: The Brontës and David McKee

1. J.D.Moorehead, p.12.
2. S.D. Wright, p. 7.
3. Wright, p. 274.
4. *ibid*. This quotation in Wright is in inverted commas, suggesting that it is verbatim. The informant must have been present, and either or both Mrs McKee and Annie, her daughter, were in the manse at the time.

Chapter 22: Patrick Brontë Abandons his Irish Harp

1. The Belfast Harp Festival was held in July 1792. Edward Bunting, a celebrated organist, was deputed to take down as many of the melodies as possible. He published *A General Collection of the Ancient Irish Music* in 1796. Thousands of Irish songs, dances and 'slow airs' have been published since. I should be very surprised if the Pruntys or McClorys did not know some of these.
2. Patrick's poems were published in Horsfall Turner's *Brontëana* and in Smith Elder's editions of *The Professor*.
3. 'The Maid of Killarney', in *Brontëana*, p. 134.

Chapter 23: Patrick Gives an Edited Account to Mrs Gaskell

1. Patrick Brontë to Mrs Gaskell, 20 June 1855. Text from Green, p. 233.
2. *Notes and Queries*, 5th Series, Vol. 12, 12 July 1879. Of course this writer wishes to distance himself from Patrick's unqualified teaching, but he may well be correct.
3. An accessible copy of this article may be found in Smith, pp. 589ff.
4. T. Wemyss Reid, *Charlotte Brontë: A Monograph*, (London, 1877), pp. 215-16.

Chapter 24: Charlotte, Emily, Anne and the Irish Language

1. John O'Donovan's letters are in the library of the Royal Irish Academy. Copies of a printed version by Brown and Nolan, Dublin (nd) are in the Linenhall Library, Belfast.
2. Ó Casaide, p. 41.
3. Ó Casaide, Aguisin (Appendix), p. 67.
4. Constable, p. 62.

Chapter 25: Charlotte's Juvenilia

1. Bibliographical details of Ms Alexander's main contributions to this area are in the bibliography. Winifred Gerin also published *Five Novelettes, Passing Events, Julia, Mina Laury, Henry Hastings, Caroline Vernon* (London, 1971), with reasonably accurate texts.
2. One wonders if there is any significance in Charlotte's choice of O'Neill as a name. We recall that the O'Pronntaighs were a family linked to the O'Neills, and that an O'Neill family lived at Bannvale, near Hilltown.
3. 'The Northern Kirk' is obviously a reference to Presbyterianism. Surely this was part of Patrick's family information to the children, who then make it part of their fictional narratives.

4. *Mina Laury* in Gerin, *Five Novelettes*, p. 147.
5. *Scribner's*, in Smith, p. 592.

Chapter 26: The Uncles Visit England

1. Ramsden, pp. 36ff. This passage seems romanticised, but it is interesting that many very early observers of the Irish Brontës claim a positive appearance and carriage in the relatives.
2. Lock and Dixon, p. 86.
3. *The Sketch*, Vol. 17 (March 1897), p. 288.
4. Ramsden, p. 161.
5. J.C. Holt, *Robin Hood*, second edition (London, 1982) p. 23, tracing the origin to the Percy Folio.
6. Ramsden, pp. 161-2.
7. *The Bookman*, Vol. 11 (March1897), p. 65.
8. *The Sketch*, Vol. 17 (10 February 1897), p. 118.
9. Lady Wilde, p. 247. The volume includes many other customs etc., likely to have been known to the Pruntys, but most of her collection, as in many of these early books, deals very little with County Down.

Chapter 27: Patrick: His Irishness in England

1. Lock and Dixon, p. 25.
2. D. Green, *Letters*, p. 317.
3. Barker, pp. 41ff, pp. 70ff deals with Patrick's impetus to write, apparently under the influence of Revd John Buckworth for the *Cottage Magazine*.
4. R. Scruton, *Thornton and the Brontës* (Bradford, 1898), pp. 59ff.
5. 'Signs of the Times', in *Brontëana*, p.227.
6. 'A Brief Treatise on the Best Mode and Time for Baptism' in *Brontëana*, pp. 233ff.
7. See Griffith's 'Valuation'.
8. Barker, p. 838n.
9. She is said to be a 'twin' of Sarah. I am continuing research about her, but have nothing yet to report.
10. Gaskell, *Letters*, p. 245
11. *Brontëana*, p. 294. It is quite hard to understand what is meant by this 'Scottishness' in the accent. Ulster English was clearly affected by Scots diction, but one might think this applied to all or most inhabitants. There was, obviously, some kind of refinement in Alice's way of talking.

Chapter 28: Moore as well as Wellington as 'Respectable Irish'

1. Kelly, p.13.
2. See Smith and Rosengarten's edition of *The Professor*, p. 333, where quotations in CB's work are listed.
3. Alexander and Sellars, p. 15.
4. Kelly, p. 275.

Chapter 29: Charlotte, Jane Eyre and David McKee

1. *Jane Eyre*, Vol II, Chapter VIII.
2. Wright devoted Chapter 28 to this issue, apparently contradicting himself. He talked of three volumes tied up in a red handkerchief, but on another page talked of single-volume edition. It seems to me that once he had asserted this early knowledge of the novels he had to skew evidence to support his assertion. Though this was unfortunate, it should not impugn his veracity in many of the details he gave in the rest of the book.
3. He certainly did contact Ellen Nussey, who was by this time wary of writers on Brontë matters, and I'm not sure that 'often' is accurate.
4. Wright, p. 274.
5. MacKay, pp. 146ff.
6. Wright, pp. 275ff.
7. Green, *Letters*, p. 214.

Chapter 30: Gondal Princes and Revolutionaries

1. e.g. in *Brontë Facts and Brontë Problems* (Macmillan, 1983). Here I lay out some evidence, but the major issue that those who think the poems are all Gondal have to address is why Emily used two disparate notebooks when she copied the poems in 1844, labelling one of the booklets 'Gondal Poems'.
2. Ratchford, *Gondal's Queen*, pp. 23ff. We need to remember, too, that Ms Ratchford was a pioneer in the study of Emily's poetry.
3. Tillyard, Chapter 4.
4. 'Gormal' and 'Grummal' with 'goblin' mixed in?
5. Wright, Chapter XVI.
6. Barker, p. 454.
7. In the 'Preface' to *Wuthering Heights*, 1850 edition.
8. Hewish, p. 60.

Chapter 31: Queen Mab and the Western Wind

1. See *A Life of Emily Brontë*, Chapter 12.
2. R. Holmes, *Shelley, The Pursuit* (London, 1974), especially pp. 200ff.
3. Smith and Rosengarten, *The Professor*, p. 333.
4. Alexander and Sellars, pp. 385-7.
5. *ibid.*
6. Roper's edition, p. 122, No. 85; Hatfield, p. 165, No. 148. It is surprising how many of Emily's poems begin with mention of the prevailing wind.
7. *Shirley*, Vol. III, Chapter II.

Chapter 32: *Shirley*, Charlotte and Irish Curates

1. Barker, pp. 341-2.
2. Mr Collins was probably from County Antrim. There are detailed notes about him in Smith, pp. 214-5 and other references in the same.

3. Smith, recording CB – EN, 4 April 1847.
4. Barker, pp. 427-8, 432, 438.
5. ibid., pp. 438-9.
6. *Shirley*, Chapter 1.

Chapter 33: Branwell and Anne

1. J. Reaney, 'The Brontës: Gothic Transgressor as Cattle Drover', in *Brontë Studies*, Vol. 29, part 1', March 2004, pp. 27ff.
2. Alexander, *Early Writings*, p. 205
3. Gerin, *Branwell Brontë*, p. 90.
4. Wright, p. 186.
5. S. Griffiths, 'Branwell Brontë, Agnes and Mary Riley', in *Brontë Studies*, Vol. 36, part 4, November 2011, pp. 358ff.
6. Wright, Chapter 26.
7. C. Flaherty, 'A Recently Discovered Unpublished Manuscript: the Influence of Sir Humphrey Davy on Anne Brontë' in *Brontë Studies*, Vol. 38, part 1, January 2013, pp. 30ff.
8. Wright, pp. 160, 164.

Chapter 34: The McAllisters, William Wright, Emily Brontë and *Wuthering Heights*

1. Wright, p. 8.
2. See Chitham, *The Birth of Wuthering Heights* (London, and Basingstoke, 1998), Chapter 2.
3. Robinson, pp. 50-51.
4. Wright, p. 276.
5. 'Biographical Notice of Ellis and Acton Bell'.
6. C. Boyce, 'A Map, Plotting 300 Pages of Longitude against 300 Years of Latitude' in *Brontë Studies*, Vol. 38, part 2, April 2013, pp. 93ff. C.P. Sanger's well-known chronology was read to 'The Heretics' in Cambridge and published by the Hogarth Press of London in 1926.
7. Facsimile in *Brontë Society Transactions* No. 72 (1962) facing page 32; discussion on pp. 24-6 by D.R. Isenberg.

Chapter 35: Objections and Questions

1. 'Eight Mile Br[idge]' is marked on Taylor and Skinner's map of 1778, near to 'Clanduff Ch[urch]' (the new church at Hilltown, though no Hilltown was yet shown). On the east of the Bann two dwellings are shown, one on each side of the road. That on the east is Bannvale, home of the O'Neills.

Appendix 1 – Hugh Prunty and Irish Storytelling

1. Hyde, p. 626.
2. O'Casaide, p. 13.
3. Originally propounded by L.P. Murray in *County Louth Archaeological Society Journal*, Vol. VII, No. 1, 1929, pp. 106-7.

4. British Library MS Add. 18747.
5. Royal Irish Academy, MS 23 A 10, MS 24 P 7, MS 24 L 25.
6. H. Morris in *County Louth Archaeological Journal*, New Series, Vol III, p. 189. British Library MS Egerton 172.
7. Wright, p. 132
8. O'Casaide, p. 56.

Appendix 2 – The Walshes, Cattle Exports, Liverpool and Slavery

1. Wright, p.17.
2. ibid., p. 23.
3. C.E.F. Trench, *Riocht na Midhe, Journal of the Meath Archaeoligical and Historical Society*, Vol. VIII, No. 4, 1992-3, p. 142.
4. Brendan Hall, at www.jbhall.freeservers.com.
5. *The Liverpool Directory for the Year 1766.*
6. W. Moss, *Guide Book to Liverpool*, 1797, reissued with commentary by David Brazendale, 2007, p. 135n.

BIBLIOGRAPHY

1.   Books Referring to the Brontës' Irish Ancestry or to the Brontës' Works (Especially in an Irish Context)

Alexander, C., and J. Sellars, *The Art of the Brontës* (Cambridge, 1995)

Alexander, C., *The Early Writings of Charlotte Brontë* (Oxford, 1983)

Allott, M. (ed.), *The Brontës: The Critical Heritage* (London, 1974)

Barker, J. *The Brontës* (London, 1994)

Brontë Society Transactions, later *Brontë Studies* (1895-present)

Cannon, J., *The Road to Haworth* (London, 1969)

Chadwick, E.A., *In the Footsteps of the Brontës* (London, 1914)

Chitham, E., *The Brontës' Irish Background* (Basingstoke, 1986)

Constable, K., *A Stranger within the Gates* (Lanham, Maryland, 2000)

Crowe, W.H., *The Brontës of Ballynaskeagh* (Dundalk, 1978)

Gaskell, E.C., *The Life of Charlotte Brontë* (London, 1857)

Gerin, W., *Branwell Brontë* (London, 1961)

Gerin, W., *Charlotte Brontë* (London, 1967)

Gerin, W., *Emily Brontë* (London 1971)

Harrison, G.E., *The Clue to the Brontës* (London, 1948)

Hatfield, C.W. (ed.), *The Complete Poems of Emily Jane Brontë* (Columbia, 1941)

Hewish, J., *Emily Brontë* (London, 1969)

Lock, J., and W.T. Dixon, *A Man of Sorrow* (London, 1965)

MacKay, A., *The Brontës: Fact and Fiction* (London, 1897)

O'Byrne, C., *The Gaelic Source of the Brontë Genius* (Edinburgh, 1933)

Ramsden, J., *The Brontë Homeland, or Misrepresentations Rectified* (London, 1897)

Robinson, A.M.F., *Emily Brontë* (London, 1883)

Roper, D., (ed), *The Poems of Emily Brontë* (Oxford, 1995)

Shorter, C.K., *Charlotte Brontë and her Circle* (London, 1896)

Turner, J. Horsfall, *Brontëana* (Bingley, 1898)

Wright, W., *The Brontës in Ireland* (New York, 1893, reprinted Belfast, 2004)

2. Background Books on Irish History and Literature

Bardon, J., *The Plantation of Ulster* (Dublin, 2011)

Boylan, H., *The Boyne, A Valley of Kings* (Dublin, 1988)

Chapman, B., *A History of Newtownbutler* (Dublin, 2005)

Corkery, D., *The Hidden Ireland* (Dublin, 1924)

Day, A., and P. McWilliams (ed.), *Ordnance Survey Memoirs of Ireland* Vols. 1 (County Armagh), 3, 7, 12, 17 (County Down), 4, 14 (County Fermanagh), 30 (parts of Louth, Cavan, Monaghan) (Belfast, 1990-1998)

Fitzpatrick, B., *Seventeenth Century Ireland* (Dublin, 1988)

Gregory, I.A. ('Lady Gregory'), *Gods and Fighting Men* (London, 1904)

Gregory, I.A. ('Lady Gregory'), *Visions and Beliefs in the West of Ireland* (London, 1920)

Hyde, D., *A Literary History of Ireland* (London, 1899)

Kelly, R., *Bard of Erin* (London, 2008)

Lewis, S., *Topographical Dictionary of Ireland* (London, 1839)

Mannin, E., *The Wild Swans* (London, 1952)

McKay, P., *Place Names of Northern Ireland*, Vol. VIII, County Fermanagh (Aghalurcher) (Belfast, 2004)

McLysaght, E., *More Irish Families* (Dublin, 1960)

Macpherson, J. (ed.), *The Poems of Ossian* (London, 1806)

Muhr, K., *Place Names of Northern Ireland*, Vol. VI, County Down IV (Belfast, 1996)

Ó Casaide, S., *The Irish Language in Belfast and County Down* (Dublin, 1930)

O'Sullivan, S. (ed.), *Folktales of Ireland* (London, 1966)

Pender, S., *A Census of Ireland, c. 1659* (Dublin, ND)

Rollason, T.W., *Myths and Legends of the Celtic Race* (London, 1911)

Stevenson, J., *Life in Down* (Belfast, 1920)

Stout, G., *The Bend of the Boyne* (Dublin, 1997)

Tillyard, S., *Citizen Lord* (London, 1998)

Wilde, J.F.A. ('Lady Wilde'), *Legends, Charms and Superstitions of Ireland [Short title]* (London, 1919, reprinted New York 2006)

3. Locally Produced Histories and Pamphlets

Bradshaw, T., *The General Directory of Newry, Armagh, etc.* (Newry, 1819)

Clarke, E.M., *City Set on a Hill* (Rathfriland, 1979)

Clarke, E.M., *Round about Rathfriland* (Rathfriland, 1981)

Cowan, J.D., *Donaghmore: Past and Present* (London, 1914)

Lowe, H.N., *Lowe's Fermanagh Directory* (Enniskillen, 1880)

McKee, J.Y., *A History of the Descendants of David McKee of Annahilt* (Philadelphia, 1892)

McNeill, L., *The Diocese of Dromore, Past and Present* (Lisburn, 2004)

Martin, M., *Magherally Presbyterian Church, 1656-1982* (Banbridge, 1983)

Moore, R., *A Life of William Dobbin* (Belfast, ND)

Moorhead, J., *First and Second Anaghlone* (Belfast, ND)

Paterson, T.G.F., *Harvest Home* (Armagh, 1975)

Presbyterian Historical Society, *A History of Congregations in the Presbyterian Church of Ireland* (Belfast, 1982).

Wright, S.D. (Uel), *The Rev. Dr William Wright of Damascus* (Belfast, 1986)

Wright, S.D., *A History of Ryans Presbyterian Church, 1835-1985* (no location given, 1984)

4. Brontë Works

Brontë, A., *The Tenant of Wildfell Hall* (London, 1848)
Brontë, C., *Jane Eyre* (London, 1847)
Brontë, E.J., *Wuthering Heights* (London, 1847)
Brontë, P., *Cottage Poems* (Bingley, 1811)
Brontë, P., *The Maid of Killarney or Albion and Flora* (London, 1818)
Gerin, W. (ed.), *Five Novelettes [of Charlotte Brontë]: Passing Events, Julia, Mina Laury, Captain Henry Hastings, Caroline Vernon* (London, 1971)
Green, D. (ed.), *The Letters of the Reverend Patrick Brontë* (Stroud, 2005)
Hatfield, C.W. (ed.), *The Complete Poems of Emily Jane Brontë* (New York, 1941)
Roper, D. (ed.), *The Poems of Emily Brontë* (Oxford, 1995)
Smith, M. (ed.), *The Letters of Charlotte Brontë* (3 vols, Oxford 1995-2004)
Turner, J. Horsfall, *Brontëana* (Bingley, 1898)

INDEX

www.thehistorypress.ie

The History Press Ireland